HOUSING AND THE STATE

HOUSING AND THE STATE

1919–1944

by

MARIAN BOWLEY

B.Sc.(Econ.), Ph.D.

LONDON

GEORGE ALLEN & UNWIN LTD

FIRST PUBLISHED IN 1945
REPRINTED . . 1947

THE PAPER AND BINDING OF THIS
BOOK CONFORM TO THE AUTHORIZED
ECONOMY STANDARDS

PRINTED IN GREAT BRITAIN
in *11-Point Baskerville Type*
BY C. TINLING & CO., LTD.
LIVERPOOL, LONDON AND PRESCOT

CONTENTS

PREFACE

It is not the purpose of this book to lay down categorically what the scope of housing policy should be after this war in Great Britain, or what particular building programme should be adopted. My aim in writing it has been more modest. It has been to describe and explain some of the more important conditions which must be satisfied if certain types of housing policy are to be successful. It is only if the main difficulties and problems involved by different policies are known that a sensible choice can be made between them. This method of approaching the housing question has led me into a discussion of housing policy between 1919 and 1939. During these years the local authorities built over a million houses. This was perhaps the outstanding peace time experiment in state intervention in this country in the provision of a necessity of life, which had formerly been supplied almost exclusively by independent private enterprise. It is obviously impossible to examine all the aspects of this experiment, or rather series of experiments, within the limits of one book. I have confined myself to considering how far the duties imposed on local authorities, and the various subsidies given to local authorities and private builders in order to stimulate the provision of new houses, achieved their objects, in what ways they failed, and why. This approach has led, in particular, to some inquiry into the question of whether a system of subsidies of uniform size, and available on uniform terms, throughout the country was reasonable.

During the period of twenty years between the end of the Great War and the outbreak of this war, housing policy went through three quite clearly marked stages. Each of these I have treated as a separate experiment in state intervention in the provision of houses. The examination of these three experiments forms the first part of the book. The second part is an attempt to summarise the conclusions reached in the first part and to show their relevance to housing problems after this war. Starting from this basis, an attempt has been made to outline the problems which demand solution, and the conditions which must be satisfied in the cases of two possible types of post-war housing policy.

The main body of the book is concerned only with England and Wales, but the most important points of difference between housing problems in Scotland and in England and Wales are discussed in an appendix. For this procedure I feel that I owe an explanation to my friends in Scotland, for it was while I was lecturing in Scotland that much of the data for this book was collected. Perhaps still more important, I was startled by the striking differences between housing conditions north and south of the Border. This convinced me of the need for considering whether the application of an approximately uniform system of housing subsidies to the whole of Great Britain was reasonable; inquiry into this question indirectly led to this book. There are two reasons for discussing separately the housing problems of Scotland. In the first place, the central authority for housing in Scotland is the Department of Health for Scotland, not the Ministry of Health; in consequence the information available, and in particular the form of the statistics, is different in Scotland. In the second place, the actual housing problems in Scotland between 1919 and 1939 differed from those of England and Wales. In my opinion they still do. To mix up discussion of Scottish questions with those of England and Wales would not only have necessitated cumbersome statistical explanations, but would have obscured the differences in the problems themselves. By dealing with Scottish questions in an appendix, however, it has been possible to concentrate attention on these particular differences and on their implications for housing policy.

This book was completed at the end of 1943, that is, before any indication had been given of the Government's plans for housing policy, even for the first few years of peace. It has not been practicable to introduce a discussion of these while the book has been in the press. Similarly, it has not been possible to take into account the damage to houses by air-raids, flying bombs and other strange missiles, during 1944.

No claim is made that this book provides a complete study of even those aspects of housing policy which are discussed in it. It is hoped, however, that it will at least provoke some serious discussion of them. I am only too well aware that the book suffers seriously from both incompleteness and defects in presentation. Both these faults are in part due to the circumstances in which it has been written. The whole book has been written, and much of the material included in it has been analysed between 1941 and 1943. The only times available for work on it have been after dinner at night and the week-ends. Inevitably it suffers from all the defects of discontinuity of writing, and it has been impossible to fill certain gaps in the material originally collected earlier. Completion even in its present form would not have been possible without the invaluable assistance of my father, Professor A. L. Bowley. Not only has he advised on the diagrams and tables, but he has worked out many of the calculations and checked others. He has also spent many tedious hours checking material collected before the war. He has also read the whole book in proof. Needless to say he is not in any way responsible for the use I have made of his advice, or for the conclusions I have drawn from his calculations.

Finally I should like to take this opportunity of thanking those officials of the Ministry of Health who have been responsible for providing me with the figures of the numbers of houses built in individual counties and county boroughs. I am also grateful to them for several interesting talks on housing questions. Naturally they are not responsible in any way for the use I have made of their figures, or of their advice.

MARIAN BOWLEY.

LONDON, *November*, 1944.

PART ONE

THE THREE EXPERIMENTS IN STATE INTERVENTION TO IMPROVE THE SUPPLY OF HOUSES, 1919-1939

Chapter I

THE BACKGROUND OF HOUSING POLICY

I. THE NATURE OF THE PROBLEM IN 1919

THE real break with the nineteenth century came rather late in the housing field. The ideas of the housing reformers of the Victorian Age dominated and paralysed the first few years of this century before the Great War. The housing problem was still basically the problem of the health of towns, and was part and parcel of the sanitary school of thought associated with Edwin Chadwick. Interest in housing as a social problem was not an independent growth; it had sprung from the realisation of the connection of drains, water supplies and lack of fresh air, with epidemics and death rates. The earliest efforts to impose minimum standards of housing were all negative and all directed from the angle of the health of towns. They were intended to prevent people living in insanitary conditions by prohibitions, by building regulations or by actual destruction of houses. The reformers would have swept the towns clean, if they could: they rampaged destructively through the congested centres of the industrial towns tearing down the rookeries. They tried by building regulations to prevent new working-class houses being crowded together in a sordid ruined countryside and probably by doing so limited, to some extent, the numbers built. The forces of law and order and the churches were behind them. It had been noticed that, as well as disease, crime and vice accumulated in the labyrinths of the slums. The police and the priest were as unable to penetrate as the sunshine.

Superimposed on the belief in the desirability of destruction in the interests of public health, law and morals, was the discovery that overcrowding was also an evil which the mere destruction of houses tended to increase and spread. The housing problem involved not merely pulling down houses, but also putting up houses which the ordinary working-class family in the congested areas of the big towns could afford. This was the special problem of finding ways of providing more houses for the families, particularly the very poor families, in the hearts of the large towns where land was expensive. It was realised that if this problem was not solved the clearance of insanitary property would increase overcrowding among the poorer families. For this nineteenth century doctrines provided no solution;

policy became confused. Private pseudo-philanthropic bodies, " the 5 per cent. philanthropists,"[1] erected blocks of tenements only to find that they were adding not to the supply of houses for the poor but to the supply of houses for the artisan class. Octavia Hill tried to reform tenants and property owners by a new theory of estate management. Local authorities were given permissive power to build houses for rehousing purposes and to defray the expenses out of the rates. The housing problem was the slum problem, the problem of people living in insanitary conditions. The official housing policy, as far as one existed, was limited to making it legally possible for the local sanitary authorities to deal with the slums at their own expense if they liked. Broadly speaking, the fundamental idea remained negative. The object was primarily to prevent or destroy insanitary housing conditions rather than to create good conditions. The actual provision of houses by local authorities remained a step taken only in the last resort.

The brief interlude of the Great War changed all this. In four short years the old interests and ideas were pushed into the background to be replaced by a medley of conflicting aims, theories and hopes.

Housing policy became a national issue. It was no longer the special interest of isolated groups of social reformers. It had graduated into the world of party politics. With the slogan "Homes fit for Heroes," it started its career as a pawn in the political game of bribing the electorate with vague promises of social reform. Let me hasten to add this was not necessarily a bad thing: most of the great reforms have been brought about in this way. In the case of housing, the apparent change was sudden and largely the accidental result of the war, which introduced a series of complicated economic problems in its train. It was not the outcome of a gradual growth of relatively clear ideas. For the twenty years between the Great War and the present war, housing policy consisted of a series of partially thought-out and partially understood experiments.

The immediate cause of the change was the combination of the introduction of rent control in 1915 and the low level of building during the Great War. It must not be supposed, however, that the outcry against rising rents in Glasgow in 1915, which was the immediate cause of the Rent and Mortgage Restriction Act passed in 1915, was due to any conscious change in outlook. It was merely the expression of popular determination not to be exploited by war

---

[1] This description was applied to the various housing trusts of the latter part of the nineteenth century by the Royal Commission on the Housing of the Poor, 1884/5.

profiteers. The introduction of rent control must be seen in perspective as part of the war-time machinery built up piecemeal to control the prices of the main necessities of life. At the end of war, the question of decontrol of rents had to be faced in common with the questions of the decontrol of the prices of other goods. It was clear, however, long before the end of the war that the problem would be especially complicated in the case of rents. The houses built were insufficient to keep up with the needs of the growing population. There was growing dissatisfaction with the pre-war standards of working-class life in general and of housing in particular. The government, now that it had interfered in the housing question, would be expected, perhaps illogically, to take some responsibility for housing conditions in the future. Responsibility for the post-war housing had become a government matter, and " Homes fit for Heroes " was to be a popular election cry.

The basic problem of decontrol of the price of any commodity after a war was, and is, theoretically very simple. Price control is normally introduced, with or without rationing, in order to prevent the scarcity of supplies causing an increase in prices. The scarcity of any particular thing may have been caused by an actual decrease in supplies below normal peacetime levels, by increases in demand with increases in population, or increases in money income, without concurrent increase in supplies, or owing to the scarcity of other goods for which it can be used as a substitute. In general, of course, the apparent scarcity of any commodity in war-time arises from some combination of all these factors. As long as the scarcity continues decontrol of prices will tend to produce just the sort of increase of prices it is the purpose of control to avoid. Decontrol, therefore, can only safely take place after supply has been readjusted to demand. The mere cessation of war does not produce an automatic and adequate increase of supplies immediately. The economic system takes time to switch back from war to peacetime conditions. Appropriate increases in raw materials, readjustment of channels of trade, repair of plant and increase of capacity, demobilisation of labour from the fighting services and war-production all take time. The supplies of skilled labour may have decreased owing to casualties in the field and ordinary wastage may not have been replaced by new entrants and apprentices during the war years; this will also help to hamper readjustments. Decontrol of prices, therefore, depends on the solution, or partial solution, of the economic problems of readjusting the system to peacetime conditions for the production of the goods and services required by a community in peacetime.

Those responsible for this decontrol have to decide at what stage control can be abolished without precipitating increases in price which may be socially, economically, or politically undesirable.

On paper this problem looks very neat, the economists' dream. In practice, it may be exceedingly complicated. There may be difficulties in increasing production; it may be impossible to forecast demand; tastes may have changed; the composition and location of the population may have changed. Last, but not least, semi-political factors may have intruded into the field. Consumers may have developed definite ideas as to the prices they ought to pay, irrespective of economic factors. The old confused semi-ethical belief in a " fair " price may reappear. There may be a nostalgia for the good old days and its prices. There may be a belief that peace should herald a new era of peace and plenty in which the sordid necessity of going without something, because it is too expensive, would have disappeared. There may merely be a belief, grown out of government price-fixing during the war years, that the prices actually sanctioned by the government in the war have some lasting ethical justification. Whatever the origin of ideas about " fair " prices, decontrol may have to be postponed indefinitely if they have political importance, simply because supplies will not be available in sufficient quantities at " fair " prices to satisfy demand, *unless* producers are subsidized in some way. Similar complications may arise, *mutatis mutandis*, if producers develop similar uneconomic ideas as to " fair " prices for their labour and capital. The problem of decontrol may in practice become inextricably mixed up with problems of social policy as well as with problems of production.

After the Great War nearly all the possible complications developed in connection with control of rents. The decontrol question was gradually swamped by the problems of production, " fair " prices and social policy. During the war rents had been controlled at the level reached at the outbreak of war.[1] At the end of the war this level had no sort of connection with the rent which would be needed to make the building of houses to let profitable. This created a dilemma to start with, for the return to peace could not be celebrated by the provision of houses at rents far above those

---

[1] During the war rent had been controlled by the Increase of Rent and Mortgage Interest (War Restrictions) Act of 1915. This applied to all houses with rateable values, not exceeding £35 in London (Metropolitan Police District), £30 in Scotland and £26 elsewhere. To all intents and purposes the rents of the houses included in this control were fixed at the rents at which they were let at the outbreak of the war (or at the rent at which they were first let during the War, if not previously let). Control was extended to more expensive houses in 1919 and 1920.

prevailing during the war. There was an idea, too, that in the post-war era working-class standards of housing should be improved. On the other side, workers in the building industry became wedded to the idea that they should be paid more and work less hard than during or before the war.[1]

There were still other difficulties to take into account. Houses have certain very tiresome and peculiar economic characteristics. From the point of view of economists they are neither " fish, fowl, nor good red herring." They are consumers' goods because they are used directly by the people who live in them. Once built they do not need any additional labour and material to make them usable. The great difference between houses and most other consumers' goods is that they are much more durable, they last for an indefinite length of time. True, they may need mending just as clothes do, but they last much longer than even the best mended clothes. Under the pressure of clothes' rationing during this war, many of us are feeling compulsorily virtuous about ' making do ' with the clothes bought before the war or even in the first year of war, but most of us still buy such clothes as we are allowed to. We do not feel, however, that there is anything very virtuous or surprising with making do with our pre-war houses. We do not even regard postponing repairs to houses, except perhaps to those which have been blitzed, as a virtuous economy. It is this extreme durability of houses which makes the difference between houses and most other consumers' goods a distinction really of kind rather than of degree. Moreover, this characteristic is particularly important in war-time, for there is no need for the houses of the community to be replaced each year in war-time in order to provide the current essential consumption, a procedure necessary in the case of food and even to some extent in the case of clothes. The provision of new houses to replace old houses and to accommodate additional families emerging during the war can in general be postponed to the end of the war. Postponement involves some inconvenience and discomfort, of course; people may be more crowded together, but this does not precipitate any immediate disaster. There are in any case good commercial reasons for not building large numbers of new houses in war-time, as it is impossible to foresee where all the families shifted about during the war will ultimately settle.

In the Great War house building was postponed in just this way with the natural result that the need for houses accumulated. Most of the families who would normally have had new houses during the

[1] See Chapter II. p. 29.

war years, but did not get them, still wanted them afterwards. As the Government had introduced rent control during the war, it had to decide how to deal with this post-war situation. With other consumers' goods this accumulation of demand could not take place on the same sort of scale. No one could accumulate all their unsatisfied demands for perishable things like sweets, cream, eggs and meat until the end of a war. If they tried to make good for all the nice food they had done without, they would undoubtedly be very ill. The normal demand for certain other things might be accumulated to some extent, such as the demand for holidays, amusements, clothes and furniture; but in the Great War the Government had not got itself involved seriously in price control in these fields and could safely ignore any problems connected with them.

Of course if the ordinary demand for houses could accumulate, so could the demand for buildings for other purposes, for offices, factories, etc. Inevitably the accumulated demand for buildings of all sorts was greater than the normal pre-war capacity of the building industry, and also greater than the probable post-war capacity which would be needed once the deficit had been made good. The pressure of the accumulated demand on the capacity of the building industry tended to increase the real costs of building by stimulating not only the use of inefficient plant and labour, but also attempts to increase rapidly the production of building materials when industry was still suffering from the dislocating effects of the war. A scramble for labour and materials was bound to occur and would help to increase prices and costs still further. Moreover, it was extremely difficult to increase the capacity of the industry. It must take time to expand the production capacity of the building materials industry; it must take still longer to increase the supply of skilled men in the building industry itself. The incentive might well be inadequate in any case, since the extreme size of the demand would obviously be temporary and the greater the expansion of the industry the more temporary would the demand be. Neither potential investors in plant for producing materials, nor the craft unions in the actual building industry itself, would be likely to regard favourably an expansion of the capacity of the industry above whatever they believed would be needed for normal post-war demands.

Under these circumstances, there was little chance that ordinary working-class houses to let would be built in large numbers. The fact that working-class houses are normally let and not sold to their occupiers is just another, and one of the most familiar, of the complications caused by the durability of houses. In general houses cost too much for the ordinary working-class family to buy, for buying a house means paying for shelter and accommodation years in advance of actual current needs, while wages are not paid in advance at all.[1] Before the Great War, the vast majority of small houses were, therefore, rented by their occupiers from people who were willing, and could afford, to invest money in buying such houses to let for profit.

It was unlikely that the years following the Armistice would be favourable for such investments. Investment in houses to let will only appear to be profitable if there is reason to believe that prospective rents will be sufficient to provide some margin of profit as well as covering the interest charges on the capital cost of the houses, and the cost of repairs and management. If building costs and interest rates are abnormally high, this condition is not likely to be satisfied. Further, if building costs and interest rates are likely to fall, or are actually falling, prospects of profits are still more gloomy and actual losses are probable. For if either costs, or interest rates, fall it is possible to let profitably any new houses built after the fall in costs, or in interest, at lower rents than the houses built at higher levels of costs and interest rates. Competition from the new cheaper houses will tend to drag down the rents of the older houses with consequent loss to their owners. The owners have no way out at all (unless they can eliminate the competition from the new houses), for they cannot maintain their net receipts. Cutting down on current expenditure on repairs and management, the only current expenses of house owners, will not help much, because these are small in relation to gross receipts from rents. Incidentally, it would be socially highly undesirable for such economies to be made, as it would lead to deterioration of the houses. There are, in fact, no important current costs of producing shelter; once built the mere existence of houses provides the shelter and accommodation with some reinforcement from repairs. It is evident then that falling costs and interest rates are highly unfavourable for investment in new houses. Stable low costs and interest rates are, on the other hand, favourable; they make it possible for investors to receive profits while charging low rents without fear of competition from houses built at still lower levels of costs.[2]

---

[1] House purchase on the instalment system was relatively undeveloped at this time. See pp. 83 et seq. on the development of building societies and instalment buying.

[2] This distinction between the effects of falling and stable low prices and interest rates is familiar to students of business cycle theory. Sufficient attention does not seem to have been paid to it, however, in discussions of the possibility of utilising expansions of house building activity to counteract trade depressions. For unless special measures are taken

It was almost certain that the years immediately following the Armistice would be characterised by all these conditions unfavourable to investors in houses to let. Building costs were, we have seen, certain to be abnormally high, and would to start with, at least, probably be so high as to make building of working-class houses to let at profitable rents impossible. They would moreover certainly be recognised as abnormally high and as likely to fall. The existence of old houses with rents fixed under the Rent Restriction Act at practically pre-war levels might provide still more discouragement to investment in new houses which could only be let profitably at rents far above pre-war levels. People might hesitate to move into new houses which were so much more expensive, even though more comfortable than those they were already crowded into. Moreover, if rent control continued, it would support the idea, rightly or wrongly, that the controlled rents were the " fair " or normal rents for working-class houses. The belief that sooner or later costs and interest rates would fall to the levels corresponding to the controlled rents would be strengthened. Obviously, this would be a fatal discouragement to investors.

The dilemma confronting the Government in 1918 was therefore serious. If rent control was abolished, as of course the property-owners hoped, there would be a great political outcry from tenants faced with notices of rent increases. Increases in rents staved off in deference to public opinion during the War could scarcely be regarded as an appropriate form of peace celebration. In any case, it was quite uncertain how quickly, and to what extent, investment in new houses would develop in response to such a stimulus. On the other hand, if rent control was maintained, it would reinforce the belief, as we have seen that the existing controlled rents were the " fair " and appropriate rents for working-class houses for all time.

As the Government had once meddled in the house market, it could not abandon all responsibility for the supply of houses. It was politically necessary to make some effort to control and organise the supply of new houses, particularly of working-class houses to let. The problems of supply were extremely complicated, however. It might prove impossible to provide conditions under which private investment in working-class houses to let would start again. In the

to counteract the depressing influence of the actual process of declines of prices and interest on investors in house property, we ought to be sceptical about the usefulness of building programmes as a method of preventing a general downswing of employment as distinct from stimulating an upswing.

B

end it might well become necessary for the Government to create some new organisation to take the place of the old individual investor. The whole question of control or decontrol of houses at the end of the war was inextricably involved with much wider questions of the organization of the supply of new houses.

In the political atmosphere after the war, the housing question thus inevitably became a major national issue of social policy. The opportunist introduction of rent control in 1915 had served as the key to a veritable Pandora's box of difficulties and dangers. In fact of course the whole thing was an illustration of the generalisation so frequently made by economists and equally frequently disregarded by the general public. If the Government controls prices it will sooner or later have to interfere in supply and distribution. In the case of rents, the annual price paid for the use of houses, the Government had been able to evade the consequence of control for a time because the supply of houses could be regarded as fixed for the duration of the war. As soon as the war was over, this condition broke down. Supply could and must be increased and some sort of responsibility for supply could no longer be evaded. The economic consequences of Government actions are like curses, sooner or later .hey come home to roost.

II.   The Size of the Problem

No doubt all the difficulties inherent in the housing situation after the Great War would have remained matters of academic interest only, if the shortage had been relatively small. In fact, it was large, both absolutely and in terms of the capacity of the building industry. The most natural way of measuring the shortage is by comparing the increase in the number of families with the increase in the number of houses during the war period.   As the married couple is the foundation of the ordinary family, the increase in the numbers of couples provides a sound basis for estimating the numbers of additional houses needed.   But married couples are not the only groups of the population who need houses for themselves. Widows as well as some of the unmarried adults also want, and will get, separate houses for themselves if they can. The Registrar-General suggested, in the Housing Volume of the 1931 Census, that a maximum figure for the growth in the number of families who might want separate houses should include increases in the numbers of widows, widowers and divorcees under 65 years of age, *plus* 10 per cent. of the increase in the numbers of single persons between 20 and

45 years of age, as well as the increase in the number of married couples. This is obviously a sensible way of estimating the number of additional families for whom additional houses are needed over any period[1] and it has been used consistently throughout this book. After the experience of the trials of sharing houses during the present war, few people would have the hardihood to deny that every housekeeper wants a house of her own. Nearly every married woman is a housekeeper, a very considerable proportion of the widows under 65 have children growing up and living at home, and are therefore, housekeepers too, while others want to keep on their own home. The only point that people may be disposed to query is the allowance made for the single people. Some will say it is too small and others that it is too big. It is, of course, a reasoned guess; in fact, as the increase in married couples was obviously much the most important element in the total estimate of needs both between 1911 and 1921 and between 1921 and 1931, it would not matter very much if the allowance for single persons were made rather larger or rather smaller.

On this basis the total number of additional families who required additional houses between 1911 and 1921 was 1,093,000 compared with 994,000 between 1901 and 1911.[2] To keep pace then with just the increase in families between 1911 and 1921 more houses would have had to have been built during the war decade than in the preceding one, i.e. just over an average of one hundred thousand a year instead of just under. Whatever might have happened if there had been no Great War, the low level of building during the war years resulted in an increase in the number of houses by only 288,000 between 1911 and 1921, including about, 50,000 houses built between January 1919 and March 1921.[3] In 1921 there was thus an actual

---

[1] A full explanation of the way in which the Registrar-General reached his conclusions is given in the Housing Volume of the 1931 Population Census for England and Wales. The Registrar-General was inclined to reduce his total figure of requirements for additional houses by assuming that after the Great War a number of the additional families would wish to share houses as other families had before the war. In fact, we do not know how many of the families who were sharing houses at the time of the 1911 Census did so because they were unable to get separate houses or because they preferred sharing, and there seems little point in making what must be a purely arbitrary guess at a figure. I have therefore made no reduction in the total of requirements on this score. Similarly no allowance is included in the estimates for increases, or changes in the number, of vacant houses. Normally the number of vacants increase in proportion of some sort to the number of houses. See Statistical Appendix, p. 270.

[2] All the figures quoted in this section come from the Housing Volume of the 1931 Census op. cit. or are derived from figures in it, unless otherwise stated.

[3] 29,264 houses were built with Government subsidies, the numbers built without subsidy are not known but according to Ministry of Health estimates must have been about 20,000. See Statistical Appendix, Table 2.

deficit of 805,000 houses, and at the time of the Armistice the deficit was probably about 600,000.[1] These figures are set out in Table I.

TABLE I.—Housing Requirements (England and Wales) from the end of the Great War up to 1931.*

Thousands.

(1) Increase in the number of families, 1911–18	..	..	..	..	848
(2) Increase in the number of houses, 1911–18	..	..	..	..	238
(3) Shortage of houses at the beginning of 1919	..	..	..	..	610
(4) Increase in the number of families, 1919–31	..	..	..	..	1,339
(5) Number of additional houses required, 1921–31	..	..	..	..	1,949

* See Statistical Appendix, pp. 269–272, for further details and explanations.

Before the War, between 1901 and 1911 the annual average increase in the number of houses had been 84,000. If this rate of increase had been maintained from the Armistice onwards it would have taken approximately seven years to make good the deficit outstanding at the Armistice, without any provision being made for the needs of the continuing increase in the numbers of families after 1919. In fact, the number of families increased by about the same amount between 1921 and 1931 as during the War decade, so that current needs from 1919 to 1931 averaged just over 100,000 a year without any allowances for replacements. A clearer idea of the magnitude of the problem can be got from calculating the number of additional houses needed each year, if the war shortage was to be made good and current requirements satisfied, at a given date. The total requirements for new houses between 1921 and 1931 amounted to about 1,900,000, that is 805,000 needed to make up the shortage outstanding in 1921 and the rest to balance the increase in the number of families between 1921 and 1931. If supplies and needs were to balance by 1931 the average increase in the numbers of houses needed each year would have been just under 190,000, i.e. an increase more than twice as great as the average annual increase between 1901 and 1911. If a more ambitious attack on the shortage were to be made, if 1925 was chosen instead, the average increase needed each year up to 1925 would have been just over two hundred thousand. In short if the housing shortage were to be overcome in five or even in ten years after 1921, an immense

[1] This result is reached by simple arithmetic. If the increase in families took place fairly evenly throughout the decade, it would have amounted to rather more than 800,000 between 1911 and the end of 1918 compared with an increase in the number of houses of about 240,000. See Statistical Appendix, Table I.

expansion in the capacity of the building industry over pre-Great War levels would be required.

All the figures of requirements used so far have referred to total requirements. The problem which threatened most difficulty, however, was that of providing additional working-class houses. Ordinary working-class houses are houses with rateable values of not more than £13,[1] Class C houses as they came to be called later on. At the end of the Great War about two-thirds of all the houses in the country came into this category, and it was natural to assume that two-thirds of the requirements for additional houses at the end of the Great War were for working-class houses of this type. This assumption agrees quite well with the estimates of the proportion of working-class families to all families in the country. This is usually estimated at between two-thirds and three-quarters.[2] As some working-class families of the artisan type often live in houses above the £13 rateable value line, it is quite reasonable to take the lower figure of two-thirds as giving the proportion of houses needed to be of the ordinary working-class type. On this basis between one-and-a-third and one and a half million working-class houses were needed between 1921 and 1931.

It will have been noticed that none of the estimates used have made any allowances for houses needed to replace old or insanitary, or worn-out or inconvenient houses, nor to replace houses converted into shops and offices, or actually pulled down. On the other hand, no compensating allowance has been made for additions to the supply of houses by the conversion of large houses into flats. Unfortunately there was no reason to expect that such additions to the supply would make up for the houses converted to other uses or pulled down. The reason for the omission is that there are no data on which estimates of the need for replacements can be made. Nor is it at all easy to give any satisfactory definition of this need for replacement in 1919. It is of course possible to define the need for replacement as the need for houses to replace those "unfit for human habitation," though the interpretation of this typically official phrase have been in practice neither uniform nor consistent. The phrase implies, however, a very narrow view of replacement needs. It ignores the need to replace houses which have become inconvenient or old-fashioned, or houses converted to other uses, yet these are important reasons for replacing houses even though they are not

[1] Not more than £20 in London Metropolitan Police Area.
[2] See *Wages and Incomes since 1860*, by A. L. Bowley and *The Home Market*, 1939 Edit., by G. Harrison and F. C. Mitchell. Chaps. 13 and 17.

susceptible to hard and fast statistical measurement. It will be much more convenient to deal with the replacement question as we go along, particularly as it did not form part of the main, specifically post-Great War problem on which policy was based. In any case, it is only too obvious that the magnitude of the need for houses, even ignoring the whole complex of replacement needs, was sufficiently great to provide plenty of opportunity for the development of all the difficulties which we have seen were implicit in the situation at the end of the Great War.

Chapter II

THE FIRST EXPERIMENT, 1919–1923

I. Policy and Intentions

On July 31, 1919, the Housing and Town Planning, etc., Act was passed. The series of experiments in State intervention to increase the supply of working-class houses began. The general attitude was optimistic ; the man-in-the-street did not believe that the housing problem was excessively difficult or complicated. A subsidy could be used to offset high building costs and interest rates ; after all subsidies had been used to keep down the price of bread during the war. The local authorities, already responsible for dealing with slums, could be given the job of providing the working-class houses which were so urgently needed, for it was assumed that temporarily private enterprise would be neither willing nor able to do so. In the meantime, while the shortage lasted landlords could be prevented from taking advantage of the situation by extension of the life of the Rent and Mortgage Interest Restriction Act.

At this point two schools of thought emerged.

According to one school, the housing problem, apart from the traditional slum problem, was a temporary result of the war. Once the crisis was over, private enterprise would be willing and able to provide all the houses required as before the war. Everything would return to normal again. This simple and obvious interpretation of the needs of the situation was widespread. The great majority of the witnesses who gave evidence before the Committee on the Rent Restriction Acts in 1920[1] held it, and it was still held by the Conservative Party in 1923, and even in 1933.

The other point of view was held by people who considered the housing problem in more fundamental terms. They believed, not so much that private enterprise would not re-enter the market, as that its achievements before the war had not been satisfactory and would not be in the future even after the immediate crisis was over. The Report of the Royal Commission on Housing of the Industrial Classes in Scotland of 1917 provided powerful if partial support to this view. It made it crystal clear that the houses provided by private

[1] Evidence taken by the Committee appointed to consider the Operation of the Rent Restriction Act, 1920. The evidence contains the most authoritative description of the house market before the Great War that I know of.

enterprise in Scotland before the war could not, on any interpretation of the term, be called satisfactory; on the contrary the standard of housing in Scotland was intolerable. The main conclusion of the Report was that, as a matter of urgent necessity, the local authorities in Scotland should be made entirely responsible for providing decent working-class houses on a scale sufficient to make good the war shortage, *and to bring the Scottish standard up to a level approximating to that already achieved in England by private enterprise before the Great War.* As it would be impracticable to charge rents in Scotland sufficiently high to cover the costs of the new houses, someone would have to fill the gap. The local authorities would not build houses if an attempt were made to push the financial burden on to them. The only alternative was the Treasury, in other words, the taxpayers of United Kingdom. The Report therefore recommended that the whole net cost of the scheme should be met by subsidies provided by the Treasury. If these recommendations were reasonable for Scotland, why should they not be adopted for ensuring sufficient supplies of new houses and for *raising the general standard* south of the border? An attractive case could be made out for this. Working-class houses were needed in large numbers all over Great Britain, but the level of building costs and interest rates would make economic, and *a fortiori* commercial, rents prohibitive. Someone would have to fill the gap between the rents that people could, or would pay, and at least the economic rents. That was just the same dilemma faced by the Commission on Scottish housing. *Ergo* the same remedy should be applied.

The first post-war housing experiment was in part an attempt to put this theory into practice. The Housing and Town Planning Act of 1919 imposed on local authorities the duty of surveying the needs of their districts for houses and making and carrying-out plans for the provision of the houses needed. The approval of the Ministry of Health was to be obtained for the plans before they were carried out. The first surveys were to be completed within three months of the passage of the Act, and later surveys were to be made whenever they seemed needed.[1] After an interval of thirty years the permissive powers given to local authorities by the Housing Act of 1890 had been made obligatory; moreover they were now to be used for general housing purposes instead of merely being available as originally intended for slum clearance. There was no suggestion

[1] *Housing and Town Planning, etc., Act, 1919.* 9 and 10 Geo. V. chap. 35. This was popularly known as the Addison Act after Dr. Addison, who had been responsible for it a President of the Local Government Board.

in the new Act that whenever possible the provision of houses should be left to private enterprise, and that local authorities, once the crisis was over, should confine their activities to slum clearance. The Act of 1890 had made it possible to open the door to the introduction of state provision of houses, and state responsibility for housing conditions. In 1919 the door was kicked wide open. In the next twenty years, up to the present war, it was to swing erratically in the winds of party politics and Treasury economy campaigns. Each time the wind shifted the interpretation of policy changed or a new experiment started.

The special interest and importance of the first experiment of the series is due to the type of subsidy offered to the local authorities to enable them to carry out their new duties, and to the rules laid down for the determination of the rents of the houses built. The principle of the subsidy was borrowed from the Report of the Royal Commission on Housing in Scotland. All losses in excess of a penny rate incurred by local authorities were to be borne by the Treasury, provided the schemes had been approved by the Ministry of Health.[1] The local authorities were guaranteed against any serious losses on their schemes and the state had taken financial responsibility for the provision of working-class houses.

The rules for fixing the rents of houses built with this subsidy reflected a belief in the temporary nature of the difficulty of the gap between the economic rents of new houses and the rents that working-class families in general could and would pay. Up to March 1927 rents were to be fixed independently of costs, that is, the economic rents were to be ignored in fixing actual rents. The level of the controlled rents of working-class houses was to be taken as a guide to rents to be charged for the new houses, but only in a very general way. On the one hand the superior amenities of the new houses were to be taken into consideration, on the other the capacity to pay rent of the particular tenants, or classes of tenants, for whom the houses were intended. In short, those tenants who could afford it would pay rather more for the new houses than the prevailing controlled rents, those who could not would be charged any rent considered suitable. It was apparently expected that the economic rents of houses built after March 1927 would be within the reach of a considerable proportion of working-class families. Wherever possible after this date, therefore, rents of subsidised houses were

---

[1] Effectively, this token contribution by the local authorities was equivalent to putting the whole financial responsibility on the Treasury as the Royal Commission had recommended in its Report. op. cit.

to equal the economic rent of houses built after this date, irrespective
of the date at which the houses in question had actually been built.
Tenants who could not afford that rent, however, would be charged
whatever seemed appropriate as before.[1] Though the local authorities were responsible for fixing rents in the first place, they had to
obtain the approval of the Ministry of Health. If the local authority
and the Ministry failed to agree the matter was referred to a tribunal.

Financially these rent rules were heroic. It was explained in the
last chapter that the problem of losses on houses built while costs
and interest rates were abnormally high would necessarily arise in
connection with any scheme for building houses to let during the
immediate post-war years. The rent rules implied that no attempt
would be made to make the tenants of subsidised houses pay rents high
enough to prevent such losses occurring, at least as far as the houses
built before 1927 were concerned. In other words, the financial loss
on the scheme would not be borne by the tenants in the form of high
rents. As under the terms of the subsidy losses would only be borne
by the local authorities to the extent of a penny rate, the Treasury
would accept financial responsibility for the greater part of any
losses which might arise for this or other reasons. There can be no
doubt that the choice of this solution in advance was consistent with
the purpose of increasing the supply of houses for those people
most in need of additional accommodation, irrespective of their
ability to pay the abnormally high rents which would be needed
to cover the costs. Local authorities would not be tempted to safeguard their investments by charging rents which would limit the
availability of the new houses to the better off. From the point of
view of the short-term difficulties of the housing situation, this
particular form of the subsidy, combined with the rent rules, clearly
had very great merits. This does not, of course, necessarily mean that
the particular limit set on the losses of local authorities was the right
one.

The decison that the Treasury, not the local authority, should
carry all residual losses on housing schemes, was important as a
contribution to long-period policy besides being intended to help
solve the problems of the emergency. After all it had been suggested
by the Royal Commission on Scottish Housing as part of a long-
period policy. It has been explained that both before and after

---

[1] i.e. The rents of houses built before March, 1927, were to be fixed at a level which
would cover costs of management and the costs of interest, depreciation and maintenance on what would have been the capital cost of the houses if they had been built after
that date. *Housing and Town Planning Act, etc.*, 1919. op. cit. These rent rules were worked
out in the *Local Authority (Assisted Housing Schemes) Regulations, 1919*.

March 1927 the local authorities were to take into account *inter alia* the class of tenant for whom the houses were intended in fixing rents. If the local authorities were to carry out the duties imposed on them by the Act, by making adequate provision for the supply of working-class houses, they would have to provide houses for the poor as well as for the well-off. Possibly at some stage they would find that the only families for whom it was necessary to provide houses were the poorest in their areas. This would naturally involve charging lower rents to the poorer families at least. The losses on the housing schemes would mount.

If the local authorities had to make good these losses out of the rates they would naturally fight shy of building houses for these poorer groups. Moreover in some areas the burden entailed might be much heavier than others. Inadequate housing is not evenly distributed about the country. Frequently, if not always, those areas where the need for better houses is relatively greatest, the ability to pay anything approaching the economic rent on a decent house is relatively least and the need for subsidies greatest. The financial strength of local authorities, the ability to provide subsidies out of the rates, is also frequently inversely proportionate to need.[1] If the principle of using a subsidy to increase the supply of working-class houses and to improve the general standard of housing is accepted, it is only natural to choose a type of subsidy which will provide help where it is most urgently needed. The provisions of the subsidy of the Housing and Town Planning Act met these needs in a rather rough and ready way. The magnitude of losses incurred on their housing schemes by the various local authorities would determine the amount of subsidy received from the Treasury. As the losses incurred by each authority would mainly be due to the combination of two factors, the numbers of houses required and the extent to which tenants were unable to pay economic rents, it was not unreasonable to assume that the size of the losses would indicate the amount of assistance needed.

It is, of course, easy to criticise the choice of this particular criterion of need for assistance. It made, for example, no distinction between losses which arose from inefficiency or extravagance on the part of local authorities, and genuine losses due to the inability of tenants to pay economic rents. It removed all the incentive to local authorities

[1] Two studies of the rate problems of local authorities have been published during the present war, viz., *Standards of Local Expenditure* by J. R. Hicks and U. K. Hicks, and *The Problem of Valuation for Rating*, by J. R. Hicks, U. K. Hicks and C. E. V. Leses. Publ. as *Occasional Papers* for the National Institute of Economic and Social Research, Cambridge University Press.

to search for the most economical methods of building and managing their housing estates. Only if the Ministry of Health exercised sufficient control to prevent inefficiency and extravagance and to enforce economies, could this weakness be entirely eradicated. The criterion, too, took no accurate account of the differing abilities of local authorities to provide subsidies out of rates. This, however, is a criticism of a rather different type for it is based on the assumption that as a matter of principle the provision of adequate housing should be at least partially a local burden. This is of course an open question about which people will argue indefinitely. It will be as well to postpone consideration of it.

These criticisms do not touch, however, the most important principle embodied in the subsidy, the principle that subsidies should be progressive with need. The importance of this can perhaps be most easily shown by analogy with the principles of taxation generally accepted in Great Britain, for there has been much less discussion of the principles on which subsidies should be given than of the principles on which money should be taken away by the Government. A great deal of thought and effort has been devoted in this country to creating a progressive tax system under which it is intended that the heaviest taxes should be borne by those who can most easily pay them. The financial burden increases under this system progressively with apparent ability to pay. However imperfectly the system may work in practice, that is the accepted intention; it is argued that this minimises the inconvenience and distress caused by transferring a given sum of money from the taxpayers as a whole to the Government. The parallel argument in the case of subsidies is as follows : the benefits derived from giving away a certain amount of money as a subsidy will be maximised if it is distributed on a scale progressive with need for help. In short, a subsidy will be more useful if it is concentrated on those who need help most than if it is given to all and sundry irrespective of needs. The significance of the incorporation of this principle in the 1919 housing subsidy arises from the fact that it had not formerly been the accepted basis of subsidies to local authorities. It was first generally accepted in the Local Government Act of 1929. It is one of the ironies of government in this country that by that time the principle had been abandoned as far as housing was concerned; it has not since been re-introduced as a principle of general housing policy.

The fundamentally progressive nature of the 1919 subsidy has received much less publicity than the question of financial control of the activities of local authorities claiming the subsidy. Superficially at least, the scheme appeared to divorce financial responsibility from administrative responsibility. Local authorities decided the number of houses they would build, what rents they would charge and to what people they should be let. The Treasury, to all intents and purposes, footed the bill. It is this reversal of the accepted principles of financial relations between the Treasury and the local authorities that has received most attention from critics. The question of whether this was the real reason why the scheme worked so badly in practice that it was abandoned, has hardly ever been discussed. This is important because in theory at least the Ministry of Health, and through it the Treasury, had been given powers, which could have been used, to control the activities of local authorities by administrative action.

It has already been pointed out that not only did each local authority have to obtain the approval of the Ministry of Health for the plans of the houses it wanted to build, but it had to obtain approval for the rents at which the houses were ultimately let. This meant in fact that the Ministry of Health could hold up plans, and with a little imagination and determination it could have forced local authorities to conform to a reasonable time-table for actual building. Its power to disallow the contracts themselves could have been used to disallow not only extravagant building but contracts let at high prices. In fact, as the Ministry of Health was jointly responsible with the Treasury for drawing up the conditions on which the subsidy was available, a definite stop could have been put to the cost at which houses could be built and qualify for the subsidy, and local authorities obliged to queue up and wait their turn for materials and labour. Individually the local authorities were powerless to achieve any sort of controlled or orderly demand for building resources. Each had a duty to perform. Each needed building resources from what to a considerable extent was a national market. If one moderated its claims, it would not benefit, but another authority would. If the central departments concerned had chosen to take broad administrative control of the housing activities of the authorities, it might have been just possible for them to do so. If they did not, then in practice it would work out that he who paid the piper did not call the tune. The general criticism can be justified not of the actual Act, nor of the type of subsidy, but of the way that administrative provisions were made to carry it out.

The Housing and Town Planning Act, and its subsidy, formed the keystone of the policy of the first experiment. It was reinforced under the Housing (Additional Powers) Act, 1919, by a small lump sum subsidy per house[1] provided for houses built by private enterprise which conformed to certain conditions as to size. The subsidy was intended to help the small man who might be in a position to buy a new house if suitably assisted. Steps were also taken to maintain the control of rents of old houses. The original 1915 Act controlling rents was replaced in 1920 by a new Act which *inter alia* prolonged control until 1923. The field of control was also extended in two stages so that by the Act of 1920 houses built before the summer of 1919 with rateable values up to £105 in London, £90 in Scotland, and £78 elsewhere were included. Certain maximum increases in rent had been made possible. The general effect was to permit by July 1921 an increase of 15 per cent. of the net rents of all controlled houses *plus* an increase of 25 per cent. if the landlord was responsible for all repairs *plus* an increase corresponding to the increases in the rates payable on each house since August 3rd, 1914.[2]

By comparison with the efforts made to make it financially possible for local authorities and private individuals to have houses built, practically nothing was done to make it physically possible. The Housing (Additional Powers) Act of 1919,[3] it is true, gave local authorities power to stop private building in their areas which interfered with the supplies of materials and labour available for building schemes, but it appears that there was practically no use made of this. A number of schemes were also discussed for increasing the supply of skilled building labour by modifying apprenticeship regulations. As, however, only a small measure of agreement had been reached by the time housing policy was fundamentally altered in the summer of 1921, the projects were dropped.[4]

The death sentence of the policy embodied in the Housing and Town Planning Act was pronounced in July, 1921. It was decided that building houses with the subsidy was too expensive and that the total number to be completed under it should be limited to about 170,000. The number was only a little in excess of that of the houses for which contracts had already been agreed. Officially it was considered that completion of these houses would occupy the building industry for another year. In the meantime, in that all too familiar

---

[1] 9 & 10 Geo. V. Chap. 99. Section 1 & 2.

[2] *Increase of Rent and Mortgage Interest (Restrictions) Act, 1919*, and ditto, 1920. For a more detailed account of the provisions of the Acts see the pamphlet issued by the Ministry of Health in 1920. *Summary of the Principal Provisions of the Increases of Rent and Mortgage Restrictions Act, 1920.* It was also made possible for the interest on mortgages to be raised by 1 per cent. subject to a maximum rate of 6½ per cent.

[3] Sect. 5 (1).

[4] See the *Report of the Departmental Committee on the High Cost of Building Working-class Dwellings*, Cmd. 1447, 1921, pp. 32 & 33, and the *Ministry of Labour Gazette, 1921*, p. 394.

terminology, " It was the intention of the Government to keep the whole housing situation closely under review."[1]   In reaching the decision without providing for any modified or new subsidy, the Government disregarded the spirit of the recommendation, if not the letter, of the Report of the Departmental Committee on the High Cost of Working-class Dwellings. That Committee had suggested a large number of improvements in the administration of the 1919 scheme. The majority report suggested that insofar as state financial aid should be necessary in the future, the local authorities should bear a *percentage* of the losses incurred in order to establish community of financial interest between them and the state. It was suggested, however, that the principle of a progressive subsidy should be maintained by varying the percentage of loss to be carried by local authorities to the circumstances of each authority.[2]

No new policy was inaugurated until the spring of 1923. By that time building by local authorities had dwindled to an insignificant level as the permitted number of subsidised houses was completed, nor had plans been made for the future. During these two years no serious attempts at all appear to have been made to deal with the outstanding problems of building costs and supplies of skilled labour. The alarm engendered by the fact that the Treasury had nearly burnt its fingers had turned into inertia, doubtless to the relief of those who were root and branch opposed to State intervention. It was a dismal story.

II.   THE 1919 SUBSIDIES IN PRACTICE

The practical effect of the subsidies provided under the 1919 Housing Acts, is easily described. In total 213,821 houses were built with them; the local authorities contributed 170,090 and public utility societies 4,545 under the main subsidy and private enterprise 39,186 under the lump sum subsidy of the Additional Powers Act. All of these except for about 15,000 of the local authority houses were completed before the end of March, 1923, that is, before the second experiment started. Altogether between the Armistice and this date about 252,000 houses were built, including approximately 54,000, built by Private Enterprise without any subsidy. It will be seen from Table II that this grand total of new houses were equivalent

---

[1] *Ministry of Labour Gazette, 1921,* p. 394.

[2] Report, 1921 Cmd. 1447. op. cit. pp. 56 & 57. The main reservation by one member, pp. 61 et seq., recommended that the existing subsidy should be continued, but that greater central control should be exercised and that attempts should be made *inter alia* to control the price of building materials.

to just under half the estimated shortage of houses at the Armistice, or to just over half the requirements for the current increases in the numbers of families between the Armistice and March, 1923. The total outstanding shortage of houses was worse at the end than at the beginning !

TABLE II.—The results of the First Experiment (England and Wales) 1919 to March 1923.*

Thousands.

(A)	Additional Houses required 1919/March 1923.	
	(1) To provide for shortage at 1.1.19	610
	(2) To provide for increase in number of families 1.1.19 to 31.3.23 ..	464
	Total Requirements	1,074
(B)	Additional Houses built 1919/March 1923.	
	(1) With subsidies :	
	by local authorities	154·5
	by private enterprise	43·7
	(2) Without subsidies :	
	by private enterprise	53·8
	Total Additional Houses	252·0
	Shortage of Houses outstanding March 1923	822·0
	(i.e. A minus B)	

* For further details and explanations see Statistical Appendix, pp. 269–272.

This unsatisfactory result cannot, however, be regarded as a proof of the ineffectiveness of the subsidy scheme, as the total number of houses to be built with the main subsidy had been suddenly limited in the summer of 1921 on grounds of economy. Actually the local authorities had started off making plans and even building with praiseworthy speed. By the end of March, 1920, eight months after the original Act had been passed, the local authorities had drawn up, and the Ministry of Health had approved, plans for 161,837 houses.[1] According to the incomplete survey of immediate requirements made by local authorities, 800,000 would have to be provided ultimately:[2] the first instalment was then substantial. Still more remarkable in just over a year and a half of the passing of the Act, 17,597 houses had been completed by local authorities and public utility societies. This was a far more rapid start than that made under the Chamberlain Subsidy of 1923.[3] By the summer of 1921 when the decision to shut down the scheme was reached, local authorities were building at the rate equivalent to 70,000 houses a year, and in

[1] In addition plans for 4,420 houses to be built by Public Utility Societies had been approved. *Ministry of Health Annual Report, 1919/20.* Part II, p. 14.
[2] *Ministry of Health. Annual Report, 1919/20.* Part II, p. 12.
[3] See Statistical Appendix Table 2.

the year ending in September, 1922, they completed 85,976 houses. In the far more favourable building conditions after 1925 the volume of building by local authorities was consistently below this level, except during the year preceding the first cut in the Wheatley and Chamberlain subsidies of the second experiment in October, 1927, and the last year and a half before the present war. Even allowing for the fact that the Ministry of Health had prepared the ground before the Housing and Town Planning Act was passed in 1919 by pamphlets, the circulation of model building plans, etc., this must be regarded as a remarakable achievement.

A similar degree of willingness to carry out the spirit of the Act was displayed with regard to rents. Although the average rent, excluding rates, was between 9/– and 10/– a week, there was a wide range of variation. In some cases, chiefly in rural areas, rents were below 5/–, in others, chiefly in the London area they were over 11/– and 12/–; in between a considerable proportion of the houses in urban areas must have been let at rents between 7/– and 9/– a week.[1] These do not compare unfavourably, in view of the high level of wages in 1921, with the rents of controlled houses which were not intended to change. After 1921, controlled rents, excluding rates, in urban areas probably averaged between 5/6 and 6/–, between 8/– and 9/– in the London area and between 4/6 and 5/– in rural areas. There is less information about the *range* of controlled rents, but the upper limits were certainly above 10/–.[2]

There can be little doubt that the elasticity of the subsidy encouraged this rent policy. Comparison with the difficulties over rents during the second experiment will make this clear, but it may be worth illustrating the financial effects of the subsidy. In Manchester, for example, the yield of a penny rate was £26,213 in the year 1924/5, in Rochdale on the other hand the yield was only £2,252. The Treasury contribution to the housing scheme equalled

---

[1] *Ministry of Health Annual Report, 1920/21*, p. 112, and the *First Report of the Rent Tribunal appointed under Article VII (4) of the Local Authorities (Assisted Housing Schemes) Regulations, 1919*. List of rents settled by the Tribunal. Among the information contained in the Report are lists of the weekly rates payable on houses whose rents were under arbitration. The rates frequently were well above 4/– or 5/– for houses with rateable values up to £13. By 1925, local authorities were trying to lower the rents of these houses in conformity with the fall in wages. The Ministry of Health and guardians of the Treasury's interests in many cases tried to prevent this. (See 2nd Report of the Tribunal.)

[2] The average levels of controlled rents were estimated for the Ridley Committee on the Rent Restrictions Acts, 1937, see p. 17 of the Report, Cmd., 5621. The range of working-class gross rents before the Great War is indicated in the Board of Trade Inquiry of 1912 into the Cost of Living in towns (see p. 119 below), and calculations with regard to permitted increases in rents and rates on the basis of the data of that enquiry justifies the statement above.

C

£131,134 and £29,669 respectively.[1] If instead the Treasury contribution had been on the conventional basis of a uniform proportion of the losses, say 66·6 per cent., the increased burden for the local authorities would have been equivalent to an additional 1·0 pence on the rates in Manchester, and in Rochdale an additional 3·7 pence. The incentive to charge higher rents, or limit the scale of the housing schemes, would obviously have been much greater in the latter than in the former.

The reason for abandoning the scheme was not that it was not achieving its purpose in getting working-class houses built and let at rents corresponding to current incomes. On the contrary it was being rather too successful and therefore becoming too costly.[2] If homes for heroes could only be provided in this way then the heroes would have to go without. This decision has given rise to most unfortunate misunderstanding of the effects of the particular type of subsidy on which the scheme was based. It has been frequently assumed that as the scheme was abandoned for good on grounds of expense, the type of subsidy on which it was based must always and inevitably produce excessive increases in building costs. The special merits of the subsidy which have already been described have apparently been sacrificed forever without hesitation. As it is more than probable that the housing situation after the present war will in some respects resemble that following the last war, it is worth trying to discover whether this is justifiable. It is one of the minor ironies of the

---

[1] Calculated from *Local Taxation Returns, Part II*. Tables of income and expenditure of rate fund services of County Boroughs. In considering differences in expenditure in terms of rates in the £, it must be remembered that methods of assessing rateable values of property differ in different boroughs and this affects the yield of rates in some cases.

[2] The annual cost to the Treasury of the scheme increased from £20·5 thousand in 1919/20 to a maximum of £7,951·6 thousand in 1924/5. The increase of cost was mainly due, of course, to the inclusion of all the houses built with the subsidy in the latter year instead of only the first few; it was due, however, to some extent, to the reduction in rents made after the fall in wages (see note 1, page 25 above). The average annual cost to the Treasury from the time building with the subsidy came to an end in 1924/5 to 1938/9 was £6796·1 thousand—equivalent to about £40 per house per year. (*Ministry of Health Annual Report, 1938/9*, Appendix XVIII, gives complete statistics of the Treasury subsidies.) The Ministry of Health gave details of the rents of, and losses on, these houses in its report for 1930/31, p. 112, *et seq.* In this year the total average loss per house was £44, of which the Treasury contributed £38 15/– and local authorities £5 5/–. Average rents had fallen from £25 a year in 1924 to £24 in 1930/31. The high local authority burden per house was due, of course, to the fact that they were obliged to contribute the equivalent of a penny rate before the Treasury paid anything, irrespective of the numbers of houses; if the scheme had been continued, if, for example, three times as many houses had been built, the local authority contribution per house would have been divided by three and reduced to £1 15/–. It is important to bear in mind that the interest on the capital borrowed for building these houses was 6·56 per cent., including sinking fund payments of 0·45 per cent. According to the Ministry of Health Report only a quarter of the capital had been borrowed on short term, and only this had been converted to rates of 5 per cent. to 5½ per cent. by 1930/31.

CHART I.—Tender prices, and subsidised building, and Index numbers of building material prices and wage rates, 1919–1923.*

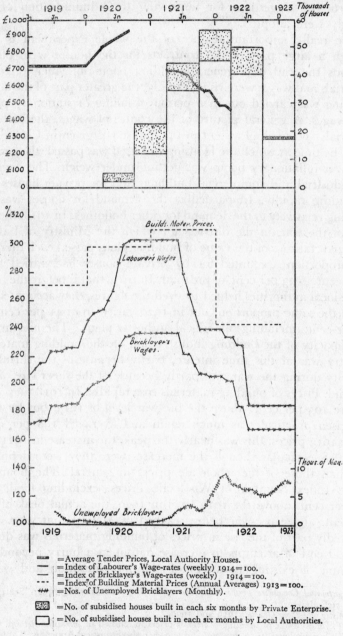

= Average Tender Prices, Local Authority Houses.
= Index of Labourer's Wage-rates (weekly) 1914 = 100.
= Index of Bricklayer's Wage-rates (weekly) 1914 = 100.
= Index of Building Material Prices (Annual Averages) 1913 = 100.
= Nos. of Unemployed Bricklayers (Monthly).

= No. of subsidised houses built in each six months by Private Enterprise.
= No. of subsidised houses built in each six months by Local Authorities.

* See Statistical Appendix, Tables 4A and 4B.

history of housing policy that although the whole question was thoroughly investigated by a Committee in 1921,[1] none of the constructive suggestions for improving the administration of the subsidy were adopted.

The really important feature of the whole experiment is that though a large part of the contracts for the houses were placed towards the end of a general building boom in which prices of materials and wages were rising rapidly, the greater part of the actual building was carried out in a period of falling or stationary prices and wages. A general picture of the course of wages, the prices of materials and unemployment in the industry is given in Chart 1.

At the time at which the Housing Act itself was passed, the general post-war inflationary boom was getting under weigh. The demand for industrial and commercial buildings and for private houses was expanding rapidly. In particular the demand for houses was expanding relatively to the demand for other buildings. In 1918, the last year of the war, in the districts for which the Ministry of Labour collected statistics of the value of building plans passed each quarter, the proportion accounted for by private houses had varied from 8 per cent. to 23 per cent. of the total. In 1919, that is before the plans of the local authorities helped to swell the figures, they accounted for much the same proportion, but in 1920 varied from 41 per cent. to 52 per cent., including some local authority plans.[2] The pressure on the capacity of the building industry and on the building materials industry was at this time intense, partly because of the shrinkage capacity during the war and partly because of the sheer size of the demand. Prices of building materials rose rapidly. In 1918 they were a mere 105 per cent. above the pre-war level of 1913, but by 1920 had risen practically as much again and averaged 198 per cent. above 1913 prices; this was nearly the peak, the increase in 1921 was small.[3] Spectacular though the increases were they were definitely less than those of the wholesale prices in general. The Board of Trade Index Number of Wholesale Prices, excluding food, was 228 per cent. above the 1913 level in 1920, the actual peak of 258 per cent. above pre-war being reached in May of that year. Undoubtedly part of the rise in prices of building materials was due to the real cost of attempts to increase output in a hurry beyond the optimum of existing resources of plant, organisation and skilled

---

[1] *Departmental Committee on the High Cost of Working-class Dwellings, 1921.* See pp. 22 et seq. etc., above.

[2] *Ministry of Labour Gazette,* 1919 and 1920.

[3] G. T. Jones' index of building materials prices, published in *Increasing Returns.* Cambridge University Press, 1933, pp. 268 and 269. See also Statistical Appendix, Table 4c.

labour. Equally certainly, however, the pressure of demand created a sellers' market for both materials and labour; it would be totally contrary to all experience if the resulting prices and wages had not been favourable to producers.

Wages in the actual building industry also rose rapidly after the Armistice, making up for the relative lack of increase during the war years. Between January 1919 and the end of the year labourers' wages per week had increased from 107 per cent. above 1914 levels to 146 per cent. above; in the autumn of 1920 they reached their peak, 203 per cent. above pre-war for a shorter week. Increases in wages of skilled men were considerable, but not quite so rapid; the comparable figures for bricklayers being 72 per cent., 97 per cent., and 137 per cent.[1] Labour costs of building increased still more than wages. Not only was the working week reduced, but the productivity of labour was less than before pre-war, probably by between 20 and 50 per cent.[2]

Actual building costs probably rose still more than material prices and wage rates. There were constant delays due to the scarcity of materials and skilled labour, and to the dislocation of transport. The penalty of trying to produce beyond the capacity of the industry, of spreading resources too thinly over too large a field, is inevitably waste and high costs. There were still other factors tending to increase costs by more than the increases in costs of labour and materials. The building contractors too, like building labour and the owners and producers of materials, were in a position to obtain specially favourable terms on contracts. This was undoubtedly the case as far as contracts for local authority building schemes were concerned. The Committee on the High Cost of Working-class Houses explained in 1921 that especially favourable contract terms had been found necessary to induce contractors to take up the local authorities' housing schemes. This fact provides a definite indication that contractors were finding ordinary private building highly remunerative.[3]

It was in these circumstances that the first group of local authority contracts under the subsidy scheme were placed and the first houses

---

[1] See Statistical Appendix, Table 4A. Wages of the other skilled trades moved in a way similar to those of bricklayers. The figures quoted relate to the summer working week; this was reduced to 44 hours in May, 1920, from an average summer working week of 50 hours in 1914.

[2] *Report of the Departmental Committee on the High Cost of Working-class Houses, 1921.* Cmd. 1447, p. 31. According to C. T. Jones' *Increasing Returns*, op. cit. p. 92, the records of a large London building firm showed that whereas between 1895 and 1915 a bricklayer laid on the average 60 bricks per hour, in 1920 he averaged only 44 and from 1921–1924 only 36!

[3] *Report of the Departmental Committee.* op. cit., pp. 44 and 45.

started. The average price to be paid for each house reflected the optimism of the contractors in the immediate future of the building industry as much as the level of current costs. By the end of April, 1921, contracts had been placed for 160,000 houses at an average all-in cost of about £1,000. The actual building contract prices of houses had increased from about £740 in the summer of 1919 to about £930 in the autumn of 1920; after that they had started to decline.[1] The competition between local authorities and private persons for the services of building contractors no doubt helped to bring about this situation, for it must be remembered that there was no effective form of rationing or priorities. It seemed probable, moreover, that if expectations current about the future of the building activity had been fulfilled the competitive pressure of the local authority demands would have pushed prices and wages still higher. Building contractors seemed to expect this, for they generally insisted on being safeguarded by the terms of their contracts, against increases in prices of materials and in wages. Not only were the local authority programmes as such competing with each other for the limited resources available, but individual contractors working for the same authority might, in badly organised areas, have competed against each other. The additional pressure on the resources of the industry might also have increased real costs of production.

The general post-war boom broke with violence in the summer of 1920. World prices and trade collapsed. The demand for new buildings, industrial, commercial and private fell in sympathy. Building projects already planned were abandoned.[2] Unemployment in the building industry increased, slowly at first and then rapidly. The building boom had started as part of the general post-war boom. As the chart shows the main increases in wages and decreases in unemployment in the building industry, as well as the main increases in prices of building materials, had taken place during the general boom in trade, before the local authorities had become actual purchasers of building resources on a large scale. The declines took place in sympathy with the collapse of trade in general, despite the fact that the local authorities had really started building early in 1921. Although 94,000 houses had been begun by March, 1921, and 34,000 had been completed in the following six months, the numbers and percentages of building workers unemployed increased steadily through the summer. Worse was to come, month for month unemployment was higher throughout the

---

[1] Ibid. pp. 8 and 44.
[2] *Ministry of Labour Gazette, 1923*, p. 85.

year October 1921 to September 1922 than in the previous year. These were the months in which the local authority building reached its peak, and in all of 85,000 houses were built of which at least half were built entirely during that time. It was only after the local authority programmes were practically completed by the summer of 1923 that unemployment began to fall, and it was not until 1925 that anything approaching another boom occurred. As far as comparable figures are available, it appears that the same thing happened in the building material industries.

Prices of building materials and wages exhibited similar features. In nearly all cases prices ceased to rise after 1920; in 1921 they were either stationary, or falling, and declines continued, or started, in 1922, reaching bottom in 1923. After 1923 prices of building materials in general tended to be stationary or slightly rising.[1] In the case of wages, the peak was reached in the autumn of 1920; decline set in in the early summer of 1921; the bottom was reached in 1922. Even such information as is available on the contract prices of houses for which local authorities let contracts conforms to this general pattern. The main decrease took place while the local authority building was at its maximum and bottom reached by the time the experiment was drawing to a close in March 1922, at a figure £436 per house, a contract price similar to that prevailing in the first years of the second experiment.[2]

The behaviour of all the main elements in building costs did not in fact support the idea that in practice the housing schemes of the local authorities had a markedly inflationary effect. By the time they had really got going they did not involve any major strain on the capacity of the industry. The experiment of the main 1919 subsidy turned out to be *inter alia* a partially successful and entirely un-expected experiment in using public investment to stave off depression.[3]   In fact though the housing schemes of the local

[1] Details of prices for individual building materials are given in G. T. Jones' *Increasing Returns*. op. cit.

[2] See Chart I and Statistical Appendix Tables 4A and B and C. As the great bulk of the contracts had been let before the prices and wages, etc., had fallen substantially, the ultimate cut of the scheme was determined more by the conditions at the time contracts were made than the conditions prevailing when they were completed. The local authorities did not, it seems, succeed to a major extent in securing downward revisions of the contracts already placed.

[3] During the year 1919/20 to 1922/3 capital expenditure on houses by the local authorities amounted to 49 per cent. of their total capital expenditure. Increases in expenditure on houses accounted for 63 per cent. of the increase in their total capital expenditure between 1919/20 and 1920/21, and for 81 per cent. of the increase between 1920/21 and 1921/22. Similarly the decline in expenditure on houses between 1921/22 and 1922/23 accounted for the greater part of the total decline, i.e. 92 per cent. These calculations are based on the figures given in Tables 5, 27, and 30 in *Public Investment and the Trade Cycle*, by Bretherton, Burchardt & Rutherford, Oxford University Press, 1940.

authorities helped to maintain employment in the building industries, the resulting demand for labour and materials was insufficient to compensate for the collapse of private building. This cannot be regarded as in any way surprising; the maximum rate of building achieved by the local authorities, 85,000 houses a year, required only about 15 per cent. of the total number of skilled men in the building crafts including 32 per cent. of the bricklayers, and about 50 per cent. of the output of bricks in 1921.[1] Although these actual figures must be regarded as only approximations, there is no reason to doubt the validity of the general conclusion to be drawn from them; the local authority housing schemes were not the main source of demand for building resources. This conclusion is entirely consistent, of course, with the changes in prices and unemployment described.

It is only possible to conclude that the course of building costs and employment was on the whole determined by the private or industrial demand, rather than by the demand of local authorities, for building resources in the four years following the Armistice. The conclusion needs careful interpretation. It certainly does not justify the assumption that housing schemes financed by subsidies of the 1919 type could always be carried out with such relative impunity. All the conclusion shows is that disastrous results may be avoided if such schemes are carried out when there is an adequate supply of building resources. If after the last war the pressure of the private demand for building resources had continued at the 1920 height, successful efforts by local authorities to obtain control of a sufficient quantity of building resources to carry out their schemes must have had the effect of driving prices up. The authorities' schemes probably would not have absorbed even half of the resources of the industry, but they would have been the proverbial last straw. On the other hand if the local authorities had not been provided with highly elastic financial resources, the danger of price increases would obviously have been less, but the chance of the schemes being carried out would also have been very much less. Regarded from this angle the 1919 subsidy was a financial substitute for administrative control of the use of building resources—consequently the high contract prices of 1920.

The effectiveness of the subsidy as a means of getting houses built,

---

[1] These estimates are based on the calculations in the *Report on the Present Position of the Building Industry with regard to carrying out the Full Housing Programme*, Cmd. 2104, 1925, and on the estimates of the capacity of the building industry in 1921, and the *Report on the High Cost of Building*, etc. op. cit.

or at least started, despite high and rising costs was indisputable. In considering this point it must be remembered that the great idea was to build working-class houses. If this pressed the industry beyond capacity and created a sellers' market, the local authorities, unaided by administrative control of the market, would only obtain sufficient resources to build large numbers of houses by outbidding the other competitors in the market. Competitive bidding is the only automatic machinery for distributing scarce resources, but there is probably little need to emphasize this point in the middle of a world war. The whole situation, the high contract prices and the pandering to contractors cannot be taken as damning the peculiar type of subsidy, though perhaps it can be used to damn the whole idea of building at that time. Nor must it be forgotten that the main increases in prices and wages had taken place by 1920 before the local authorities had started building on a large scale; building materials are not normally bought a long time in advance of use, and labour never can be. The local authority schemes cannot be saddled with the responsibility for the increases in wages, and prices which took place before they actually started building on a serious scale.[1] They were only partially responsible for the prices of completed houses envisaged in the contracts they placed.

If local authorities had had to face carrying the costs of the schemes on the rates it is improbable that they would have planned to build on an adequate scale. We all know that they are among the most parsimonious bodies if their ratepayers may have to foot a bill. The truth is that the country was faced with the dilemma of having large numbers of working-class houses built at immense expense or having very few houses of this type built and saving the public purse. Public opinion, local and national, wanted the houses. The Government's promises to provide homes for heroes and the Ministry of Health's pressure on the local authorities to carry out the Government's wishes reflected this decision. Without control of the market, expense was therefore inevitable. The situation could only be eased as building capacity increased, and both the real costs of production and the strength of the sellers' position declined. The Committee already quoted took a gloomy view of the extent to which, under

[1] It would, in fact, be very difficult to apportion responsibility for increase in building costs between the local authorities working with the main Addison subsidy and private builders working with the lump sum subsidy of the Additional Powers Act. The former completed 3,542 houses by September, 1920, and a total of 16,201 by March, 1921, the latter 2,585 and 13,063 respectively. It was only in the six months up to September, 1921, that local authorities really outstripped subsidised private enterprise, and, of course, by this time prices and wages were well on the way down.

existing contracts, such decreases in costs would be realised in diminished cost of building. They pointed out that neither contractors nor local authorities had any real incentive to take the greatest possible advantage of any favourable turn in the situation.[1]

Before going on to the second experiment there is another aspect of the 1919 subsidy to consider. Did the peculiar type of subsidy, its extreme elasticity, lead to extravagance and inefficiency on the part of local authorities? Was the control exercised by the Ministry of Health a sufficient safeguard? Was it an adequate alternative to a financial incentive to economy such as that had been as provided by a subsidy based on a given proportion of losses incurred? It is impossible to make an independent investigation twenty years after the event, but as the Committee of 1921 on the High Cost of Building Working-class Dwellings went into the question with some care, this does not matter much.

It seems that the Ministry of Health were at least morally responsible for the use of contracts which gave contractors no incentive for economy. The model contracts drawn up by the Ministry included clauses to safeguard contractors against any risks of increase in costs of material or labour. While local authorities might have been unwilling to adopt these clauses, if they themselves had not been in turn safeguarded against loss by the subsidy, it was argued at the time that it was impossible to place contracts except on these terms. This particular loophole for extravagance seems therefore to be part of the basic problem of lack of control of the market. It seems clear, however, from the Report that the Ministry of Health failed to exercise sufficient control over the types of houses built and the lay-out of estates. The Report pointed out that the Ministry had not prevented the local authorities selecting more elaborate models and more expensive lay-outs than seemed necessary. It seems too that insufficient guidance was given on other points, such as costs, possible economies in materials, etc., or in planning the placing of contracts in some relation to local building resources. The local authorities on the other hand, were only too apt to make use of the freedom from effective control to select the expensive type of plans and layouts. Nor did they in general display any obvious interest in trying to secure economy in building either by insisting on the use of the cheaper type of materials, or by general supervision of their contracts to secure cost reductions. The Committee absolved the local authorities of charges of spectacular

[1] *Report of the Departmental Committee on the High Cost of Working-class Houses, 1921.* op. cit. pp. 56–8.

extravagance or gross inefficiency.[1] It seems that apart from the basic problem of lack of control of the market, the Ministry of Health did not display sufficient determination or imagination in exercising its powers in circumstances in which the type of subsidy made central control particularly necessary. It seems reasonably certain, however, that the lack of financial incentives to economy on the part of local authorities raised new and difficult problems of administration.

The lessons of the first post-war experiment in state intervention to increase the supply of houses will stand out more sharply when the results of the second experiment have been discussed. It will be useful to sum up provisionally the main conclusions which may be relevant to housing problems in the future. First, the 1919 scheme main subsidy, by relieving local authorities of practically all financial responsibility for their housing schemes, created conditions financially highly favourable to a policy of providing houses to let at rents within the reach of those families most in need of houses. The progressive character of the subsidy was probably particularly useful in this connection. At the same time the need for providing a substitute for the financial incentive to economy by means of a purely administrative control of the activities of local authorities, created administrative problems which were not solved during the life of the experiment. The experience of the four years after the Armistice brought to the forefront the difficulty of evolving a subsidy scheme, compatible with administrative efficiency, which would overcome the difficulties of building during periods of uncertainty about costs and interest rates, and would also be of a progressive character. From the point of view of the effects of subsidies on building costs, the experiment demonstrated an obvious but frequently forgotten principle. If a given number of houses are wanted they can only be obtained either by paying the market price, determined by supply and demand, or by the introduction of an efficient administrative control of the use of resources. If the building industry is fully occupied in satisfying private demand, the resources needed by local authorities to build additional houses can be obtained with the aid of a highly elastic subsidy, but at high prices. A subsidy is, in these circumstances, an expensive and clumsy substitute for deliberate control of the use of building resources. It is important that this obvious principle should not be forgotten again at the end of the present war.

[1] *Report of the Departmental Committee on the High Cost of Working-class Houses, 1921.* op. cit., particularly Part VII of the Majority Report. There were, of course, a number of instances both of extravagance and serious inefficiency, but it must be remembered that the local authorities were inexperienced and in a hurry.

Chapter III

THE SECOND EXPERIMENT
1923–1933/4—POLICY

THE second experiment was inaugurated in July, 1923, by the Conservative Government which came into office in 1922. The new policy was contained in Neville Chamberlain's Housing Act. The previous experiment had ended with the panic-stricken rejection of the financial innovations of the original Act of 1919. The new one naturally conformed to the principles of sound conservative finance. A new subsidy to be paid by the Treasury was fixed at a maximum of £6 a house a year for twenty years. It was to be available for any house built by either private enterprise or the local authorities, which satisfied certain conditions. No subsidy from the rates at all was required. Houses would be eligible for the subsidy if they were up to, or above, a defined minimum standard of size, equipment, etc., but did not exceed an over-riding maximum size. No limitations whatever were put on the use of the houses; they could be let at any rent or sold at any price. The subsidy was to be strictly temporary; it would only be available for houses built by October 1st, 1925.[1]

There were also provisions intended to encourage owner-occupation. Local authorities were given powers to advance money to people wanting to buy new houses but unable to provide the initial payment down needed to obtain advances from the building societies; they could help further by guaranteeing payments to be made to building societies by purchasers. Advances for landlords undertaking repairs and reconstruction of houses was also made possible.[2] In short, local authorities could help finance improvements and increases in the supply of houses made by private enterprise as well as building themselves.

Obviously, Chamberlain's Act had the great merit of simplicity. Any person and any organisation, practically speaking, could build a house of the appropriate size within the two years after it came into force and claim the subsidy. At the end of two years (all being

[1] *Housing, etc., Act, 1923.* 13 & 14, Geo. V. Chap. 24. Section 1 & 2. The local authorities could pay out the subsidy as a lump sum recovering it from the annual payments to be made by the Treasury. The capital value of the subsidy reckoned at 5 per cent. interest was £75, and could be given as a lump sum to private builders.
[2] Ibid. Sect. 5. Use of these powers was urged on the local authorities. (Ministry of Health Circulars, 555 and 571, 1925.)

well), it was assumed that no more subsidies would be needed and houses would be built as they had been before the Great War, by the unaided efforts of private enterprise. The whole policy was based on the hypothesis, for which there was no supporting evidence at all, that the housing crisis would be over and done with quickly. It was assumed that only remedies of an emergency type were needed. Consistently with this attitude, a deliberate attempt was made to prevent the permanent establishment of the local authorities as suppliers of working-class houses in general. The main Act of 1919 had opened the door for the treatment of the provision of working-class houses as a sort of social service. The door was now closed as far as possible by a clause that only allowed local authorities to build houses themselves *if they succeeded in convincing the Minister of Health that it would be better if they did so, than if they left it to private enterprise.*[1] This was the price of relieving the local authorities from the necessity of making any contribution at all from the rates. The Act was really an Act to encourage private enterprise to build small houses either for sale or for letting. The local authorities were to be merely " also rans." If the supporters of Chamberlain had their way, the provision of working-class houses would not become a social service.

It was perfectly clear that what little had been learnt from the experience of the preceding few years had been learnt with the wrong emphasis. It had been decided that the inflation of buildings' costs during the life of the 1919 subsidy to local authorities, had been mainly, if not entirely, due to the particular form of the subsidy. The basic cause of the high costs of building had not been grasped. The advocates of the new policy either had not realised, or had been unwilling to realise, that the resources of the building industry were too small to provide both the houses and the other buildings of all sorts wanted in a hurry. As long as this situation existed, such resources as were available would go to whoever offered the highest prices, unless some system of priorities or rationing were introduced. Chamberlain's Act was altogether too simple. It made no attempt whatever to grapple with these problems by trying to increase the capacity of the industry: rather the reverse. The short life proposed for the subsidy together with the amendments of the Rent Restriction Acts introduced at the same time[2] certainly created the impression that by 1925 the shortage of houses would be over. Anyone following the official lead might argue that there was no point in trying to

[1] Housing, etc., Act, 1923: op. cit. Section 1.
[2] See p. 22 above.

increase the capacity of the building industry merely to cope with so temporary a problem.

True, Chamberlain's subsidy had two apparent advantages over the 1919 subsidy, apart from its simplicity. It would safeguard the position of the Treasury and it would not have the same inherent power to create a crescendo of inflationary increases in costs. The latter would in some circumstances be an advantage to those families with limited fixed incomes trying to buy houses. These advantages were not gained without sacrifice.

The risks of decreases in returns on, and loss of, capital invested in houses to let during periods of unstable building costs and interest rates has already been described at length. The 1919 subsidy had protected local authorities entirely from these risks. The new subsidy gave protection only in certain cases though it extended it to private enterprise. The protection would be complete only if, when the subsidy was withdrawn, building costs and interest rates on new mortgages fell not more than enough to balance out the subsidy, and then ceased to change. In this case, there would be no change in rents. If costs fell further than this, the economic rents of new houses would fall below the subsidised rents of the older houses and would tend to drag them down to their own level. Nobody knew whether this would happen or not. If it did, sooner or later losses would occur unless special steps were taken to prevent the benefits of the fall in costs being passed on to consumers in lower prices.[1] In the abnormal circumstances of the post-war years, investment in houses to let meant taking on risks of loss of an unknown order of magnitude, not compensated by any reasonable chance of additional profits. Any normal local authority or private person would take care to avoid such a proposition as far as possible.

The inflexibility of the subsidy had another disadvantage. Houses would be subsidised irrespective of the varying capacity of the families needing houses either to rent or to buy, and irrespective of the capacity of local authorities to add to that capacity by subsidies out of the rates. The poorer a family, the smaller was the chance that it would be able to pay the balance of rent or purchase price not covered by the subsidy. It followed that the poorer the family, the less its chance of benefiting directly from

---

[1] It will be appreciated that if the life of the subsidy were prolonged, losses would tend to occur as soon as costs of building fell perceptibly. The rents or prices would always be reckoned after taking the subsidy into account and the economic rents of new houses would fall by the full amount of the fall in costs, dragging down the rents of the more expensive houses with them. (See p. 8 above.)

the subsidy by getting a subsidised house. Worse still, they would not benefit even indirectly for some time. Old houses would not necessarily be left vacant by the better-off families moving into the new subsidised houses, until so many had been built that provision had been made for all the relatively well-to-do families who had temporarily been obliged to share houses during the crisis as well as extra families which emerged in the natural course of events. Only when the better-off families began shifting into the new houses, not because they needed houses as such but because they thought they would prefer to live in modern houses, would old houses be left vacant in substantial numbers. At this stage the poorer families would begin to benefit indirectly from the increase supply of houses encouraged by the subsidy.[1] Similarly, the better-off districts would tend to benefit from the subsidy more than the poor districts. Those areas where the numbers of families able to afford subsidised houses were relatively small would receive a relatively small share of the total amount paid out by the Treasury in subsidies.

In discussions of taxation, the use of the terms regressive and progressive has served the useful purpose of crystallising the question of who suffers most from a tax. We can equally appropriately use them in discussing problems of subsidy. We can legitimately say that subsidies which benefit the rich more than the poor are "regressive" just as in an earlier chapter we described as "progressive" subsidies arranged to benefit those in greatest need of assistance most. By thinking in these terms, it may be possible to focus rather more attention than has been customary on the important question of who benefits from a subsidy. We can make a start by saying that the Chamberlain subsidy would be "regressive," both between families and between places.

The subsidy intended to increase the supply of small houses was supplemented by an extension of the life of the Rent and Mortage Interest Restriction Acts until 1925. Consistently with the apparent belief that the housing crisis would be over or nearly over in two years,

[1] As the Chamberlain Act defined the minimum type of house which was eligible for the subsidy with some precision, it would be difficult for the inelasticity of the subsidy to be counteracted, for example, by economies in expenditure on building by cutting down the size of the house. (Although certain deviations from the standard were to be permitted in exceptional cases (Sect. 1(2)) they were not of the type to give real elasticity to the standard.) The standard set up by the Act was in many ways admirable and provided the standard for the family house built by local authorities since. But it certainly limited the possibility of large families or families not belonging to the aristocracy of the working-classes getting new houses. It provided for a considerable rise in standards without providing the means for paying for it. It reversed the theory that it is better to have half a loaf than no bread at all. The effect of this on the housing situation in different areas is discussed in Chapters IV and VI below, and in the Appendix on Scotland.

an important concession was made to landlords. In future all houses becoming vacant and reverting to the landlords' possession, were to be freed from any further restriction of rents.[1] As people moved from the houses they had lived in up to 1923, the house market would gradually become freed from Government control. By moving, of course, a family would deprive itself of any protection from the Rent Restriction system, for any house it could move into must have previously come into the landlord's possession and therefore be free from control. If the assumption that the housing shortage would be over in two or three years had been reasonable, such a plan of gradual haphazard decontrol might perhaps have been justified. It might have been useful in helping to settle appropriate new levels of rents. In practice, of course, the assumption was not justified and the continuance of the system was extended first to 1927 and then each year until the whole scheme was revised in 1933. This revised scheme belongs properly to the period of the third experiment and is described in Chapter VII. The system introduced in 1923 completed the acceptance of the views of the housing problem held by the majority of property owners who gave evidence to the Committee on the Rent Restriction Acts in 1920.[2]

The pure Chamberlain policy did not remain undiluted for long. In 1924 the Labour Party took office and Mr. Wheatley as new Minister of Health introduced another Housing Act and another subsidy.[3] The Chamberlain policy was partially scotched though his subsidy was not repealed. The most significant change made perhaps was the restitution of the powers of the local authorities. They were given back their powers to provide ordinary working-class houses without first having to prove that they could not be provided by private enterprise.[4] The controversy was settled. The local authorities were established as part of the permanent machinery for providing working-class houses; they were not mere intruders. No government since has dared to try openly to alter this: in fact, the position was reaffirmed in the codifying Act passed in 1925 when the Conservatives were back in office.[5] The job of providing houses could once more, if the local authorities or the local electors liked, be

---

[1] Rent and Mortgage Interest Restriction Act, 1923. Powers of eviction continued to be restricted.

[2] See p. 15 above.

[3] Housing (Financial Provisions) Act, 1924. 14 & 15. Geo. V. Chap. 35.

[4] Ibid. Sect. 1(2).

[5] Housing Act, 1925. 15 Geo. V. Chap. 14. Sect. 57 to 62. In 1933 an attempt was made to revise the position by administrative action following the Housing (Financial Provisions) Act of that year. See pp. 138 et seq. below.

developed as a social service. The door to at least partial socialisation of the field was definitely propped open. It remained to be seen whether the threshold would be crossed.

The second important change was the introduction of a long-period housing programme. The Chamberlain subsidy was now made available for houses completed before October 1st, 1939[1] and a new and larger subsidy for the same period for houses satisfying stricter conditions was introduced. If the building trade unions relaxed their rules so that the number of skilled men could be increased, there would in future be a reasonable prospect of employment for the additional men. On this basis Wheatley was able to make the famous " gentleman's agreement " with the building trade unions which made a rapid increase in the numbers of houses built each year possible. The programme envisaged by Wheatley and the Unions involved an increase in the number of houses built each year from between 63,000 and 95,000 in 1926 to between 85,000 and 127,000 in 1928 or 1929, reaching a maximum of between 150,000 and 225,000 in 1934 or 1935.[2] After five years' delay the most essential step in any attack on the war-created shortage of houses had been taken. The length of time needed to get to this point had been rather longer than the whole period of inadequate building during the Great War which had created the particular problem to be cured. In fact, on reasonable estimates the actual shortage of working-class houses in 1924 was larger than in 1919.[3]

The new subsidy introduced by Wheatley and the conditions under which it was to be available are of prime importance. They represented a curious marriage of some of the ideas of 1919 with the principles of orthodox finance. The completeness of the ignominious retreat of 1921 which had been confirmed by Chamberlain in 1923 was modified, not reversed. The subsidy from the Treasury was to be available for houses satisfying approximately the same standards as to size, etc., as those laid down in the Chamberlain Act, but only if the houses were let. Houses built by local authorities and public utility societies would be eligible for the subsidy. It was fixed initially at £9 per house per annum for 40 years in urban parishes and £12 10/– per house per annum for 40 years in rural

---

[1] *Housing (Financial Provisions) Act, 1924.* op. cit. Sect. 1 (1).

[2] The Trade Unions agreed to certain relaxations in their apprenticeship rules which would make this programme possible. See Report op. cit. Cmd. 2104, published in 1925, and *Housing (Financial Provisions) Act, 1924*, Sect. 4 and 1st Schedule. To safeguard building wages, a fair wage clause was inserted in the Act of 1924 (Sect. 3).

[3] See pp. 23–24 above.

D

parishes.[1] This differentiation between urban and rural was the sole concession to the varying needs and difficulties of different areas.

An attempt was made to lay down rules for fixing the rent of houses built with this new subsidy. In this matter, there was a partial return to the ideas of the original 1919 Act. Rents were to be fixed in relation to the prevailing controlled rents of houses built before the Great War. The assumption that these rents were those appropriate to the post-war period, from which departure should only be made for specific reasons, had a new lease of life. There was, however, an important innovation. The current controlled rents were only to be the criterion for the average rent charged by each local authority. This *average* rent was not to exceed that which would be obtained for similar houses coming under the Rent Restriction Acts, *unless* it was necessary to charge more to cover the estimated annual expenses incurred by local authorities, after the equivalent of £4 10/- per house for 40 years had been contributed from the rates.[2] In other words, the local authorities were to contribute not less than this amount in the effort to prevent the average level of rents for new working-class houses rising above the level of the controlled rents of similar pre-war houses. They were under no obligation to contribute more than this, and provided the general rule for average rents was satisfied, the rents of individual houses could be varied as they liked.

Obviously, the question of what were the appropriate pre-war houses for use as a basis of comparison was difficult to decide. Should houses of the same standard as those being built by the local authorities be used ? These, of course, would be the best houses in the working-class market and the most expensive. If not, what sort of houses should be used for the purpose ? The Wheatley Act gave no guidance on this important point beyond explaining that the existing houses could be divided into groups for the purpose of comparison if the local authorities liked. There was no clear decision

---

[1] *Housing (Financial Provisions) Act, 1924.* op. cit. Sect. 2 & 3. The subsidies were to be reviewed in 1926 and every subsequent second year.

[2] The actual text of the rent rule for houses built by local authorities is as follows: "the rents charged in respect of the houses shall not in the aggregate exceed the total amount of rents that would be payable if the houses were let at the appropriate normal rents charged in respect of working-class houses erected prior to the third day of August nineteen hundred and fourteen, except where the estimated annual expenses to be incurred in connection with the houses exceed, so far as the sums are borne by the local rate, an amount equivalent to four pounds ten shillings a year for each house payable for forty years for each house and then only to the extent of such excess; no fine, premium or other like sum shall be taken in addition to the rent." (Section 3(1) e.) For convenience, this rule has been paraphrased in the text above into terms of average rents, but it means, of course, just the same thing. A similar rule applied to houses built by Public Utility Societies, etc., but they did not receive a subsidy from the rates.

as to whether the average rents of the new houses were to correspond to the highest controlled rents of working-class houses or not. The basis of rent policy was left entirely vague.

One thing was, however, entirely clear. The maximum loss from their housing estates which the local authorities could be required to carry was the equivalent of a subsidy of £4 10/– for 40 years on each house built under that Act. The Treasury undertook to contribute, on the other hand, £9 for each new house for forty years. Average rents could, therefore, be fixed at a level which would prevent any loss in excess of an average of £13 10/– per house per year (in rural parishes, £17).

The local authorities or rather the ratepayers were apparently thoroughly safeguarded. They were relieved of any obligation to incur losses on their housing schemes beyond a fixed amount. No suggestion had been made, however, as to what the local authorities were to do if building costs, or the rate of interest on new capital for building houses, fell. As this would reduce the economic rents of new houses, it would threaten to drag down the rents obtainable from any houses built at higher levels of costs.[1] The local authorities were left free to do what they liked in such a contingency. They were not obliged to shoulder any additional loss on the old houses if they could devise ways of avoiding it. Of course it was possible, though uncertain, that the subsidy would be revised downwards proportionately to decreases in costs and interest so that any effect of the fall of costs on the rents of new houses would be offset. There would be no tendency for rents of any house to fall. It is worth pointing out again that the unorthodox financial provisions of the original 1919 Act expressly recognised this problem. By providing that losses should be carried by the Treasury, it made sure, as far as possible, that consumers should benefit from decreases in cost.

Before leaving the question of the losses which might be incurred or avoided by local authorities, there is one further aspect of the problem which needs pointing out. It is usually assumed that the burden of housing subsidies to be carried by the rates is equivalent to the contribution paid out from the rate fund. This is not necessarily true ; in fact, it is probably frequently not true. It is quite possible that the maximum net burden which would fall on the ratepayers would be much less than this. The tenants of local authority houses have to pay rates which go into the same rate fund from which the subsidy out of the rates is supposed to be paid. Pro-

[1] See p. 38 above. This difficulty might also arise with houses built with the Chamberlain subsidy.

vided that the houses built by each local authority increase the total rateable value of their own area, part at least of the subsidy will be offset by the increased yield of rates. Blessed is he whose left hand knoweth not what his right hand doeth !

The difference between the conditions of the 1919 subsidy and those of the 1924 subsidy were not confined to these general questions of high finance. The rent rules of the 1924 Act referred only to average or aggregate rents, the local authorities were entirely free to fix rents of individual houses as they liked. They were not pre- vented from introducing some form of differential renting, but they were not obliged to do so. The rules of the 1919 Act, on the other hand, had contained a definite instruction that rents were to be fixed according to the class of tenant for whom the houses were intended. The Wheatley subsidy was not, in fact, likely to encourage differential rents, for they could only be introduced at the expense either of the ratepayers, or of some tenants who would have to pay higher rents to finance the lower rents charged to others. Nor was the legal position clear. It is true that neither the Chamberlain nor the Wheatley Acts prohibited differential rents, but they did not explicitly sanction them. As late as 1935, the position was so un- certain that a case on the matter went right up to the Court of Appeal.[1] In view of the failure of the Act to give a clear lead, local obstruction might be expected.

The total effect of these rent rules was to leave entirely unsettled the principles on which the rents of individual houses were to be fixed. Even the basis on which average rents were to be determined was so vaguely defined that for all practical purposes they, too, were left to the discretion of local authorities. In addition no attempt had been made at all to work out the policy to be adopted if building costs and interest rates fell. An almost infinite variety of rent scales might grow up under the Act. In this absence of any definite rent policy, the combination of a rigid subsidy with a rigid standard of building left the question of who would benefit directly from the Wheatley subsidy almost as uncertain as in the case of the Chamber- lain subsidy. Wheatley's subsidy might or might not, in practice, be as regressive between families as Chamberlain's. It would depend on how the local authorities behaved. Almost certainly, however, it would be regressive between areas.

It is impossible to know exactly how Wheatley would have dealt with these problems—possibly in the same way as that suggested by

---

[1] Leeds Corporation v. Jenkinson, 1935: see *Rent Rebates*, by Geoffrey Wilson, Fabian Research Series, No. 28, 3rd edition.

Greenwood, the second Labour Minister of Health in 1930–31. Between Wheatley and Greenwood, however, there was a Conservative Government and a Conservative Minister of Health and no progress was made with these outstanding questions. Local authorities were urged, it is true, to concentrate on the cheapest type of house for the lower-paid workers.[1] It was also pointed out that they would avoid competing with private enterprise by doing so. No incentive was offered and no compulsion applied to ensure that this advice was followed. Interest in this interval was concentrated more on the size of the subsidies than on the determination of rent policy. It appears to have been argued that on the one hand the subsidy ought not to be allowed to drive costs up, and on the other, if costs fell, the subsidy should be reduced.

The first argument led to the reduction of both the Chamberlain and Wheatley subsidies on all houses completed after September 30, 1927.[2] The second led in 1928 to another decision to reduce the subsidies. This time the Chamberlain subsidy was to be abolished except for houses completed by September 30th, 1929, and the Wheatley subsidy further reduced as from the same date.[3] The reduction of the Wheatley subsidy was frustrated by the return of the Labour Party to office in the summer of 1929, with Greenwood as Minister of Health.[4]

With Greenwood at the Ministry a more clearly defined housing policy began to emerge. His Slum Clearance Act of 1930 was intended to deal with the problem of the worst housed sections of the community for whom the ordinary subsidy was of little use. The Ministry of Health meanwhile began to urge local authorities to take advantage of the fall in building costs to charge lower rents, pointing out that there was no need for uniform rents to be charged for all their houses.[5] In 1931 the first clear statement on rent policy was made. Local authorities were informed that the time had come to reconsider their rent policies. It was explained that the goal of the subsidy policy was the provision of new houses to let at rents similar to those paid for the ordinary working-class houses. They

[1] Ministry of Health Circulars: No. 755, January 1st, 1927, and No. 954, January 1st, 1929.
[2] The Chamberlain subsidy was reduced to £4 per house per year for 20 years, the Wheatley to £7 10/- per house per year, for 40 years from the Treasury in urban parishes (and £11 in rural), while the local authorities' contribution could be reduced proportionately to £3 15/-.
[3] i.e. in urban areas, to £6 per house per annum for 40 years from the Treasury, and in rural parishes to £9 10/-, the local authority contribution being reduced to £3.
[4] The second reduction of the Wheatley subsidy was prevented by the *Housing (Revision of Contributions) Act, 1929.*
[5] *Annual Reports of the Ministry of Health, 1929/30,* p. 82; and *1930/31,* pp. 97–99.

were told that in calculating the appropriate average rents for their houses they should work out an average, taking into account all the different types and rents of old houses in proportion to their relative numbers of each in their districts. If they preferred, they could work out a series of averages based on rents of special classes of old houses, or on rents in individual districts. They were further told that the time had come when in working out rent schemes they should, as far as practicable, regard the houses built at the new low levels of costs as quite separate from the houses built when costs were higher. The average rents of their newer housing schemes should therefore be lower than those of their old ones, and within these, differential renting should be introduced. Tenants, moreover, should be selected according to their real need for houses.[1] The contrast between this effort at the beginning of the 'thirties to induce local authorities to reduce rents and the efforts made ten years earlier to make local authorities charge higher rents than they wished, suggests a moral. In housing, just as in other matters, local authorities are more anxious to be progressive at the expense of the ordinary tax-payer than at the expense of the rate-payer and local popularity.

The policy of differential rents urged by Greenwood was continued. It received on the whole the blessing of the Committee on Local Expenditure in 1932. In the interest of economy, the Committee went further. They decided that it was a waste of public money to let families who could afford to pay economic rents live in houses with subsidised rents, and that such families should be obliged to pay the economic rent of their houses or quit; the subsidy should be concentrated on those who really needed it. The local authorities were urged to adopt this policy.[2] The Committee also suggested the complete cancellation of the general housing policy of the Wheatley Act as interpreted by Greenwood. It was argued now that as it was possible to build houses without subsidy to let at rents comparable with the subsidised rents of the houses built in 1927, there was no reason for continuing the subsidy. This meant the end of the second experiment. New building schemes, except in connection with slum clearance, ceased to be welcomed by the Ministry of Health. In the following year, the Housing (Financial Provisions) Act, 1933, repealed the Wheatley subsidy on all houses for which plans had not been approved by the end of December, 1932.

[1] *Circular on the Housing (Financial Provisions) Act, 1924, No. 520 (revised)*, August 14th, 1931.
[2] *Report on Local Expenditure, 1932*, par. 94–97. Ministry of Health Circulars, No. 1311. March 22nd, 1933, and No. 1334, May 22nd, 1933.

The end of the second experiment was also in practice the end of attempts to increase or improve the supply of houses for ordinary working-class families. Greenwood's rent policy became merely a method of distributing the existing pool of local authority houses among possible tenants, instead of a method of increasing the total supply of modern houses to let at rents within the reach of ordinary working-class families. The final stage of the process was reached in 1936 : by the Housing Act of that year Local Authorities were obliged to lump together into one housing account all the receipts from, and all the expenditure on their ordinary houses built with the general subsidies of the 1919, 1923 and 1924 Housing Acts. These final developments, however, are really an intrinsic part of the third, and last, experiment, and are better dealt with later.

The cost of the second experiment has not in fact been large compared to the costs of other social services. The Treasury contribution for houses built with the Chamberlain subsidy has averaged since the end of new building with it in 1929, £2·6 mn. a year, and has worked out at just under £6 a year per house. The Wheatley subsidy has naturally been more expensive; the Treasury contribution has averaged £4·3 mn. a year since the completion of building with it in 1934, and has worked out at an average cost of £8 5/– a year per house. In total the two subsidies have cost the ordinary tax-payers £6·9 mn. a year since 1934; in 1936 it was equal to about 1·8 per cent. of the income and super taxes and of the estate duties. The cost to the rate-payers has been still more modest, totalling only £1·9 mn. in 1935/6, and equivalent to 0·9 per cent. of the total rate expenditure.[1]

[1] Calculated from summary tables of expenditure on rate fund services in the *Local Taxation Accounts, 1935/6*. Separate figures of the cost to the rates of the Chamberlain and Wheatley subsidies are not available after 1935/6.

Chapter IV

THE SECOND EXPERIMENT IN PRACTICE
1923–1933/4

I. Total Supplies of Houses in Relation to Requirements.

During the eleven and a half years during which either one or both of the Chamberlain and Wheatley subsidies were available, private enterprise and local authorities together built a total of 2,207 thousand houses. This seems impressive and indeed it is; it is equivalent to 28 per cent. of the total number of houses existing in 1921! In the first full year of the period, October 1923 to September 1924, about 110 thousand houses were built; in the last year, October 1933 to September 1934, nearly three times as many, 298 thousand.[1] The average number of houses built each year of the period was 192 thousand, a figure unequalled probably in any other previous period of similar lengths, and well in excess of the figure of 170 thousand per annum contemplated by the Committee of the building industry in 1924. It had been made possible by the increase in the numbers of skilled men. The number of bricklayers, for instance, increased from 58,000 in 1924 to 75,760 in 1927, and to 85,190 in 1933.[2] Output of materials had increased in proportion.

Even in relation to the requirements of 2,047 thousand additional houses to make good the deficit inherited from the past and provide for additional families emerging during these years, the number of houses built is impressive. Theoretically there would have been a surplus of about 160 thousand houses at the end of September, 1934, if no other changes had occurred. In fact, of course all sorts of things had happened to upset this result. Some houses had been divided up into flats, some had been pulled down and others had been converted into offices. The number of houses built is not the same thing as the increase in the number of separate houses. We know in fact that the net wastage caused by these changes in the number

---

[1] For all practical purposes, only the Chamberlain subsidy was available for the first year of the period, and in 1933/4 the Wheatley subsidy was available only for houses of which the plans had been approved by December 7th, 1932. Houses built for slum clearance purposes are excluded from these figures and all others used in this Chapter unless they are specifically mentioned. The totals given above include a few houses finished late under the Addison subsidy and a few houses built by local authorities without subsidies.

[2] See Statistical Appendix Table 8A.

of houses available as dwellings was just over 200 thousand between 1923 and 1931, and it is probable that there was a further net wastage of at least 80 thousand houses in the following three and a half years. As soon as account is taken of this, the apparent surplus of September, 1934, is transformed into a deficit of over 100 thousand. The figures are set out in detail, Table III, below.

TABLE III.—General results of the Second Experiment (England and Wales) April 1923 to September 1934.*

Thousands.

(A) Additional Houses required April 1923 to September 1934.
    (1) To provide for shortage at 1 April 1923   822
    (2) To provide for increase in number of families 1 April 1923
        to 30 Sept. 1934   1,225

                Total Requirements   2,047

(B) Additional Houses provided April 1923 to September 1934.
    (1) Total number of new houses built   2,207
    (2) Net Wastage by demolition, conversion, etc.   ..   ..   ..   −287

                Total additional Houses   1,920

(C) Shortage of Houses outstanding in September 1934   127

* Excluding houses built under slum clearance schemes. For further details and explanations see Statistical Appendix pp. 269–272

Although if considered in terms of numbers of houses and in relation to numbers of families things were infinitely better than eleven years earlier, there was practically no margin available for improving the general standard of pre-war housing. Worse still, except for those fortunate families which had got new houses, and those who no longer had to share houses, the general standard of housing must have deteriorated both absolutely and in relation to modern needs. For just over twenty years replacement of old houses had been negligible. It is probably safe to assume that little more than a quarter of a million houses had been demolished or converted to business uses. If we took the optimistic figure of half a million this would only be equivalent to an annual rate of replacement of the houses existing before the Great War of about 0·33 per cent. for the twenty years.[1]

The fashionable denigration of modern jerry building and the enthusiasm for genuine Tudor and Georgian houses must not be allowed to obscure the implications of this. Apart from the fact that

[1] Replacement of houses under slum clearance schemes was so small relatively to the total that no specific allowance for it has been made here. See Chap. VIII below. It will be appreciated that as there was still in fact a shortage of houses in 1934, some of the replacement was at the expense of overcoming the shortage.

architectural gems are often most inconvenient to live in, the majority of houses fail most lamentably to provide æsthetic pleasures in compensation for their inherent lack of convenience and comfort. Most of the houses existing in 1911 and still existing in 1934 after more than twenty years of additional wear and tear were working-class houses built in the nineteenth century. That is to say that they were built without respect to architectural merit, without regard to modern ideas of town planning, of convenience or of sanitation. They were built when sunshine and fresh air, baths, indoor sanitation and gardens were generally regarded as luxuries to which only the most aristocratic of the working-class families could aspire. Even the houses built in the great Victorian age for middle-class families are now considered unsatisfactory and inconvenient. Since the great bulk of the houses in this country were built population has shifted, towns have grown, customs, needs and fashions have changed, inventions and science have created new criteria. In short, the great majority of houses in the country in September, 1934, were as out-of-date as the customs and clothes of the Victorian era. And these houses were being replaced during a period of twenty years at the rate which was probably less than a third per cent. per annum!

Looked at from this angle the outstanding needs for new houses in September, 1934, were enormous. Twenty years' arrears of replacement had to be made up and a tolerable rate of current replacement achieved. Apart from this the number of houses was almost certainly inadequate, taking into account the inconveniently low number of vacant houses, while some provision was needed for those sharing families who wanted separate houses and for the current needs of additional families emerging each year. Even so, it might perhaps seem that the policy of the preceding eleven years had been successful. The acute crisis was certainly over. It might be time to switch over to direct efforts to replace the worst of the old houses and to reduce overcrowding. The conclusions of two Committees cast doubts on this. The Marley Committee on the Rent Restriction Acts in 1931 declared that the control of the rents of small working-class houses could not be abolished in the near future because of the shortage; even six years later the Ridley Committee decided that decontrol to be tolerable must be gradual.[1] It must strike the least critical observer as odd that

[1] *Report of the Inter-Departmental Committee on the Rent Restriction Acts, 1931.* Cmd. 3911. Part IV. (Chairman, Lord Marley), and the Report of a similar Committee in 1937. Cmd. 5621. Part VI. (Chairman, Lord Ridley.)

despite the new building and the subsidies specifically intended to increase the supply of working-class houses there were still insufficient to make decontrol politically possible. Perhaps after all the wrong types of houses had been built or the wrong people had got the subsidies. Perhaps the tendency to concentrate on the total numbers of houses built has been misleading. These questions are so important that they must be considered at some length.

II. Who Benefited from the New Houses?

Even if there had been no shortage of houses in September, 1934, the questions just raised about the types of houses built and about replacement would be important. Without knowing more about them, we cannot decide whether the second experiment was really successful or not, or even whether the subsidies were necessary. Nor is it possible to understand the course of house building in the five years before the present war without considering the period up to 1934. These inquiries are not merely of historical interest; they should provide some of the data needed for formulating post-war housing policy. For this we need to know, *inter alia*: first, how particular types of subsidies, which have already been tried, worked in practice; second, whether after this war there is any likelihood of private enterprise providing the houses which will be needed or, if not, whether the local authorities can be relied upon to do so. Naturally the information available for answering these questions is incomplete. It will be necessary to use both indirect methods of inquiry and statistical estimates.

It was explained in Chapter I that the need for additional working-class houses, that is houses with rateable values up to £13 (£20 in the Metropolitan Police Area), amounted to not less than two-thirds of the total needed. The need for houses with rateable values from £14 to £26 (£21 to £35 in the Metropolitan Police Area), that is, houses rather bigger and more pretentious than the ordinary working-class houses, probably accounted for most of the rest of the requirements. Table IV summarises the information available about the numbers of houses built with, and without, subsidies, between the Armistice and September, 1934. The startling feature of the figures is that out of nearly two and one half million houses built, less than one-third were built by the local authorities, while out of approximately one and three-quarter millions built by private enterprise only about one-quarter were built with the assistance of a subsidy. In consequence rather less than half of all the houses built received subsidies of one sort or another. Considering the fuss and excitement and the amount of legislation, these results are extremely surprising. The total supply of houses and the reduction of the shortage turned out to be more dependent on private enterprise than on the state acting through the local authorities, and only dependent on state financial assistance to a limited extent.

TABLE IV.—Types of houses built between 1 January, 1919 and September 30, 1934. (England and Wales).*

	Thousands of houses built			% of total built
	Rateable value up to £13†	Others	Total	
By Local Authorities	763	—	763	31·0
By Private Enterprise :				
(a) with subsidy	20	418	438	17·8
(b) without subsidy	249	1,009	1,258	51·2
Total	269	1,427	1,696	69·0
Grand Total	1,032	1,427	2,459	100·0
Additional houses required	1,532	767	2,299	—
Surplus or deficit at Sept., 1934 ..	—500	+660	+160‡	—

*Excluding houses built for slum clearance. For further details and explanations, see Statistical Appendix, Tables 1, 2 and 3A.
†Up to £20 in London Metropolitan Police Area.
‡The apparent surplus emerges because no allowance has been made for wastages.

The next table shows the distribution of the new houses between three categories, ordinary working-class and intermediate and others. This table, too, is surprising. It might have been expected perhaps that the bulk of the new houses built would have been of the ordinary working-class type which it was the primary purpose of the subsidies to increase. This expectation was not fulfilled. This group of houses increased relatively less than the intermediate group, by 19 per cent. compared with 60 per cent., though the absolute increases were similar, 1032 thousand and 983 thousand, respectively.[1] All, except the ordinary working-class houses, were built by private enterprise and were in general for sale to owner occupiers; while most of the working-class houses were built by the local authorities and were for letting, of those built by private enterprise in this group the great majority were for sale.

[1] See Statistical Appendix, Table 3A.

TABLE V.—New houses of different types as percentages of total built and percentage increases 1 January, 1919 to 30 September, 1934 (England and Wales).

	Houses with Rateable Values†			
	Up to £13	£14 to £26	£27 to £78	Total
Houses in each Rateable Value Group as Percentages of :				
(a) All houses in 1919	67·6	20·9	11·5	100
(b) New houses built, January 1919 to September, 1934	41·9	40·1	18·0	100
Percentage increase January, 1919/September, 1934* ..	19	60	48	31

*No allowance has been made for wastage. See Statistical Appendix, Tables 3 and 3c below for further details and explanations.

†Up to £20, £21, £35 and £36—£105, respectively, in London Metropolitan Police Area.

Taken altogether these changes represented something like a revolution in the house market, but the supply of working-class houses had not increased sufficiently. Even if none of the old houses, apart from the limited numbers included in slum clearance schemes, had been demolished thus offsetting new houses, the new houses built fell short of requirements by nearly 500 thousand. Against this deficit there was, however, an apparent surplus of all other houses of about 660 thousand.[1] These apparent surplus was available for use in three ways. The better-off working-class families might make an effort to buy them. Middle- and upper-class families might move out of their old houses into the new ones. These old houses might remain empty or be pulled down, or, alternatively, they might be occupied by less well-to-do families and working-class families moving into them, " filtering-up " as it is called. It is certain that the migration of the upper middle-class families into new houses took place on a considerable scale; thus the extent to which the apparent near disappearance of the shortage[2] represented the real facts of the situation depended on the extent to which this filtering up process was practicable and successful.

The situation etched in by these statistics obviously meant difficulty for the ordinary working-class family in search of a house. For example, a family who would normally have expected to rent a house with a rateable value not exceeding £13 was faced with

[1] This surplus of larger houses over the shortage of working-class houses is only apparent. We have not taken demolitions and other wastage into account. See Table IV above.
[2] See Table III p. 49, above.

four alternatives. It might get one of the relatively rare new houses of this type which were available for renting, but the chances were obviously not particularly good. Alternatively, it might buy a new house through a building society if it had sufficient capital to pay the initial lump sum required, and if its credit was sufficiently good to satisfy a building society and if it had sufficient confidence about its own future income to take on the commitments involved. There are a lot of " ifs " about this alternative. As an alternative it might be lucky and find an old house of the intermediate group to rent in a suitable district after another family, able and willing to buy a new house, had moved out, or had disappeared for some reason. This solution would probably necessitate higher rent and rates than the first. The only other alternative was that of finding an old working-class house to rent in a suitable place, but this depended of course on some other family having broken up, or, having opted for one of the other three alternatives. After 1923 the rent of such a house would be de-controlled and the family would, therefore, in most cases pay a rent higher than that of a similar family who had not had to look for a house since 1923. The last two solutions it will be noticed also depended on a lot of " ifs " for it must be remembered that as a result of demolitions there were still not enough houses to go round in 1934.

It cannot be denied that the whole business of getting suitable houses for those who could not buy was very chancey. We should scarcely tolerate such erratic methods of satisfying other everyday needs in peace-time. Even in war we are apt to be querulous about the vagaries of the supply of things like fish and fruit. We are inclined to suggest that something is wrong with the policy of the Ministry of Food. There seems by analogy some justification for suspecting that there was something wrong with housing policy. It will be sensible, as a first step towards finding out if this suspicion was justified, to see how far the housing policy worked equally well or equally badly in different parts of the country.

III. The Second Experiment in the Regions

It became customary in the two decades before this war to divide England and Wales up into regions based on their main economic characteristics. At one stage it was fashionable to speak of the Inner Regions, and the Outer Regions. The former covered the prosperous areas, the Home Counties and the Midlands ; the latter the areas of the depressed or relatively depressed industries, textiles, coal and shipbuilding. This distinction is too broad for the present purposes, and it is more useful to use a more detailed and equally familiar sub-division of economic regions: the Home Counties, the Midlands, the Textile Regions, the two outlying and depressed regions of South Wales and the North-East[1], and the rest of England.

Between 1921 and 1931 the Home Counties and, in slightly different degree, the Midlands, exhibited all the economic character-istics popularly associated with building activity; they were pros-perous and population was increasing both from natural causes and by immigration from other areas. The other regions suffered to varying degrees from economic depression and lost part of their natural increases in population. From the point of view of housing policy, it will be useful to distinguish between these varying degrees of prosperity and depression.

There are other reasons for choosing the more detailed break-up. The size of towns has, it is usually assumed, important effects on housing conditions. The ease or difficulty of providing working-class houses to let depends on the availability of cheap sites within easy reach of places of work and of shopping centres. In the bigger towns the available sites tend to be both further away from the centre and more expensive. The situation may be further complicated by the centrifugal effects of big towns on the well-to-do. From time to time the upper classes living in large towns have become inspired by impulses to migrate to the outskirts, or sometimes further. The impulse may come from a wish to have a modern house, or get into more rural surroundings, or to avoid high rents. The important point at this stage, however, is not the exact reason for the move, but the effects. The old large houses are left vacant in the centre, and convenient sites on the outskirts of the towns are used up. These are the peculiar difficulties in the way of providing cheap houses which concentrations create, whether they consist of individual big towns or several small towns. Against this, must be set the greater possi-bilities of providing efficient local authority services in big towns, the possibility of employing the specialised services of good architects, sanitary engineers and town planners.[2] Under the existing system of

---

[1] The Home Counties are taken as: Bedfordshire, Berkshire, Buckinghamshire, Essex, Hertfordshire, Kent, London, Middlesex, Surrey and Sussex; the Midlands as Derby-shire, Leicestershire, Northamptonshire, Nottinghamshire, Staffordshire, Warwickshire and Worcestershire; the Textile Region as West Riding of Yorkshire, Lancashire and Cheshire; the North-East as Northumberland and Durham County; and South Wales as Monmouthshire and Glamorganshire.

[2] For a discussion of the greater apparent efficiency of the health services in big towns than in small, see the *Report of the Royal Commission on the Distribution of the Industrial Popu-lation, 1940.* Cmd. 6153. Chap. V.

local government these possibilities only exist, however, if the big concentrations are single units for local government purposes. The economies of large scale organisation may be realised in Birmingham but not in the Tyneside concentration which is made up of towns of varying sizes.

The big towns and/or concentrations are not distributed evenly through the country, and each concentration has its own peculiar features. The Home Counties are dominated by the great town of London. In the Midlands the largest town, Birmingham, had a population less than one-fifth of that of the County of London in 1931, and does not occupy the same dominating position, nor is it surrounded to the same degree by a densely built-up concentration. In the Textile Region, on the other hand, the great concentration of Merseyside clustered round Manchester and Liverpool dominates Lancashire and Cheshire. In the North-East, though Tyneside resembles Merseyside in some respects, the scatter of the industrial population in the colliery villages of Durham introduces another element which may complicate or ease the housing problem. The type of urban concentration thus varies from region to region; this is another good reason for examining them individually.

Partly from historical reasons, the regions have in effect different types of local government. As the responsibility for building working-class houses to let was thrown on to the local authorities, this is worth keeping in mind. The form of local government in the County of London, with its complex divisions of responsibility between the County Council and the Metropolitan Boroughs is unique. Outside the boundaries of the County, however, the local government system conforms more to those of urban or rural areas than to those of other great built-up areas. It is practically dependent on urban and rural district councils. Municipal boroughs are relatively rare, and of the nine county boroughs in the Home Counties four are seaside resorts, three (East Ham, West Ham and Croydon) are in Greater London; one, Canterbury, is the smallest county borough in the country, and the ninth, Reading, is the only ordinary semi-industrial town. In contrast, the Midland and the Textile regions are dominated by the county boroughs, always substantial. Their size varies from 49 thousand people to one million averaging 132 thousand in the former, and in the latter from 41 thousand to 855 thousand averaging about 170 thousand. Finally, neither South Wales, nor the North-East, nor *a fortiori* the " Rest of England " are dominated by county boroughs. In the two former 66 per cent. and 59 per cent. respectively lived outside the county boroughs, while in the whole of the " Rest of England " there were only seventeen county boroughs and the majority of the population lived in rural or urban districts.[1] This distinction in connection with county boroughs may be of significance. In general, towns achieve the status of county borough only when they have been separate urban entities for a considerable period. Only one new one was created between 1921 and 1931, and in consequence they were nearly all towns which were accustomed to possess and use powers. The minor stars in the local authority system, municipal boroughs, and urban and rural districts, were given far more independent powers as housing authorities than they had in respect to social services generally.

(a) The Regions.

In discussing the effects of the first two experiments for the country as a whole we found it useful to use the Registrar-General's method for estimating the requirements for additional houses. There is no reason why the same method should not be used for the various regions, or for any other areas for which statistics are available, and we shall use it throughout this section. The only difficulty is that it is impossible to make estimates for parts of the whole country except in the years of the Population Censuses of 1921 and 1931, for there is no adequate information about the movements of population from place to place between intermediate years. Fortunately this does not matter very much as the greater part of the building by local authorities under the second experiment was over by 1931, and the building under the first experiment after 1921 was not large enough in relation to the total to affect the general comparison between areas.

The requirements for additional houses in each region for the period 1921/31 are shown as percentages of the total for England and Wales in Diagram I, together with other useful information. The three regions with the largest populations, the Home Counties, the Textile Region and the industrial Midlands, accounted for 36·6 per cent., 21·2 per cent., and 17 per cent. respectively, of the total requirements for additional houses. The two other industrial regions accounted for between 3 per cent. and 4 per cent. each and the " Rest of England and Wales " for about 18 per cent. Diagram II gives a picture of the situation in each region separately. In the Home Counties the number of additional houses needed was equivalent to about one-third of the houses existing there in 1921; in the Midlands, the other main prosperous area, it was equivalent

[1] Census of Population, England and Wales, 1931. Volume of General Tables.

E

DIAGRAM I.—Regional Distribution of Requirements, Deficits 1931, and New
Houses built 1921-31, as % of Totals for England and Wales.*

□ = Home Counties (incl. London)   ◩ = Midlands
▨ = Textile Region   ◫ = N. East.
▩ = " Rest of England and Wales."   ▤ = S. Wales.

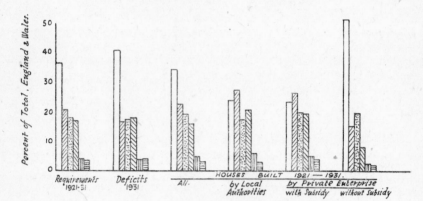

* See Table 9.A. Statistical Appendix.

DIAGRAM II.—Requirements 1921 to 1931 in each Region as % of number of
houses in each Region 1921 and Additional Houses provided by
Local Authorities and Private Enterprise 1921-32 and Deficit 1931
in each Region as % of Requirements of each Region.*

□ = Home Counties (incl. London)   ◩ = Midlands.
▨ = Testile Region.   ◫ = N. East.
▩ = " Rest of England and Wales."   ▤ = S. Wales.

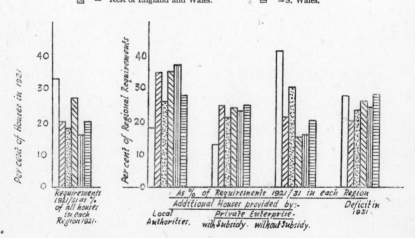

See Table 9.B. Statistical Appendix.

to just over a quarter, and in both the Textile Region and South Wales, rather less, about one-fifth; in the North-East it was rather lower still. Despite these considerable differences in the proportionate increases in the numbers of houses needed, about three-quarters to four-fifths of the requirements in the various regions had been satisfied by 1931, after allowing for net wastage by demolition, etc.

The second diagram brings out the fact that these apparently similar results were reached in very different ways. There were broad differences between the Home Counties and the " Rest of England and Wales " on the one hand and the other regions on the other as well as minor differences between each. Private enterprise was obviously relatively more important in the first two than in the others. About 41 per cent. of requirements in the Home Counties, and 30 per cent. in the " Rest of England and Wales," were satisfied by unsubsidised private building, compared to between only 15 per cent. and 21 per cent. in the others. On the other hand, in the case of subsidised building a much smaller proportion of requirements was met by private enterprise in the Home Counties than in the others, 13 per cent. compared with between 21 per cent. and 25 per cent. As there is no reason to suppose that the willingness to accept subsidies differed in different parts of the country, it must be assumed that an exceptionally large proportion of the new houses in the Home Counties were too big to qualify for the subsidies available.[1] In total, private enterprise provided for 50 per cent. and over in the Home Counties and in the " Rest," but in the other regions was lower varying between 38 per cent. and 46 per cent. The contributions of the local authorities varied in a different way. In the Home Counties they provided only 18 per cent. of the houses needed, and in the " Rest " 26 per cent.; in all the other regions, however, their contribution amounted to between 28 per cent. and 37 per cent.

These differences are important because they suggest that the type of family who got new houses differed between different places. In each region, as private enterprise provided more houses than the local authorities, the better-off and middle-class families tended to have their needs satisfied more completely than ordinary working-class families. This tendency was, it appears, more pronounced in some regions than in others, but there is no evidence to show that the social structure of the population varied sufficiently between the regions to justify this. Indeed, such evidence as there is suggests that

[1] There is no evidence that a greater proportion of building in the Home Counties took place after the abolition of the Chamberlain subsidies than in other regions.

between these large regions the variation in social structure was remarkably small, although lower-middle and middle-class families probably are slightly more important in the Home Counties than in the other regions. The only estimates available give the proportion in the former as just under a third, and elsewhere as between a quarter and a fifth.[1] This difference is certainly insufficient to explain either the differences in the proportions of unsubsidised and subsidised houses built by private enterprise in the various regions, or, the differences between the contributions of local authorities. Thus, while it is clear that in each region there must have been some necessity for filtering up, as over one-third of the requirements were met by private enterprise in each,[2] it is evident that this must have been relatively most pronounced in the Home Counties and the " Rest " than elsewhere.

There is another point of some importance. There were considerable differences between the way in which the requirements were met in the two most prosperous areas, the Home Counties and the Midlands. Similarly there were quite marked differences between the two most depressed regions, the North-East and South Wales. On the one hand the prosperous Midlands and the depressed North-East had several points in common in the matter. It is evidently impossible to jump to conclusions as to any clear relation between the way the second experiment worked and the economic prosperity or depression of various places. This conclusion appears to be confirmed by the record of building after 1931. The figures given in Table 9A in Appendix II show that the geographical distribution of new houses, provided by local authorities and private enterprise respectively, was much the same after 1931 as before. All the regions except South Wales shared in the expansion of private enterprise between 1931 and 1934, while the local authorities appeared in each to be more concerned with the economy campaign and the winding-up of the second experiment than with anything else. The regions in which the authorities' contributions had been particularly low before 1931 made no obvious spurt to catch up after that year.

This cursory inquiry into building in the regions provides little support for hasty generalisations. It leaves the question of the con-

---

[1] *The Home Market*, by Harrison and Mitchell, 1939 edition. Table XVI. The regions in the table differ somewhat from those used here, but are roughly comparable. The figures quoted in the text refer to families of which the head had an income of £4 and over, that is, broadly, to non-manual workers.

[2] It is generally accepted that private enterprise did not build a significant number of ordinary working-class houses before 1931. See pp. 79 et seq. below, and Table 3A in the Statistical Appendix.

nection between the results of the second experiment and prosperity or depression in different regions unsettled. Nor does it provide any evidence for supposing that the activity and efficiency of local authorities automatically depended on the size or type of local authority and the bigger the authority the better. We have seen that there was apparently little to choose between the Midlands and the North-East, though the former was more dominated than the latter by county boroughs. Similarly though the Home Counties were dominated by the biggest local authority in the country, the local authority activity there compares most unfavourably with that in other regions, even with that in the "Rest of England and Wales," a region characterised by large numbers of small authorities. It is clear, however, that the experiment did not work out uniformly all over the country. To discover the reasons a more detailed examination dealing with smaller areas is necessary. This is attempted in the next section.

(b) The Counties.[1]

Theoretically it would, of course, be desirable to examine the requirements for additional houses and the way in which they were satisfied within the areas of individual local authorities. In practice this is quite impossible, partly because of the development of over-flows of population from the districts of the main local authorities into dormitory towns, partly because—and this seems conclusive —it is essential to choose areas of which the boundaries have not changed to an important extent between 1911 and 1931. In fact, for the latter reason the administrative counties, including their associated county boroughs, provide the only practicable statistical basis. Even the basis of the counties is not infallible, and it has been necessary or desirable to combine some of them. For example, Warwickshire and Worcestershire have had to be combined because the City of Birmingham succeeded in acquiring a considerable piece of Worcestershire during the period. It also seemed rather obviously desirable to put Lancashire and Cheshire together, and London and Middlesex.[2]

[1] The method of statistical analysis used in this section was worked out initially for a paper read to the Manchester Statistical Society in March, 1942. *Local Authorities and Housing Subsidies since 1919*, published in the *Manchester School*, Vol. XII, No. 2. Since then it has been possible to incorporate certain improvements and revised figures. (See statistical note on p. 283 below.)

[2] The Welsh counties, other than Glamorgan, have been omitted from consideration, as their individual requirements were too small to be included in the statistical comparisons. In one or two other cases counties have had to be combined, owing to lack of separate data, e.g. Cumberland and Westmorland, and the North and East Ridings of Yorkshire.

The question of actually comparing the requirements of the counties raises a certain difficulty. It seems unreasonable to compare just the absolute size of requirements, for as between very different areas they can give little idea of the magnitude of the problem in relation to the situation in each area. Suppose, to take an extreme example, requirements amounted to 5,000 houses in each of two areas, A and B, but the number already existing in A was 100,000 while in B it was only 10,000. The difficulties in relation to building resources in the areas, in provision of the necessary ancillary services of water, sewage, roads and all the rest would inevitably be far greater in B than in A. It would be far more reasonable to compare the requirements of these areas in relation to the houses already existing in them, as we have just done in general terms in discussing the regions. The requirements in each county between 1921 and 1931 can conveniently be calculated as percentages of the houses already existing in 1921.[1] These percentages can be called *the rates of requirements*. The qualitative difference entering into the difficulties of providing the requirements, such as greater difficulties of obtaining sites in densely built-up districts, are more properly as well as more easily allowed for separately.

In Table VI the counties in each region have been arranged in order of the magnitude of their rates of requirements. It is, of course, evident that if housing requirements are measured in the way initiated by the Registrar-General they become dependent on the age composition of the population. Since the age composition of the population in any district depends partly on its past history, and partly on contemporary shifts of population from one part of the country to another in search of work and prosperity, considerable variations in the rate of housing requirements are inevitable. These factors work out in much the way we should expect from our consideration of the regions. The rates of requirements were, of course, on the whole highest in the Home Counties, in most cases over 30. The variations were considerable, however, and reflected the uneven incidence of the movements of population. Bedfordshire, on the edge of the region, for instance, had the lowest, 22·8, Surrey the highest, 53·0. In the Midlands the counties resembled each other rather more closely; only Northamptonshire came below 20, and only Warwickshire and Worcestershire combined above 30. Requirements in the counties in the stagnating or depressed industrial regions were considerably lower, concentrated between 18 and 21, except for Northumberland. The

[1] As in the case of the regions, statistical difficulties necessitate starting from 1921 and ending in 1931 as far as detailed inquiry goes.

miscellaneous mainly non-industrial counties, lumped together as the Rest of England when we discussed large regions, break up into fairly clear sub-groups. The four counties skirting the Home Counties and the Midlands (Hampshire, Dorset, Wiltshire and Gloucestershire) had quite high rates of requirements similar to those of the Midlands; the rate of the intermediate counties of the North and East Riding taken together also come into this range. Five other counties forming a still more distant periphery to the Home Counties and the Midlands had rates between 16 and 20, rather similar it will be noticed to those of the less prosperous industrial areas. Finally, at the bottom of the scale come the remote agricultural counties, Cornwall, Herefordshire and Shropshire, Westmorland and Cumberland, together with the depressed corn counties of Norfolk and Suffolk.

The fourth column of Table VI shows the net additions made to the supply of houses in each county between 1921 and 1931 expressed as percentages of all the houses in the respective counties in 1921. The figures are thus comparable with the rates of requirements and it will be appropriate to call them *the rates of increase in supply*.[1] The differences between these two rates are given in the third column; these show the deficiency or surplus of increases in supply compared to requirements also as percentages of the houses in 1921. These can be called *the rates of deficiency or surplus*.

The rates of increase in supply repay study. It will be noticed that they tended to be relatively high in those counties in which the rates of requirement were relatively high. The correlation coefficient between the rates of requirements and the rates of increase in supply was in fact positive and very large +0·96. It is clear that the rate of increase, though not usually adequate to satisfy requirements, did at least vary in very close relationship to the rate of requirements. We can say, therefore, with reasonable certainty that supplies of additional houses did display a high degree of responsiveness to local requirements. We should have been able to be rather more definite about this if it had been feasible to use areas smaller than counties as the basis of comparison, but there is really little doubt about the general conclusion. It is not of course inconsistent with this conclusion that the actual rates of deficiency or surplus in 1931 varied considerably in the different counties. They represent, it will be realised, the rates of requirements at a single point of time and

---

[1] The rates of increase in supply are net rates, that is, they exclude new houses used to compensate for the net wastage of houses through demolition and conversion. See the Statistical Appendix, p. 283 below.

TABLE VI.—Rates of Housing Requirements and Rates of Supply, 1921–31 and Rates of Surplus of Deficit, 1931.*

| Counties (1) | Rate of Requirements for Additional Houses, 1921–31 (2) | Rate of Deficiency or Surplus in 1931 (3) | Rate of Increase in Supply of Additional Houses, 1921–31 | | |
			Total (4)	Local Authorities (5)	Private Enterprise (6)
Home Counties					
Surrey	53·0	— 10·8	42·2	6·2	36·0
Essex	45·6	— 8·8	36·8	6·4	30·4
Hertfordshire	39·1	— 4·8	34·3	11·0	23·3
Bucks.	32·7	— 4·7	28·0	5·8	22·2
Kent	31·3	— 6·3	25·0	5·6	19·4
Sussex	30·9	— 2·1	28·8	5·7	23·1
Berkshire	27·8	— 9·7	18·1	5·5	12·6
London and Middlesex ..	26·5	— 11·5	15·0	5·2	9·8
Bedfordshire	22·8	— 5·1	17·7	5·1	12·6
Midlands					
Warwickshire and Worcestershire ..	33·8	— 10·4	23·4	12·1	11·3
Leicestershire	28·6	— 6·3	22·3	6·8	15·5
Nottinghamshire	28·3	— 6·0	22·3	7·8	14·5
Derbyshire	24·7	— 6·6	18·1	7·2	10·9
Staffordshire	21·4	— 4·2	17·2	10·4	6·8
Northamptonshire ..	19·7	— 5·6	14·1	7·1	7·0
Textile Countries					
West Riding, Yorks. (including York)	19·7	— 3·1	16·6	7·9	8·7
Lancashire and Cheshire	19·3	— 4·2	15·1	6·2	8·9
North East					
Durham	18·8	— 6·0	12·8	6·4	6·4
Northumberland	10·3	+ 0·4	10·7	5·1	5·6
S. Wales and Mons.					
Glamorganshire	20·4	— 6·0	14·4	5·5	8·9
Monmouthshire	19·6	— 4·7	14·9	5·6	9·3
Rest of England					
Hampshire and I. of Wight	29·0	— 4·6	24·4	4·7	19·7
Dorset	22·2	— 2·7	19·5	3·5	16·0
Gloucestershire	21·6	— 8·1	13·5	6·1	7·4
Wiltshire	20·6	— 7·4	13·4	5·1	8·1
East and North Ridings, Yorks.	20·0	— 5·6	14·4	5·4	9·0
Devonshire	19·9	— 4·2	15·7	4·5	11·2
Somerset	18·1	— 4·3	13·8	5·9	7·9
Oxfordshire	17·2	— 3·3	13·9	5·8	8·1
Lincolnshire and Rutland	16·3	— 3·0	13·3	4·2	9·3
Cambridge and Ely ..	16·3	— 2·7	13·6	6·5	7·1
Suffolk	13·7	— 1·4	12·3	4·4	7·9
Norfolk	13·3	— 2·3	11·0	5·3	5·7
Salop	12·9	— 4·6	8·3	4·2	4·1
Westmorland & Cumberland	11·8	— 2·1	9·7	5·8	3·9
Herefordshire	10·4	— 4·8	5·6	2·2	3·4
Cornwall	9·6	— 0·4	9·2	2·3	6·9
London, Middlesex, Essex, Kent and Surrey ..	33·6	— 9·3	24·4	5·6	18·8

* For details and Explanations, see Statistical Appendix, p. 283. All rates are calculated as percentages of the numbers of houses in 1921. For definitions see pp. 62, 63 and 65.

there was no reason for them to be identical with each other, and it will be noticed that the variation was a good deal less than that of the original rates of requirements for the period 1921 to 1931.

So far we have not considered the parts played by the local authorities and private enterprise so that we know nothing whatever about the increases in supply of specifically working-class houses to let. The last two columns of Table VI provide information on this aspect of the matter. They show the supplies of houses which can be credited to the local authorities and private enterprise, respectively, expressed as usual in percentages of the number of houses in 1921. These can be called the *local authority* and *private enterprise rates of increase in supply*, respectively.[1] The advocates of Private Enterprise will be cheered by these figures. For 37 counties the average local authority rate of supply was only 6·0, but that for private enterprise was 11·9, twice as high. The private enterprise rate was higher throughout than that of the local authorities except in Durham, the agricultural counties of Shropshire, Cumberland and Westmorland, and the Midland Counties of Staffordshire, Northamptonshire, Warwick and Worcestershire. It will be noticed also that the local authority rate varied much less than the private enterprise rate. For instance the lowest local authority rate was 2·2 and the highest rather more than five times as high; in the case of private enterprise the highest rate 36·0 was about 11 times as high as the lowest.[2]

It seems that there was a certain stickiness about the rates of supply of the local authorities. They exceeded 10 only in three counties, Hertfordshire, Warwickshire and Worcestershire together and Staffordshire; the last a county without a particularly high requirement rate. In the other Midland counties and in the textiles, it was between 6 and 8. The latter, it will be remembered, had lower rates of requirements than the former. The rates of supply were still lower in all the Home Counties except Hertfordshire, and

---

[1] There is a slight complication in connection with these figures. Normally the houses provided by local authorities in each county or group of counties are those built by the actual authorities included in the counties. The L.C.C., however, built to some extent outside its own boundaries and those of Middlesex, viz.: in Essex, Surrey and Kent, particularly in Essex. These houses are included only in the totals for the L.C.C. and Middlesex, and therefore in strict accuracy all five counties should be grouped together for calculations. This procedure would, however, make no substantial difference to the results, and it has proved more convenient to treat these counties separately in some connections. An alternative set of calculations is shown in which these counties are grouped out, and is given in the Statistical Appendix, p. 283.

[2] The contrast is shown more accurately by the coefficients of variation. See Statistical Appendix, p. 283. If the Home Counties are omitted from consideration the contrast between the variations of rates of supply become much less.

TABLE VII.—Deficiencies (or surpluses) in 1931, and Additional Houses supplied by Local Authorities and Private Enterprise, respectively, 1921–31, as Percentages of Requirements 1921–31.*

Counties	Deficiency or Surplus in 1931 as % of Requirements, 1921/31	Additional houses supplied 1921/31 as % of Requirements, 1921–31	
		By Local Authorities	By Private Enterprise
(1)	(2)	(3)	(4)
Home Counties			
Surrey	−20·5	11·8	67·7
Essex	−19·3	14·0	66·7
Hertfordshire	−12·2	28·3	59·5
Buckinghamshire	−14·3	17·8	67·9
Kent	−20·0	17·8	62·2
Sussex	− 6·9	18·3	74·8
Berkshire	−35·1	19·8	45·1
London and Middlesex	−43·5	19·9	36·6
Bedfordshire	−22·3	22·2	55·5
Midlands			
Warwickshire and Worcestershire ..	−30·7	35·9	33·4
Leicestershire	−22·2	23·5	54·3
Nottinghamshire	−21·2	27·4	51·4
Derbyshire	−26·6	28·9	44·5
Staffordshire	−19·6	48·5	31·9
Northamptonshire	−28·6	36·1	35·3
Textile Counties			
West Riding, Yorkshire (incl. York) ..	−15·9	40·1	44·0
Lancashire and Cheshire	−21·6	33·9	44·5
North East			
Durham	−32·1	33·8	34·1
Northumberland	+ 3·5	49·4	54·1
South Wales and Monmouthshire			
Glamorganshire	−29·5	27·7	42·8
Monmouthshire	−23·8	28·2	48·0
Rest of England			
Hampshire and Isle of Wight	−15·8	16·3	67·9
Dorset	−12·2	15·8	72·0
Gloucestershire	−37·4	28·4	34·2
Wiltshire	−35·7	24·6	39·7
East and North Ridings, Yorks.	−28·1	27·1	44·8
Devonshire	−20·8	22·8	56·4
Somerset	−23·2	32·9	43·9
Oxfordshire	−19·4	33·6	47·0
Lincolnshire and Rutland	−17·1	25·7	57·2
Cambridgeshire and Ely	−16·3	40·2	43·5
Suffolk	−10·3	31·8	57·9
Norfolk	−17·2	40·4	42·4
Salop	−35·3	32·5	32·2
Westmorland and Cumberland	−17·9	49·8	32·3
Herefordshire	−46·6	21·2	32·2
Cornwall	− 4·1	24·0	71·9
London, Middlesex, Essex, Kent and Surrey	−27·5	16·6	55·9

* For details and explanations, see Statistical Appendix, p. 283.

practically the same as in the North-East, in South Wales and in eight of the counties included in " the Rest of England." They were lowest of all in the remainder of the " Rest of England " group. Thus not only were the local authority rates of supply low but the natural expectation that they would be highest in the counties with relatively high rates of requirements was not fulfilled. Any tendency in this direction was obscure and irregular. A glance at the last column of Table VI shows that the private enterprise rates of supply provided a sharp contrast. They were on the whole much higher than the local authority rates and they obviously tended to be highest in the counties with high rates of requirements.

Now it is just this matter of the extent to which local authorities responded to varying rates of requirements which seems so important in judging the adequacy of the local authority mechanism for providing additions to the supply of houses. It will be convenient to call the degree or extent of this responsiveness " *the elasticity of response to requirements.*" This involves some abuse of a technical meaning of " elasticity " in economic jargon which may offend economic purists but the word " elastic " was not invented by economists, and it is a very convenient word. This " elasticity of response " then needs measuring, and it is clear that it can very suitably be measured by the correlation coefficients between rates of requirements and the rates of supply of private enterprise and local authorities respectively. Both these were positive and significant, but in the former case it was very high +0·92, and in the latter relatively small +0·45.[1] The correlation coefficient of rates of requirements with the rates of total supply has already been given, +0·96, practically the same as the correlation with the private enterprise rate. It is clear, then, that private enterprise displayed a much higher degree of responsiveness to local rates of requirements than local authorities.[2]

The relatively weak elasticity of response of the local authorities was not, it appears, merely due to haphazard irregularities in the relation between rates of requirements and local authority rates of supply. The third and fourth columns in Table VII show the proportions of requirements for additional houses provided by the local authorities and private enterprise respectively. The most cursory

[1] See Statistical Appendix—Table 10.
[2] It is clear from the Table that the lack of positive relation between local authority rates of supply and rates of requirements was most pronounced in the Home Counties. If these are entirely omitted from the calculations, however, the correlation coefficient between rates of requirements and local authority rates of supply is increased to 0·64 but remains lower than that between rates of requirements and private enterprise rates of supply.

comparison of these proportions with the rates of requirements in the various counties shows that the proportions of requirements provided by the local authorities tended to be particularly low in two types of counties; those which were prosperous but had high rates of requirements and those in which requirements were low but suffered from economic depression. For instance, local authority contributions were relatively smallest of all in the Home Counties and some of the periphery counties, such as Hampshire, with high rates of requirements. On the other hand among the industrial counties they were higher in those which, like Staffordshire, Northumberland[1] and the West Riding, had relatively low requirements than in the counties with relatively high requirements. Among, however, the counties with low requirements the local authority contributions tended to be low in the industrially depressed counties, such as Durham and Glamorganshire.

The proportionate contributions to requirements made by private enterprise, on the other hand, had some tendency to increase with the rates of requirements, that is, where the proportions contributed by the local authorities tended to be particularly low. This, however, was so much more marked in the Home Counties than elsewhere, that it may be said that, except in the Home Counties, there was little indication that private enterprise compensated for the lack of building by local authorities.

The results are perhaps most effectively demonstrated by the correlation coefficient between the rates of requirements and the proportions of requirements contributed by local authorities. This was negative and significant -0.58. There is no manner of doubt that the proportion of houses provided by the local authorities was not merely not higher where the rate of requirements was relatively high, but actually tended to be lower. The parallel correlation coefficient for private enterprise was on the other hand positive and significant though not large, i.e. $+0.43$. Even if the Home Counties are left out of the calculations the negative correlation between the proportion of requirements contributed by the local authorities and the rates of requirements remains, though somewhat less pronounced, -0.42. Similarly, the positive correlation in the case of private enterprise is also reduced, i.e. $+0.29$.

[1] The case of Northumberland deserves perhaps special comment. It cannot be classed as a prosperous county, but compared to the really depressed area of Durham its position was favourable. The Commissioner for the Special Area of the North-East expressly excluded much of it from the special or depressed area on this ground. (*Report of the Commissioners for the Special Areas, 1934.* Cmd.4728, pp. 69–71.) Its requirements for houses were on the other hand the lowest but one in the country.

There is another point worth noticing about the proportionate rates of contributions. The local authorities responsible for providing working-class houses succeeded in achieving rates of supply equal to half the rates of requirements only in Cumberland and Westmorland. Even outside the Home Counties the proportion provided exceeded 40 per cent. only in four cases and was between 30 per cent. and 40 per cent. only in eight. The proportions of requirements provided by private enterprise were on the whole higher even outside the Home Counties, falling below 40 per cent. only in nine counties. Thus it seems that in most counties, if not in all, the non-working-class houses, i.e. those provided by private enterprise, were built in excess of requirements for *additional* houses of this type and considerable numbers must have been absorbed nearly everywhere by middle-class families moving from old-fashioned houses into modern ones.

It will be convenient before trying to look for explanations to summarise the conclusions so far reached:—

(1) The rate of housing requirements differed considerably between the various counties and on the whole was greater in the Home Counties and Midlands than elsewhere.

(2) In nearly all counties private enterprise made larger contributions to requirements than the local authorities, and probalby in most they were in excess of strict requirements for additional non-working-class houses.

(3) The local authority rates of supply showed considerable stickiness, particularly in comparison with those of private enterprise.

(4) The elasticity of response of private enterprise to requirements was positive and very high, that of local authorities though also positive, was considerably lower.

(5) The proportion of requirements satisfied by the local authorities appears to have been dependent mainly on two factors, the magnitude of the rate of requirements and the prosperity or lack of prosperity of individual counties. Thus local authorities made the smallest effective contributions in prosperous areas with high rates of requirements and in depressed areas with relatively low rates of requirements. There were, of course, exceptions to this rule, but it may be accepted as a reasonable generalisation.

(6) The proportion of requirements satisfied by private enterprise showed some tendency to be greatest where requirements were greatest, but on the whole it appeared much less dependent on the depression or prosperity of particular areas.

The whole analysis suggests unmistakably that between 1921 and 1931, housing policy as operated by the local authorities did not provide adequately for the very varying requirements for additional working-class houses in the different parts of the country. We cannot, however, accept the conclusion without question. It is possible that the types of families needing new houses were not uniformly distributed between the counties, and that, therefore, the rates of requirements do not reflect the differing requirements for local authority houses accurately in individual counties. This is quite possible even though there is no evidence that this was the case as far as the regions were concerned, for what is true of large areas is not necessarily true of their parts.

The period under review was characterised by a tendency for middle- and upper-class families to have their new houses built either on the outskirts of big towns or some distance away from them. Moreover, a considerable number of middle-class families who already had houses in the large towns gave them up and moved into new suburbs and into the country. In some districts, therefore, practically the whole of the increase in the numbers of families was due to these influxes of middle-class families, and requirements for new houses to balance additional families in these areas did not reflect requirements for additional working-class houses. It is important to be clear about the effects of the two separate elements of the demand for middle-class houses in connection with the geographical distribution of the need for new houses. To the extent that the new houses in one district simply represented a local concentration of the additions to the total numbers of middle-class families in a large area as a whole, the high proportion of requirements accounted for by middle-class families in the district of concentration merely meant that there was a concentration of requirements for working-class houses in other districts. It had no effect on the composition of requirements for the large area as a whole. On the other hand, in so far as the increase in middle-class families in any district was due to migration proper which involved actual substitution of the new houses for the old houses in other districts, the total number of new working-class houses needed in the whole area was reduced, on the assumption that the abandoned houses could be used by other families who might filter up into them. In short, part of the requirements for new working-class houses might be replaced by the demand for extra middle-class houses.[1]

[1] Up to 1931 the replacement element formed only a relatively small part of the demand, but by 1934 it was becoming a factor of major importance. It will be

It was probably only in the Home Counties, and their periphery that these differences in the distribution of social classes occurred on a scale sufficient to affect the composition of rates of requirements.[2] Here not only had the middle- and upper-classes already spread from London into surrounding counties in the past, but the new middle-class houses were as a rule built outside the London boundaries after the Great War. Nearly all the surrounding counties were affected by this. The middle- and upper-class suburbanisation of Surrey, Essex, Kent, Sussex and other Home Counties is too well known to need description. The middle- and upper-class element in these developments was reflected in the fact that in nearly all these counties the majority of the new houses built by private enterprise did not qualify for subsidies. The demand for the new houses was made up of two elements: the concentration of the additional middle- and upper-class families for the whole region in them and the migration of families from old houses in London to modern houses outside it.

The high proportion of private enterprise building in these reception counties, running up for instance to 75 per cent. in Sussex, can thus easily be explained, as well as the relatively small deficits in many of them in 1931, despite the low proportion of requirements provided by local authorities. It is evident, however, that the housing problem was not solved by this type of building for the region as a whole. Part of the concentration of middle-class demand in some counties was obviously balanced by a concentration of working-class demand in others, particularly in London and Middlesex. In these two counties together, private enterprise provided barely one-third of the additional houses needed, and, as the local authority only provided one-fifth, the deficit in 1931 was over 40 per cent. of the requirements. In Middlesex, where the new light industries were developing, the shortage of houses was actually greater in 1931 than it had been in 1921.[3] The requirements for additional working-

---

appreciated that there is no reason why the demand for new houses for replacing old ones should be proportionate to the demand for additional houses. In individual areas, however, the additional families may be, as we have seen, immigrants who have decided to give up their old houses in one area so as to have new ones somewhere else; in these cases the additional requirements may be proportionate to replacement requirements elsewhere.

[2] This is so, partly because the migration from London was more marked than that from other large towns, and, partly, because Cheshire has been combined with Lancashire and Warwickshire with Worcestershire in the tables, thus amalgamating the main towns with their dormitories across the county boundaries.

[3] Between 1921 and 1931 the number of families in Middlesex increased by 126 thousand, but the number of houses only by 115 thousand. Thus a deficit of 11 thousand houses accumulated between 1921 and 1931 in addition to that outstanding in 1921.

class houses here was not offset by the migration of middle-class
families from old to new houses.

The effects of the migration proper from London into surrounding counties in setting free old houses in London cannot be measured.
Undoubtedly it helped to reduce the need for additional houses in
London. On paper the reduction in the need for new houses should
have corresponded to the scale of the migration, and the shortage
of working-class houses should have been correspondingly relieved
by the filtering-up process. In practice this process has, however,
obvious limits determined by the suitability of the abandoned
middle-class houses for other types of families. It is too often forgotten
that migration may be reflected in empty or derelict houses or,
particularly where site values are high, in exceptionally high rates
of actual demolition. On the basis of rather inadequate data the
net wastage[1] of houses through demolition and conversion to non-
residential purposes may be estimated as probably about 2·9 per cent.
of the old houses in the Home Counties compared to only about
1·6 per cent. in the Midlands. Owing to the absence of proper
statistics of vacant houses in 1921, it is impossible to estimate changes
in their numbers between 1921 and 1931[2].

It is clear, in any case, that though the low proportion of requirements for additional houses provided by the local authorities may
have been due to the lack of need for working-class houses in some
of the Home Counties, this was not the case in London and
Middlesex. It cannot be regarded as a complete explanation for the
region taken as a whole. We must conclude that the shifting of
population complicated the housing problem in the region as a whole
by increasing the net wastage of houses.

The case of the Home Counties has been discussed in detail
because more data is available than in other cases of counties with
particularly high proportions of private enterprise building, and
low local authority ones. It is possible that the Sussex-Surrey type of
explanation applies to one or two of the periphery counties also,
such as Hampshire and Dorsetshire, but it cannot be applied to
counties not subject to net middle-class immigration.

It must not be assumed, however, that movements of population
complicated the housing problem only in this way. For instance,

---

[1] Theoretically net wastage can be calculated by subtracting the actual increase in
dwellings between the Census of 1921 and that of 1931 from the total number of new
houses built. Unfortunately, however, exact figures of the latter for the individual regions
(see Table 9A, Statistical Appendix) are not available.

[2] See p. 11 n. 1 above, and p. 270 n. (4) below.

there were high rates of net wastage in certain of the agricultural counties and in Northumberland and Durham also.[1] These must be attributed to the tendency of the agricultural and mining population to drift into the towns in search of higher wages or urban amenities, leaving cottages in the villages to go derelict.

This digression on the Home Counties has cleared up a certain number of doubtful points. It has shown that the low proportionate contribution to housing requirements, made by local authorities in some counties, may have been due to differences in the composition of the demand for new houses in particular areas partly caused by genuine migrations of particular classes of families. It has made it equally clear, however, that the emergence of differences in the composition of demand in particular counties are frequently merely due to the accident that single economic areas are artificially cut up by county boundaries. Incidentally, the investigation has led to the conclusion that the filtering process may lead to increases in the effective wastage of houses by demolitions and increases of vacants. Most important of all, the digression has confirmed our original conclusion that local authorities tended to be least successful in dealing with housing requirements, even in prosperous areas, if the rate of requirements was particularly high. Private enterprise building did not appear to suffer from this weakness. We have discovered that there were a few counties with high requirements to which the conclusion about the local authorities did not apply, owing to the peculiarities of the composition of their requirements which were due to county boundaries dividing up districts which were part of the same economic unit.

These conclusions apply to building activities up to the spring of 1931 as they are based partly on the data contained in the Population Census of that year. It has already been explained, however, that the greater part of the local authority building of the second experiment was completed by them. Our results have significance, therefore, as providing an indication of the effects of the policy of the second experiment and as a comparison of the apparent effectiveness of the local authorities and private enterprise in providing supplies of houses. It must be emphasised that this chapter has been devoted entirely to describing what happened. We have not yet made any real attempt to find explanations. The next two chapters deal with this more difficult aspect.

[1] e.g. The net wastage rate was 2·9 per cent. in Cornwall, 2·8 per cent. in the North and East Ridings of Yorkshire, 6·6 per cent. in Northumberland and 3·2 per cent. in the county of Durham.

F

Chapter V

THE SECOND EXPERIMENT—(*contd.*)

THE CONTRIBUTION OF PRIVATE ENTERPRISE

I. Building and Costs

Failure to supply people with what they want, provided they can pay for it, is not usually one of the defects ascribed to private enterprise. Between 1923 and 1934 there were large numbers of families wanting new houses and apparently able to pay for the houses they wanted. We need to know which these fortunate families were.

It has already been explained that an additional three-quarters of a million houses, superior to the ordinary working-class type, were needed between the Armistice and 1934. Actually nearly twice as many houses of this type were built. They accounted for about 58 per cent. of all the new houses built, instead of the theoretically correct proportion of 33 per cent.[1] There are two possible explanations of this apparent surplus. Families who would normally before the Great War have lived in the ordinary type of working-class house with a rateable value not exceeding £13, may have decided to make the effort and live in a better type of house. Alternatively, families already living in lower and upper middle-class houses may have decided that it would be preferable to live in a new modern house built as and where they liked. It will be noticed that a maximum total increase of about 660 thousand in the supply of houses with rateable values over £13 for the ordinary working-class market was the net result in any case.

It has already been suggested that some sort of exodus from the old houses might have been expected to take place sooner or later. For any family in the happy position of being able to afford to pay a builder to provide a new house, the move would naturally take place sooner rather than later. The temptation to move was probably greatest for those families living in the small, three or four bedroomed type of house, which compared so unfavourably with the small modern villas. The long dark passages, cold and depressing sculleries, sordid bathrooms and villainous scarlet brick of Victorian lower middle-class villas could, in the post-war era, be abandoned in

[1] See Tables IV and V above.

exchange for compact new houses with all sorts of modern conveniences and fittings. The new villas may be stigmatised as jerry-built, they may be despised as pseudo-Tudor or ugly by the sophisticated, but there is no denying their attraction for the young couple with a small family. Nor must it be forgotten that the improvements in transport, better trains, electrification, buses and motor coaches made the outskirts and new suburbs cheaply and rapidly accessible. It became unnecessary for the conscientious clerk to live near his work.

All these changes have conspired to encourage the natural wish to get out of old houses into new. But it would be quite wrong to jump to the conclusion that by 1934 an exodus had taken place on a fantastic scale. Even if it can be assumed that all the houses not of a normal working-class type had been entirely absorbed by the lower and upper middle-classes, the balance of new houses to spare over those required to cover the war shortage and current requirements was only sufficient to enable one quarter[1] of such families living in old houses to replace them by new ones. An exodus of this size, considered as it should be, spread over the whole period of twenty years from 1914 to 1934 is only equivalent to an average annual rate of replacement of about 1·3 per cent.! Another sixty years were still needed, at this rate, to complete the process. In fact, it would be well to ask why the exodus was not more rapid.

However attractive and desirable the new houses might seem in comparison with the old, the question of the cost of the new houses compared to the old would inevitably intrude on the housewife's dreams of modern delights. Then, too, the cost of new houses was more likely to be important to families who already had houses of sorts to live in, than to those who were in difficulties in getting houses at all. The rate of replacement, or, in other words, of moving from old to new houses, was therefore likely to be very closely tied up both with the costs of new houses, and the terms of tenure on which the new houses could be obtained. The question of costs would, of course, also affect the extent to which families from the lower income groups might be tempted to venture into the field.

Chart II gives a bird's-eye view of building by private enterprise. It shows the numbers of houses of various sorts built by private enterprise, and the changes in the annual cost of buying a house through the building societies, with, and without, the Chamberlain subsidy.

---

[1] This is simple arithmetic for there were about 2,700 thousand families of this type in 1919 excluding those who were without houses because of the shortage. These latter have been taken into account in calculating the surplus of houses in 1934.

CHART II.—Building by Private Enterprise and the cost of buying houses.
1924–5 to 1933–4.*

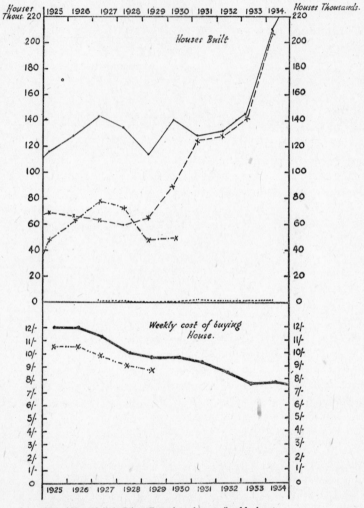

Nos. of Houses built by Private Enterprise each year ending March 31st.

```
————————    =All houses built by Private Enterprise.
- - - - -    =Houses built by Private Enterprise without subsidy.
- · - · -    =Houses built by Private Enterprise with Chamberlain subsidy.
· · · · · ·  =Houses built by Private Enterprise with Wheatley subsidy.
```

Annual Averages of minimum cost of buying a " local authority type" house.

```
━━━━━━━    =Weekly cost without subsidy.
- · - · -    =Weekly cost with Chamberlain subsidy.
```

　　　　　* See Statistical Appendix, Tables 2 and 6.

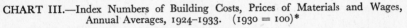

CHART III.—Index Numbers of Building Costs, Prices of Materials and Wages, Annual Averages, 1924–1933. (1930 = 100)*

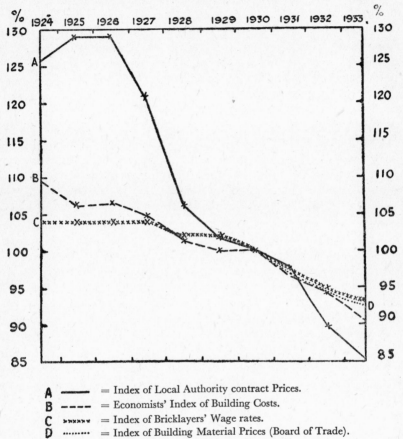

A ——— = Index of Local Authority contract Prices.
B − − − − = Economists' Index of Building Costs.
C ⋈⋈⋈⋈⋈ = Index of Bricklayers' Wage rates.
D ········ = Index of Building Material Prices (Board of Trade).

* See Statistical Appendix, Table 5.

For comparison index numbers of building costs are given in Chart III.

Chart II shows very clearly the four phases through which building by private enterprise passed during the Second Experiment. In the first, lasting up to the beginning of 1927, the number of houses built each year increased; in the second, up to the beginning of 1929 the number built each year decreased; in the third there was a gradual but unmistakable revival, while the fourth phase, starting in 1932, overlapped the opening stages of the great expansion of building which culminated a few years before the outbreak of the present war.

It is obvious that the capacity of the building industry was the main limiting factor on the output of houses during the first phase. The numbers of insured workers in the building industry increased slowly, and unemployment was negligible. Among bricklayers, for instance, not more than 2 per cent. were unemployed on an average in the summer months in 1924 and 1927.[1] Building costs remained practically stationary in 1925 and 1926, and the number of houses built with the Chamberlain subsidy increased each year, though the output of unsubsidised houses hardly changed.

The decline in the volume of building started right at the beginning of the second phase and continued to its end without interruption. It was due entirely to the collapse of building with the Chamberlain subsidy, and in the year ending March 1929 the number of houses built with it was 41 per cent. less than in the last year of the first phase. The lack of change in the rate of building without the subsidy formed a sharp contrast. The fall in total output was accompanied, however, by a major fall in costs. The cost of buying a small house of the three bedroom, non-parlour type usually built by local authorities fell by between 2/– and 3/– a week to about 9/9 without the subsidy.[2] The decrease in the cost of buying with the subsidy was, of course, smaller owing to the cut made in it in 1927. It is possible, perhaps, to argue that it was the announcement of the forthcoming cut in the subsidy that precipitated the decline in building. The cut, however, was only equivalent to a few pence a week. It is impossible to attribute the whole fall in building to so small an initial change in the weekly cost of purchase, particularly as it was followed so quickly by a much bigger fall due to the decline in actual building costs.

It is clear, however, that by 1930 the continued fall in costs had become in total sufficient to stimulate an expansion of unsubsidised building of houses of all sizes. This expansion was practically sufficient to offset the complete disappearance of new building with the Chamberlain subsidy with its abolition as from October 1929. This expansion of unsubsidised building marked the opening of the third phase, and it will be noticed that though costs fell more slowly from 1929 to 1931, the expansion continued into 1931/32. The fourth phase opened with an acceleration of the rate of building in 1932/3

[1] See Statistical Appendix, Table 8B.
[2] See Statistical Appendix, Table 6.

which developed into the great upswing of output in 1933/4. In 1932 and 1933 the cost of buying houses had fallen again, partly as a result of the further fall in actual building costs, partly as a result of the first substantial fall in the rate of interest charged on building society advances.[1]

Now all this is rather puzzling. Sometimes the volume of building seemed to depend on changes in costs, as in the third and fourth phases. At other times there seemed to be no connection as in the first and second phases. Obviously the relation between the volume of building and the costs of buying houses was not perfectly straightforward. There is no doubt that the changes in costs were genuine. As people were in general buying their own houses, they were in a position to benefit directly from the decreases, instead of only after an interval during which such decreases might be absorbed by landlords. The amount of capital purchasers had to borrow decreased with building costs as well as the amount they themselves had to provide, unless of course they decided to take advantage of the lower costs to get better houses.

The explanation must be looked for in the peculiarities of the demand for houses. The demand for houses is made up, of course, of the demands of individual families for individual houses. Since in general each family only wants one house, its demand for houses will not expand with decreases in costs as one expects to happen in the case of chocolates or clothes for instance. A family will not want two houses merely because houses have become cheaper to buy. In consequence, the current demand for houses is made up of the demands of those families which have not already got houses, together with the demands of those families who would like to give up their old houses (thereby ceasing to have a demand for them), and get new ones instead. The number of families effectively in the market for buying houses at any particular time depends, therefore, upon whether the cost of getting satisfactory houses is appropriate to the particular groups of families either without houses, or tired of their houses. If we consider the changes in the costs of buying houses between 1925 and 1934 from this angle, some of the peculiarities of building activity disappear.

For this purpose it is necessary to distinguish two groups of houses, those with rateable values up to £13, the ordinary working-class houses, and those with rateable values over £13 and up to £26,[2]

---

[1] The average rate charged on new advances fell from 5·9 per cent. in 1932 to 4·9 per cent. in 1933. (Statistical Appendix, Table 6.)
[2] i.e. up to £20, and £21–£35, respectively in London.

the houses of the better-off artisan and lower middle-class families. The controlled rents, excluding rates, for old houses of the former type ran up to a maximum of about 9/- outside London, and those of the latter type reached about 17/- outside London. [1] During the first phase of the second experiment the payments to building societies necessary to buy the cheapest and smallest type of house built was about twelve shillings a week, or with the Chamberlain subsidy, between ten or eleven shillings. Although these weekly payments were not in excess of the lower controlled rents of houses in the over £13 rateable value group, other expenses were involved which made the real cost of buying considerably higher. The weekly payments to building societies included no allowance for costs of maintenance and repairs, and in addition, at this time the initial lump sum payment required by the building societies even for the cheapest type of house would have been about £150. [2] Moreover, the house obtained with all this expense would have had only the advantage of being new and modern to offset the absence of the parlour cherished by all better-off families. To get a house with a parlour would have meant another few shillings on the weekly instalment. All things considered the cost of getting the sort of house wanted would have corresponded to the highest of the controlled rents of the old houses.

Obviously the demand for houses at this sort of level of costs must have been limited. By March, 1927, nearly half a million non-working-class houses had been built, including nearly two hundred thousand qualifying for the Chamberlain subsidy. The number of additional houses of this superior type needed to cover the war shortage and current needs up to that date was only four hundred thousand. Unless a substantial fall in costs occurred sufficient to bring new houses within the reach of families only willing or able to incur smaller liabilities, building was bound to fall off.

It was not until 1928, that the accumulated fall in costs had become really substantial. [3] By that year the smallest local authority type of house could, even with the reduced Chamberlain subsidy, have been bought for between eight and nine shillings a week. At this level of costs houses were becoming a reasonable financial

[1] Calculated from data given in the *Marley Report* op. cit. pp. 26 and 29, assuming rates were 25% of gross rents.

[2] The cost of building, land, etc., for an ordinary non-parlour three-bedroom house built by local authorities averaged £510 at this time. The normal advance made by building societies did not exceed 70 per cent. of the all-in cost of the house, so that if a private individual could get a house of this type built privately as cheaply as by a local authority he would have to find 30 per cent. of £510 himself, i.e. £153.

[3] See Charts II and III above and Statistical Appendix, Tables 5 and 6.

proposition for the whole group of families accustomed to living in houses with rateable values between £13 and £26, provided they had the capital available for the initial lump sum payment required. The next year, 1929, however, the Chamberlain subsidy was abolished. This meant that for the smallest type of house practically two-thirds of the whole fall in costs since 1927 was counteracted. There was, nevertheless, a considerable demand for houses in the same rateable value group which were too large to qualify for the subsidy, the market for these benefited from the whole fall in costs, and it is probable that the expansion in the building of unsubsidised houses with rateable values up to £26 occurred here.

It seems fairly clear that the very high rate of correlation, noticed in the last chapter, between building by private enterprise and requirements, between 1921 and 1931, was due to the fact that the fall in costs enabled private enterprise to build houses for sale for successively lower sections of the market for houses with rateable values between £13 and £26. In the earlier years the Chamberlain subsidy partly made this possible; in the later years the fall in costs helped particularly for houses of a type not qualifying for the subsidy in any case.

It was not until the end of the third phase in 1933 that the further fall in costs and the reduction in interest rates was sufficient to offset the cancellation of the Chamberlain subsidy on the costs of buying really small houses. It is thus not surprising that there was a failure to realise a major expansion in building parallel to the fall in costs until after 1932. Unfortunately, we do not know at what date private enterprise really penetrated into the working-class market proper. In 1933/4, however, 94·5 thousand houses of this type were built by private enterprise, and of these just under a third were intended for letting.[1] It is evident that by this time the market for the largest type of houses was dwindling in importance relatively to that for the small houses. Houses with rateable values over £26 had fallen from 21 per cent. of the total built by private enterprise in 1930/1 to 12 per cent. in 1934/5.[2]

Other conditions had also become favourable to a new expansion in the rate of building, particularly of small houses by the end of the third phase. Real income had increased during the Great Depression for those who had remained in jobs, with the fall in the

---

[1] October 1933 to September 1934. See Ministry of Health Report, *Housing*, 1935.
[2] As there are no figures available about the rateable values of the Chamberlain houses, it is impossible to say whether the decline started before 1930/1. See Statistical Appendix, Table 3D.

cost of living, and by 1933/4 prospects of employment were improving. Meanwhile the yield in gilt-edged investments remained at extreme low levels, and the belief that a new era of low interest rates had begun was spreading. Interest rates on new mortgages were in consequence low and might be expected to remain so. Finally, it seemed improbable that building costs would fall any further. They were more likely to rise than fall. The situation was favourable for investment in houses to let for the first time since the Great War, as well as for building for owner-occupation. The stage was set for a new building boom.

The history of building by private enterprise between 1923 and 1934 is in part a record of the purchase of new houses by families in successively lower economic classes. Some of the houses were bought by families who were unable to get a reasonable old house to let, others by families who had decided to abandon old houses in favour of new. Naturally the movement to substitute new houses for old lagged behind the purchase of new houses because some sort of house had to be obtained somehow. Equally naturally the movement started later among the lower than the higher income groups. It was only after 1931/2 that it began to develop on a really large scale as buying a new house became a relatively attractive financial proposition for families living in the old houses with rateable values round about £13. Some indication of the extent and timing of this exodus from old houses into new is given by the figures showing the numbers of houses which became decontrolled on changes of tenancies under the Rent Restriction Acts. It will be remembered that under the revised scheme of control instituted in 1923 houses were freed from control as soon as the families living in them in 1923 moved out. The proportion of each main type of house which had become decontrolled at various dates gives a rough idea of the extent to which the exodus from old houses of various sorts took place. Between 1923 and 1931, 37·7 per cent. of the tenants of houses with rateable values over £35 moved house, compared to only 13 per cent. of those in the houses in the next rateable value group, £14 to £35, and 12½ per cent. in the up to £13 group. By the following year all the percentages had increased, reaching 41·2 per cent., 16·1 per cent., and 17·0 per cent. respectively. It will be noticed that the increase during 1932 was most rapid among the families living in the houses with rateable values up to £13. By 1933 the percentage of families in the lowest group who had moved reached 25 per cent. It had doubled in two years, but had not caught up with the percentage of families who had moved out of the old houses in the next group above ; the latter was now 39 per cent.[1] It is clear that the move out of old houses started with families living in the most expensive old houses and that it was only after 1931 or 1932 that families in the cheaper old houses joined in the exodus on a large scale.

The history of the purchase of houses between 1923 and 1934 by successively lower income groups, has a wider significance than a record of attempts to satisfy an urgent need for houses of some sort or other. The demand for new houses was in part at least a demand for a higher standard of housing, or at least for a standard consistent with modern ideas and knowledge. It marked the first stage in the battle to break free from the pattern of housing conditions and domestic life created in the Nineteenth Century ; in all senses it was a logical part of the emancipation of women, an attempt to free themselves from household drudgery. Families in the higher income groups naturally led the way, not only because they could afford to buy new houses most easily, but also because the disappearance of cheap and uncomplaining domestic servants threatened the women in the upper classes with an intolerable burden of household work if they went on living in the old houses. The women in the lower income groups were not threatened in the same way. It was only gradually that they realised how much pleasanter their lives would be if they could get new houses. It was only gradually, as costs fell, that this ambition could be realised by the better-off among them.

II. PROBLEMS OF FINANCE AND THE GROWTH OF OWNER-OCCUPATION.

Now that we have some idea of the sort of people who got new houses between 1923 and 1934, and when they got them, it is time to go more carefully into the questions of how it was that so many people could manage to buy their own houses and why they bought their houses instead of renting them.

---

[1] These figures only give a rough indication of the trend of moves from old houses to new, for some people may have moved out of controlled houses into other old houses which had become decontrolled because someone else had already moved. It is almost certain, therefore, that the figures exaggerate the size of the moves into new houses, but they can fairly be taken as showing the timing of the exodus and the differences between its size and timing in the various groups. The figures themselves are based on estimates given in the Reports of the Marley and Ridley Committees on the Rent Restriction Acts, op. cit., pp. 19 and 14 respectively, and in a Memorandum issued by the Ministry of Health, *Statistics of Houses*, Cmd. 4208, 1932. Comparable figures for houses with rateable values over £35 are not available for 1933. The results quoted in the text are entirely consistent with those of the Ministry of Labour's Cost of Living Inquiry of 1937/8, and Inquiry into Middle Class Budgets in 1938/9 by the Civil Service Statistical and Research Bureau. See pp. 176–177 below.

The first question is relatively simple to answer in general terms. Although a very large proportion of the capital of the country is owned by a relatively small number of people, there is a large intermediate group between the capitalists in the popular conception of the term and the poorest group of the population which owns no capital worth mentioning. It has been calculated that, between 1924 and 1930, about five million adults, of twenty-five years of age and over (that is, about one in five of the women and one in four of the men) owned more than £100 each.[1] There were therefore plenty of people who could, if they wished, provide some of the capital at least for buying houses for themselves if the houses were not too expensive. There were numerous ways of obtaining any balance of capital required through mortgages ; private mortgages might be obtained, the money might be borrowed from the building societies, or it might be borrowed from the local authorities under the Small Dwellings Acquisition Acts. Of course, these people with capital could instead buy houses to let to other people ; if they wanted new houses themselves, however, they were unlikely to do so. Actually, the total sum advanced by the building societies between 1923 and 1934 was £864 million. The number of individual borrowers had grown from about half a million in 1928 the first year for which the information is available, to over one million in 1934. Although not all these new advances were made to owner-occupiers of new houses, most of them certainly were, and it is evident that part of the capital for the majority of the houses was provided in this way. There is no mystery about the source of the capital at all. In addition to the advances made by building societies, loans made for house purchase under the Small Dwellings Acquisition Acts amounted over this period to between £80 and £90 million.[2] Though small in comparison with the former, this too is a substantial sum. These developments are shown on Chart IV.

The second question is more difficult. It is undoubtedly generally considered that before the Great War the majority of houses, including those in the intermediate group, with rateable values between £13 and £26, had not been owned by the people living in them. Owner-occupation on the scale of the period of the second experi-

[1] *Distribution of the National Capital*, by G. W. Daniels and H. Campion. Manchester University Press, 1936, pp. 30 and 31. The authors suggest, as a rough estimate, that the small capitalists, owing between £100 and £500 each, numbered between 2,700 thousand and 3 million.

[2] Including advances made by local authorities under the Housing Acts of 1923 and 1925. Loans to purchasers made by building societies had been guaranteed in respect of 26,775 houses also. See Ministry of Health Six-Monthly Statement, *Housing*, and *Annual Reports*.

CHART IV.—The Growth of Building Societies, 1924–33.*   (Ratio Scale).

- - - - Liabilities to Shareholders and Depositors £mn.
· · · · · · · · New Advances £mn.
▬▬▬▬ Number of Shareholders and Depositors.
─────── Number of Borrowers.

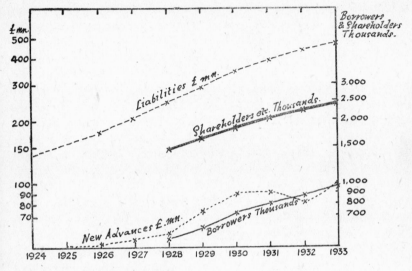

* See Statistical Appendix, Table 7A.

ment is regarded as something new. There seems no reasonable doubt about the general correctness of this view, though, to be candid we have no means of knowing statistically the extent of owner-occupation before the Great War. We must content ourselves with the general statement that both in relative and absolute importance owner-occupation increased in the years following the war. Actually, it is more important to know why the change occurred than to know its actual size, and there is no need to be led astray in a futile search for non-existent statistics. The explanation of the change is best approached by considering changes in the attractiveness of invest-ment in houses to let. This will help to dispel both much of the confusion which habitually surrounds discussions of housing pro-blems and the myth that the increase of owner-occupancy has been due either to a remarkable increase in the virtue and thrift of the population or, alternatively, to some factor of the " Act of God " type. We shall, in fact, find that the system of buying houses through building societies spread rapidly merely because it was the only way available of satisfying a particular need.

The willingness of investors to put capital into the ownership of houses for letting to other people to live in depends, naturally, on opinions about the attractiveness of the type of investment compared to others. Undoubtedly, the Rent Restriction Acts of the Great War had rather upset ordinary calculations. The owners of houses to let, that is, the effective owners of the equity in the investments, had been forcibly reduced in status. They had become more like preference shareholders in joint stock companies since their maximum incomes were limited, but they were without guarantees. They were prevented from realising the highest profits available in the market for houses and increases in their incomes became strictly controlled by the Government. They were not compensated for this control, however, by any sort of guarantee, nor were their liabilities and duties correspondingly reduced ; they were still obliged to pay the interest on any mortgages on the property. Under these conditions the relative attractiveness of investing capital in the ownership of houses to let dwindled. Few people would undertake investment in which they shouldered all the risk, but were prevented from picking up the plums that came their way.

There is a school of thought that maintains that these effects of the Rent Restriction Acts explain the absence of private investment in new houses to let after the Great War. The fact so damaging to this argument, that rents of houses built after the summer of 1919 were not controlled, is apt to be ignored. Rent Restriction, in fact, only affected part of the house market directly, and even in that part it did not precipitate losses so much as prevent extra profit. The explanation is altogether too thin to stand by itself. In any case, gradual re-emergence of investment in new houses to let occurred during the 'thirties despite the continuance of rent control ; this makes the explanation untenable.

There are, however, other far sounder reasons for the decline in the relative attractiveness in investment in houses to let for profit in the post-war period. Building costs had soared immediately after the war, but had started falling in 1921. They had risen again in 1924 and 1925 and fallen again after 1926/7. This second fall continued for the next eight years. If there was anything certain during these years about the course of building costs, and, for that matter, interest rates, it was that they would tend downwards. It was explained in the first chapter that the continuance of rent control after the war would encourage the belief that sooner or later building costs and interest rates would revert to pre-war levels.   In fact, the increases, amounting to 40 per cent. of net 1914 rents, permitted by the amendments of the Rent and Mortgage Interest Restrictions Act in 1919 and 1921, suggested an ultimate level of 40 per cent. above pre-war as the new normal; the rent rules of the Wheatley Subsidy involved this assumption also.   But even if 40 per cent. above pre-war were to be regarded as the normal, this would imply substantial falls in costs after 1924, if investment in houses to let was to become profitable.[1] The effects of initial high costs and interest rates and expectations of decreases on the prospective income from investment in houses to let, has been described at some length in earlier chapters.   It will be sufficient here to point out that the prospects are peculiarly unlikely to encourage anyone to put money into new houses to let. It is a relatively stable low level of costs and interest which makes such investment attractive, *not* the painful process by which such a position is reached.   It can hardly be regarded as surprising that these circumstances, combined no doubt with some reaction to rent control, led to the disappearance of the investor in new houses to let even outside the field covered by the local authorities.

These are short term and particular explanations which apply specifically to these years.   The fact that after building costs and interest rates reached bottom in the Great Depression, the revival of new investment in houses to let was on a small scale suggests, it seems, that there were more deep-rooted and permanent tendencies at work also.   Both the usefulness and the attractiveness of this way of investing money appeared to have diminished permanently, and we must examine more general tendencies in the investment market.

On the whole, before the Great War, the investment market in houses was local.   Local people invested money in their own locality in houses built either by themselves or by local speculative builders. This method had a number of quite formidable disadvantages. The investor put his eggs into one basket, in the form of a small or large group of houses in a particular area.   Any decline in the rents of one house was likely to be accompanied by declines in the rents of the rest of his houses, and, of course, vice versa. The possibility of realising his investment, even in favourable circumstances, depended on the existence of other local investors willing to buy them.   There was no nationally organised market such as that for stocks and shares or government securities, and the units

[1] See p. 22 above.

of investment were inconveniently large compared to shares. The
organisation of the market in the equity of houses was thus primitive
and out of line with other investment markets. Its survival probably depended on the belief that it was possible to know all about
the local market, but not about the other opportunities of investment. Socially it had the grave disadvantage that the supply of
houses in any place depended mainly on the local supply of capital.
Sooner or later it might be expected to die out like other primitive
institutions.[1]

Other tendencies were also at work, particularly in the post-
war years. The habit of indirect investment through investment
trusts or insurance companies was growing. These offered small
and rather timid investors opportunities of investment in industrials
combined with professional advice, and dispersed risks over a wide
field. Moreover, it was a form of investment free from commitments, the investors had no responsibility for mortgage interest and
repayment and no liabilities for repairs.

On the whole then it seems relatively easy to explain the apparently
mysterious disappearance of the private investor in houses to let.
Other ways of investing capital had become more attractive. It
was merely a bread-and-butter question of the ordinary economic
type.

The modern owner-occupier aided and abetted by the building
societies stepped neatly into the place deserted by investing owner.
We shall see later that he was unable to fill the gap altogether, but
the apparent popular enthusiasm for owner-occupation almost
suggests that for a large number of people it was a preferable way of
getting a house. Obviously the system has a lot of advantages, and
it has always been common among the well-to-do. An owner-
occupier can decide within fairly wide limits when and where he
will have his house built. He is not dependent on anyone else being
willing to provide a house for him. He is free of interference from
landlords and from the risk of his rent being raised against him at
the expiry of his lease. All these are specially attractive characteristics if there is a shortage of houses. The solution of the housing
problem is complete for those who can afford it. Nor must the
pleasing sensations of property ownership be overlooked, a house
after all is a very tangible form of property. No doubt appreciation of these advantages were materially reinforced after the Great
War by the pragmatic argument that as people would not invest in

---

[1] Cf. the evidence taken by the Committee appointed " to consider the operations of
the Rent Restrictions Act," 1920, p. 19 *et seq.*

houses to let, anyone wanting a house had to buy one or go without, if they wanted a modern house.

As far as it goes, this explanation is convincing. It suffers from the weakness that it does not account for the willingness for people to invest capital in houses for their own use, while investment in houses to let to other people was so unpopular. Superficially the nature of the risks involved seem similar. In fact, they were different because the purpose of investment was different. The old type house-investor invested in order to obtain a fairly secure cash income, or return on his investment, and he probably often hoped to maintain the selling value of his investment. The owner-occupier does not invest in order to obtain a cash return but in order to secure a house approximately of the type he would like to live in. Changes in the cash value of that privilege are only indirectly relevant. They neither effect the real income derived from living in a house nor directly the terms on which that real income is obtained. Changes in the market value of the house affect its owner directly only when for some reason he wants to sell the house. Alternatively, it may affect only his heirs if they want to sell or obtain a cash income from it when he dies. It is reasonable to assume that most people will buy houses for their own use only if they do not expect to need to sell. No doubt, for instance, many people who bought houses in the 'twenties and 'thirties expected to live in them until the end of their lives. The question of the ultimate selling value is apt to be just as remote a contingency as death.

These considerations naturally give owner-occupiers an attitude towards the risk of investing their money by buying houses quite different from that of people investing in houses to let. Uncertainty as to the future course of building costs and interest rates do not necessarily deter them. The whole nature of the equity risk they shoulder is different and very much smaller than in the case of investment in houses to let. The net effect should be, of course, that they get houses on cheaper and more favourable terms by buying than by renting.

It is important not to get confused at this point. Indifference, or relative indifference, to the future course of prices and interest rates does not imply indifference to the actual cost of building a house and to the interest which must be paid on any mortgage. Indeed, it is precisely these things which will decide the question of what people can afford to buy houses. The cost of building at the time of building affects the amount of capital to be extricated from existing investments and how much has to be saved in the future,

G

while the rate of interest on mortgages affects the payments to be made each year by people unable to buy outright for cash.[1]

The development of owner-occupation on the scale of the post-war period, the replacement of the private investor in houses to let by individual owner-occupiers, could only have taken place if sufficient funds were available for borrowing on mortgages on the new houses. Otherwise owner-occupation would have been limited to the families with sufficient capital to buy their houses outright or sufficient credit to raise mortgages privately. It is at this point that the building societies came in. They had been started primarily by and for small men in the nineteenth century for the very purpose of making it possible for them to borrow enough capital on mortgage to buy houses to live in; they were not started for the benefit of investors intending to buy houses to let. Unless some sort of arrangement for borrowing on mortgage such as that provided by the building societies is available, the possibility of any individual borrowing money to buy a house is dependent mainly on his happening to know someone willing to lend him enough money, or someone who knows someone else who is willing to do so. The further anyone is down the economic or social scale, the more modest his financial circumstances, the more dependent he would be on borrowing, and the less likely to have connections and acquaintances possessing money to lend and willing to lend it. The investing-owner, by making it part of his business, would normally be in a better position to make the necessary contacts through solicitors, merchants, etc., and this is important, has a better security to offer for a loan. The would-be occupying-owner can only offer his personal credit as a guarantee of his honouring the terms of a mortgage. A man with a small income and limited resources, about to put most of his capital into a house, would be able to offer little security beyond his own expectations of his income in the future. Of course, the selling value of the house would provide alternate security for the capital lent, but realisation of this is the last resort; it involves

[1] There is one other point to consider, the loss of cash income which would have been obtained from the same amount of capital put into ordinary investments. Of course the possible loss will be smaller the lower the yield on whatever sort of investment is considered to show a reasonable alternative. If, as may often be the case, this is some sort of gilt-edged investment, the uncertainty during the twenties about the time and method of conversion of the War Debt may have encouraged people to regard the probable loss of cash income from investing in houses as rather unimportant. It seems impossible, however, to dogmatise about how such a loss would be reckoned in terms of real advantage in buying a house. Some people might make careful calculations of the loss against the future savings on rents. Others may ignore the problem altogether, for if the only way to get a house is to buy it the actual cash-loss involved may well be considered irrelevant.

foreclosure and the premature termination of the mortgage investment. Any reasonably cautious lender would make careful enquiries
about the character and prospects of the borrower.

The investing owner of houses to let would offer something
stronger. Unless things went wrong with the investment the interest
on the mortgage would be provided for out of the rents for which
the houses would be let. If one tenant failed to pay, another might
be found, and the bother of doing so would fall on the owner. If
rent failed to come up to expectations, the result would normally
merely be that the owner, not the mortgagee, received a smaller
income. Of course, if rents fell below that amount required to pay
the interest on the mortgage, the income of the mortgagee would
come into the danger zone. But even at this stage there would be
a last line of defence, the one which was the first line of defence in
the case of the owner-occupier, the personal income and security of
the owner. The combination of owner-occupation and private
mortgage could not take the place of the combination of investing
owner and private mortgagee on a large scale.

The system of collecting and pooling the capital of lenders and
pooling investments worked out by the building societies provided
a solution for the problem of people trying to borrow capital for
buying their own houses. The investor was offered a much better
security for the investment. In the first place the risks were decreased. Neither the safety of, nor the income on, the capital of an
individual lender was tied up with the reliability of a particular
indivdual borrower or with the value of a particular house. The
capital was put into a pool which was invested in the mortgage on
a large number of houses often scattered over different parts of the
country. The system of repayment of loans by instalments also
reduced the risk of loss on any particular investment made by a
building society : it also increased the liquidity of a building society's
assets : some money was always being repaid. This made it possible
for small investors to be paid back their capital when they needed
it, so increasing the liquidity of the individual investor's positions.[1]
In any case, the building society and its resources stood as a buffer
between the individual investor and losses, and any losses actually
made, would be spread over all the investors if the worst came to
the worst. The system had still other advantages for investors, they

[1] It should be pointed out that private mortgagees would usually not benefit from
the additional security from repayment by instalments. The perpetual repayment of
small sums would involve perpetual search for new investment opportunities; apart
from the trouble and inconvenience of the process it would almost certainly involve
some loss of time between investments and consequent loss of interest.

were not limited to their home towns or districts which they individually knew. Through the societies they could invest in a national market for mortgages and put in small sums if they had them available. It was almost, if not quite, as easy as investing in a savings bank, and the return was rather higher.

The building society system offered correspondingly great advantages to borrowers. The societies collected the savings of large numbers of small investors, pooled and organised them, making them available for advancing to the borrower. The borrower was freed from dependence on private and local contacts. The improvement in the security offered no doubt increased the amount of money available for lending, and enabled it to be borrowed at lower rates of interest than would have been possible under a system of private mortgages.

The system seems to be better suited to owner-occupation than to investing ownership for letting. The fact that the great expansion of the building societies coincided with the boom in owner-occupation in the post-war period suggests this, though it does not prove it. But the system of repayment by instalment might not have suited investing owners who were only interested in the equity earnings of houses to let ; instalment repayments might have prevented them expanding the scale of their investments in equities.[1] It is fairly clear that expansion of the building societies on a large scale depended on the development of owner-occupation. On the other hand the latter was dependent on some sort of machinery such as that provided by the building societies for the supply of sufficient capital on reasonable terms. The opportunity came with the great demand for houses after the Great War. The building societies took full advantage of the opening.[2] Their success in attracting capital was at times almost embarrassing to them. The money invested with them by deposits and purchase of share increased by £385 millions between 1924 and 1934. The numbers of shareholders and depositors increased by rather over one million between 1928 and 1934.[3] During the great depression of the 'thirties they were severely inconvenienced by the number of large investors who decided that they offered the safest and most profitable method

[1] The extent to which investing owners bought houses through building societies appears to have varied in different parts of the country. See *Evidence of Committee on the Rent Restriction Acts, 1920*, op. cit., pp. 9-14 and 15-19.

[2] See Chart IV above or Statistical Appendix, Table 7A.

[3] The attraction the building societies had for small investors is illustrated by the fact that the average size of share-holding in the eleven biggest societies varied from £156 to £398, and the average size of deposit from £66 to £280 in 1933. See *Annual Reports of the Registrar of Friendly Societies*, op. cit.

of investment for the time being.   The danger to their stability of this development was among the factors leading to both the change made in the interest they offered the investors in 1932/3 and the introduction of a limit in the size of the investment that could be made by any one person. The societies were equally successful in finding suitable borrowers.   New advances in 1924 were only £40·6 millions ; by 1930 they had more than doubled, and in 1934 reached £124·6 millions.[1] Throughout the period for which figures are available, 1928 to 1934, the expansion depended partly on borrowers who required small sums ; of the total of mortgages outstanding those under £500 accounted for between 40 and 46 per cent. of the total assets of the societies and averaged between £275 and £300 each.[2] It was the development of the building society system that made the large volume of building by private enterprise possible.   The importance from the long period point of view is even greater, for this development was equivalent to the supercession of the private and local market in mortgages by a national market based on indirect investments.   As far as the mortgage market for houses for owner-occupation was concerned the industry of providing houses came into line with other industries of national importance.

[1] Statistical Appendix, Table 7A, below.
[2] See the *Economist Building Society Supplement*, July 1939, p. 18.

Chapter VI

SECOND EXPERIMENT (*contd.*)

THE CONTRIBUTION OF LOCAL AUTHORITIES

I. Local Authorities and Costs

WHY did local authorities build so few houses compared to private enterprise ? Now that we have decided how and why so many houses were built by private enterprise mainly for sale, we are in a better position to tackle this question. We can consider it from the point of view of what underlying conditions were different in the case of local authorities.

Completely final and authoritative answers could be given to these questions only after a detailed study of the individual idiosyncrasies of the seventeen hundred odd local authorities who are housing authorities: of all the hundred and one accidents and conflicts which go to make up the substance of local politics, the varying personalities of the elected councils, the efficiency or inefficiency of the permanent officials, the enthusiasm or lack of it, of city engineers, or medical officers of health, the strength of vested interests in house-property and land, the strength of public opinion. All these things help to determine the particular housing policy which has emerged in different places and the ways in which it has been carried out. Fascinating and amusing as an investigation of these matters would be, it would provide a herculean task even in peacetime. In the middle of a total war it is out of the question.

(a) Building, Rents and Requirements.

The local authorities altogether built 505 thousand houses with the Wheatley subsidy and 75 thousand with the Chamberlain subsidy. This total of 580 thousand had to be set against the shortage of about 550 thousand houses outstanding in 1923, and the further requirements each year of over 60 thousand to keep pace with the annual increase in the number of families. The local authorities' efforts left an unsatisfied gap of about 785 thousand. To meet this deficit and replace any houses pulled down, there were some small houses to let or buy provided by private enterprise, probably about 265 thousand, and the houses discarded by the families who gave up

CHART V.—Building by Local Authorities and Rents, 1924–5 to 1933–4.*

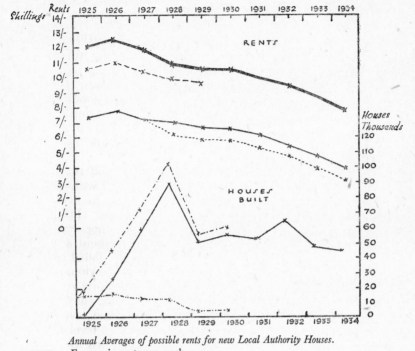

Annual Averages of possible rents for new Local Authority Houses.

━━━ = Economic rents per week.
‒ ‒ ‒ = Subsidised rents per week (Chamberlain).
▬▬▬ = Subsidised rents per week (Wheatley)
········ = Subsidised rents per week (Wheatley) if subsidy had remained at
　　　 original level after 1927.

Number of Houses built by Local Authorities during each year ending March 31st.
───── = Under the Wheatley Act.
··‒··‒ = Under the Chamberlain Act.
‒··‒·· = Total under both Acts.

* See Statistical Appendix, Tables 2 and 6.

their old houses in favour of moving into new ones. Approximately
the local authorities provided 39 per cent. of all the houses, old
and new, which became, in theory at least, available for working-
class families. [1]

Chart V shows the volume and timing of local authority building,
together with the average economic rents at which new houses
built by local authorities between 1925 and 1934 could be let. The

[1] See Tables III and IV pp. 49 and 52 above, and Statistical Appendix Table 2.

corresponding subsidised rents possible under the Wheatley and Chamberlain Acts are also shown. The outstanding feature in the diagram is the complete lack of relationship between the development of local authority building and subsidised economic rents. The lack of a close relationship between changes in costs and the volume of private building was discussed at length in the last chapter, and at first sight the lack of any close connection in the case of local authorities may not seem surprising.

But there is an important difference. We found that although building by private enterprise did not vary directly with costs, there was a strong underlying tendency for building to expand after sufficiently large changes in costs had accumulated. There was no similar tendency in the case of local authority building. It followed the same sort of trend as private building up to about a year after the cut in subsidies of 1927 ; after that it practically failed to expand. The contraction in 1927/28 compared to the previous year was partly, of course, the natural reaction to the efforts to complete as many houses as possible by the end of September, 1927, to benefit from the full subsidy. Continuation at the reduced level between 45 and 60,000 houses a year, that is at about the level of 1925/6, for the next six years cannot, however, be explained away on this ground. It is all the more remarkable in view of the fact that private building increased despite the abolition of the Chamberlain subsidy in 1929.

Examination of the changes in economic rents with the Wheatley subsidy increases the mystery, for the falls were sufficiently large to be significant. In 1926 before the subsidy was cut, the average subsidised economic rent for new local authority houses was 7/9 ; by 1928, despite the cut in subsidy, it had fallen to 7/-, and the following year to 6/8 : a decrease of 1/1, i.e. 14 per cent. in three years.[1] The decrease continued slowly, and after the fall in the rate of interest in 1932 it became possible to build new houses with the Wheatley subsidy to let at average rents of between 4/4 to 5/3.

The question of what rents families of various types can afford to pay, or ought to be willing to pay, is largely a matter of opinion. During the Second Experiment and up to the outbreak of the present war, it was generally considered that a gross rent of 10/- including rates, was the *maximum* that the families of ordinary unskilled

---

[1] See Statistical Appendix, Table 6. A fall of this size should have been significant, for it was about equal to the average weekly expenditure per head on fats and cheese of working-class families in 1937/8. Ministry of Labour—Cost of Living Inquiry, 1937/8. See *Ministry of Labour Gazette*, December, 1940.

labourers, or even in many cases of semi-skilled labourers, could afford. Rates in urban areas varied from 2/– to 4/– or more a week but were usually between 3/– and 4/– ; the maximum net rent that it was considered could be paid for new houses by these classes was therefore between 6/– and 7/–. It will be convenient to call this rent the *maximum notional rent*.[1] This conclusion was based on general experience of the sort of rents families were willing, and in practice able, to pay, and on comparison with the controlled rents of old houses. It is extremely important that it should be understood that this notional figure of 10/– gross rent represented a maximum for the lower part of the working-class market, that it formed a sort of dividing line between the really comfortably-off families and the rest. If new houses were to be supplied on an effective scale to the lower part of the market gross rents would have to be well below this figure, and it would be important to make sure that the advantages of low rents were not off-set by additional expenses, such as increased costs of travelling to and from work, and shops, and so on.

In the last resort, it is the willingness and ability of people to pay for anything which decides at what price a mass demand will materialise. This willingness can only be tested by experience, and it was this which led to the belief in the maximum of 10/–. It is possible, however, to show that for certain types of families particular prices are too high even though they may be willing to pay them for a longer or shorter time. Statisticians and dieticians have found ways of estimating the minimum income needed for keeping a family properly clothed and nourished after rent has been paid. If the payment of rent makes such a drain on family income that this minimum is not available, then one or more members of the family will go short of the essentials of food and clothing needed to keep them in full health. These estimates must be used very carefully. Incomes theoretically adequate may not be so in practice because of the individual difficulties of particular families. They may not be adequate, for instance, if there is sickness, or, if the housewife falls below the high standards of determination and efficiency needed to budget every penny to cover necessities leaving out the minor conveniences and luxuries. The calculations of the minima do not leave much balance for giving the children a little odd pocket money for sweets, or for the cinema, or to pay for minor family festivities. *It is safe to say that if these minimum amounts are not left after rent is paid,*

---

[1] In rural areas the corresponding figure would be a couple of shillings lower, and in the London area a couple of shillings higher.

there will be deficiencies more or less serious in the supply of other necessities. It is not safe to assume that wherever these minimum amounts are available there will be no deficiencies.

The sort of rents that could just be afforded, if all other circumstances were favourable, can be illustrated on the basis of a fairly widely accepted estimate of minimum income requirements. Rowntree's *Human Needs Standard* shows that a family of man, wife and one child needed 38/1 a week in 1936 to cover essential requirements after paying the rent. If there were two children, 41/2 was needed, and if there were three, 43/6.[1] Now the ordinary weekly wage of unskilled labourers at that time was between 48/– and 53/–. It is easy to see that payment of a gross rent of 10/– out of an income of 50/– would result in a deficit of expenditure on some other necessity, if the family consisted of man, wife and two children under fourteen, but in favourable circumstances there would be a margin of a shilling or two if there were only one child of school age. A period of unemployment or sickness would wipe out any possibility of a margin, even in this case.

It is clear that such evidence as there is about minimum needs shows that the idea, that a gross rent of 10/– was a maximum for the lower part of the working-class market, was no exaggeration of the position. It is obvious that the ability to pay rent, which means an ability to pay a fixed sum every week in the year, cannot be based on calculations so fine that there is no significant margin for emergencies, or human frailty. The crux of the difficulty over the ability to pay rent was the inelasticity of income in relation to the numbers of dependants, and inability to make a family income equivalent, throughout the year, to the weekly wage of an unskilled labourer.[2]

Comparisons with the rents of old controlled houses lead to similar conclusions about notional maximum rents. This confirmation is important, for not only did these houses form the majority of working-class houses, but the maintenance of control was based on the assumption that the controlled rents represented the proper rents for working-class houses. Average controlled net rents[3] for old houses varied from 4/6 in rural areas to a maximum of 9/– in London, while the averages for the county boroughs varied between 5/10 and 6/2.[4] These averages were not fully typical of the actual rents

---

[1] *Human Needs of Labour*, by B. Seebohm Rowntree, 1937. The nutritional standard used by Rowntree is now considered to be rather low.

[2] For an account of the part played by children in bringing families temporarily below the " Human Needs Standard," see Rowntree's *Poverty and Progress*, Chapter VI.

[3] i.e. without rates.

[4] *Ridley Report*, op. cit. p. 17.

paid, in which there was a considerable amount of variation. Before the Great War the size of working-class houses in each town generally varied from two or three rooms to five or six, and the rents varied of course with the size ; there was also, in most towns, considerable variation in the rents for houses of similar sizes.[1] There was thus a variation in rents above and below the average which was not removed by rent control, as the permitted increases in rents were proportionate to the actual rent of each house before the control was imposed. Thus a maximum notional rent without rates of 6/-- or 7/– was quite consistent with what might have been deduced from rents of controlled houses.

In 1927 average subsidised rents for new houses were about equal to the average levels of rents for decontrolled houses and thus above controlled rents and above the notional maximum. As early as 1929, however, subsidised rents were well below average decontrolled rents though still slightly above the average for controlled rents and the notional maximum. If the local authorities had let their new houses at the subsidised rent corresponding to the current economic rent for houses built after 1928/9, they could have provided houses for practically the whole upper part of the working-class market at rents not significantly higher than the average already being paid for old controlled houses. From 1932 onwards there is not the slightest doubt that the local authorities could have built new houses to let at rents within the reach of a very large proportion indeed of ordinary working-class families.[2]

The failure of local authority building to expand in the favourable circumstances after 1932 is very easily explained. As part of the economy campaign to reduce local authority expenditure, recommended by the Committee on Local Expenditure in 1932, the local authorities were instructed to restrict their building activities and to refrain from embarking on new projects. This decision came just at the time that the fall in building costs and in the rate of interest had reduced the economic rent of new houses to between 5/2 and 5/9 with the subsidy. In 1933 the availability of the Wheatley subsidy was limited to houses for which plans had been approved by December 7th, 1932. At the same time circulars to the local authorities explained that the new housing policy would rely on

---

[1] *Board of Trade Inquiry into the Cost of Living, 1912.* Cd. 6955. According data collected in this inquiry, the highest rent for a house of say four rooms might be 30 per cent. or more above the lowest for a house of the same size in the same town, and the highest recorded working-class rent might be more than 100 per cent. above the lowest recorded rent in the same town.

[2] See Table Xa p. 114 below and Statistical Appendix, Table 6.

private enterprise for the provision of new working-class houses in general ; the authorities were to concentrate on slum clearance.[1] The latter had not increased their rate of building despite the fall in costs earlier when there was no such official discouragement; the tailing off of their building activities after it was inevitable. The absence of any boom in local authority building when general market conditions were so favourable is sufficiently explained.

The economy campaign of 1932/3 does not, however, explain the absence of expansion in the earlier years during which costs were falling, and the Ministry of Health was urging increased building activity. It is certain that insufficient working-class houses were being built by the local authorities, for there was still a serious short-age in 1931/2. More rapid building during the previous four years of falling costs would have been an advantage. It is equally certain that the low rate of building was not due to a shortage of labour. Unemployment among skilled men in the building industry increased steadily after 1927. For instance, in the summer months, April to June of 1927 there were, on the average, only 1·4 per cent. of brick-layers unemployed ; after 1927 the percentage increased steadily each year, reaching 10·9 per cent. in the corresponding three months in 1931. The position was similar in each of the other important skilled building trades.[2]

When the local authorities fail to carry out any scheme with enthusiasm, it is usually argued that this is because to do so would place too heavy a burden on the rates. In the case of housing schemes this argument breaks down. By the end of the second experiment the net contribution from the rates was only £1·3 million, equivalent to only 0·8 per cent. of net expenditure out of the rates. Provided that only the subsidy stipulated by the Acts was contri-buted from the rates, the rate burden was too small to be regarded as a serious deterrent to building.[3]

So far, then, the lack of expansion in local authority building is unexplained. If output had been maintained at the level of 1927/8 for the remainder of the second experiment the supply of working-class houses to let would have been three hundred thousand greater in 1934 than it actually was, and the housing situation would have been materially different. It would be profoundly unsatisfactory if a similar breakdown in the middle of an acute shortage occurred again after this war. The matter is important for another and more

[1] See p. 46 above.
[2] *Ministry of Labour Gazette, 1925/31,* monthly statement of insured workers unemployed in the building industry.
[3] See p. 47 above.

general reason. In recent years much emphasis has been laid on the importance of the part played by house building in stimulating recovery from the great industrial depression of the early 'thirties, and in maintaining the level of employment.[1] Local authority building should be the sector of the industry whose activity is most easy to control for the purpose of maintaining full employment. The unexpected and unwanted collapse after 1927/8 indicates that suitable methods of control had not been evolved. We shall see that this remained true during the third experiment. The question of what determined the level of local authority building during the Second Experiment is, therefore, too important to leave unanswered. In the next section the actual magnitude of investment in houses by local authorities and the behaviour of individual authorities is investigated.

II. CAPITAL EXPENDITURE OF LOCAL AUTHORITIES

The importance of the capital expenditure on housing by the local authorities during the First Experiment has already been described. It was the largest single item in the total of their capital expenditure. During the Second Experiment the over-riding importance of investment in houses continued. For the ten years, 1924/5 to 1933/4, it averaged £35 million a year and accounted for 30 per cent. of total investment by the local authorities. The next two largest individual items, capital spent on roads and on trading services, accounted for 14 per cent. and 25 per cent., respectively.[2] These figures, if anything, underestimate the importance of investment in housing from the point of view of creating employment. Between 1929 and 1932, according to the only estimate available, only 6·2 per cent. of the capital spent on housing schemes was absorbed by expenditure on land and other general expenses which cannot be relied upon to create employment. In the case of roads 18·8 per cent. of the total was used in this way, and in the case of trading services 8·1 per cent. was used for these purposes and for buying out existing businesses.[3]

There is another point of importance. During the Second Experiment as during the First, it was the violent fluctuations in capital expenditure on houses which were the main cause of the

---

[1] For the part played by local authority building in maintaining employment in the building industry in 1921/2.
[2] Calculated from *Public Investment on the Trade Cycle*, by Messrs. Bretherton, Burchardt and Rutherford. Tables 29 and 30.
[3] Ibid, p. 127.

fluctuations in the total investment of the local authorities as a whole. These fluctuations corresponded broadly to the fluctuations in the numbers of houses built. Thus during the main expansion of the total investment of local authorities from 1923/4 to 1927/8 the expansion of expenditure on housing accounted for 46 per cent. of the total increase. During the decline in the next two years the collapse of investment in housing accounted for 79 per cent. of the total for all.[1] In the later years the fluctuations in housing expenditure accounted for a smaller but still major portion of the vagaries in the totals of investment. Evidently, if local authorities, or some substitute organisation, are to embark on investment in housing on a similar or greater scale after this war fluctuations of this importance must not be allowed to recur except as a controlled part of a general investment policy.

If control of investment in housing by local authorities is to be achieved in the future, we must know how far the fluctuations in the past have been the accidental net results of the activities of individual authorities, and how far the effect of general underlying factors affecting all or an important section of the authorities. Such an enquiry will also afford an opportunity of searching for more explanations of the disquieting conclusions about the local authorities reached in Chapter IV. Unfortunately, annual figures for capital expenditure for individual authorities are not available except for the county boroughs and for the London authorities.[2] This is particularly regrettable owing to the uneven geographical distribution of the county boroughs. As, however, this group of authorities accounted for half the houses built under the Second Experiment their activities were sufficiently important to deserve investigation.

The most striking features of the capital expenditure of the group were the variations from year to year in the expenditure of individual towns, and the lack of uniformity between the towns with regard to the timing and direction of these changes. The data summarised in Table VIII shows that during this period, out of the seventy-five[3] boroughs included, there were never more than ten which changed their capital expenditure by less than 5 per cent. between any two consecutive years. Changes were thus the rule, not the exception.

[1] See p. 101. n. 2. above.

[2] The annual capital expenditure of local authorities is published each year in the *Local Taxation Accounts*.

[3] Comparable statistics are not available for Doncaster, Barrow-in-Furness or Bootle. In five other boroughs expenditure was nil in some years, so that percentage changes cannot be calculated. The total number of boroughs included is, therefore, only seventy-five.

Moreover, they were large. In all, only 40 were less than 5 per cent., 291 between 5 per cent. and 45 per cent. and 259 over 45 per cent. of the expenditure of the previous year. The predeliction for large decreases was as marked as that for large increases. The details are shown in Table VIII.

TABLE VIII.—Percentage Annual Changes in Capital Expenditure on Housing 75 County Boroughs.

Years between which change occurred	Numbers of Boroughs with				
	Decreases		Increase or Decrease under 5%	Increases	
	45% or more	5% and under 45%		5% and under 45%	45% or more
1925–6 and 1926–7 ..	3	17	5	21	29
1926–7 and 1927–8 ..	11	19	10	19	16
1927–8 and 1928–9 ..	30	26	5	8	6
1928–9 and 1929–30 ..	14	22	4	21	14
1929–30 and 1930–1 ..	14	26	6	18	11
1930–1 and 1931–2 ..	10	19	4	15	27
1931–2 and 1932–3 ..	30	25	2	5	13
1932–3 and 1933–4 ..	22	22	4	8	19
Total	134	176	40	115	135

The instability in the investment of individual authorities was the more disconcerting because of the lack of unanimity in the direction of the changes. Even in the years in which there were clear majorities of boroughs increasing, or decreasing their expenditure, the minority was substantial, varying from fourteen to twenty-nine. On two occasions, between 1926/7 and 1927/8, and between 1928/9 and 1929/30, there was no clear majority at all. The rapidity with which the direction of the changes altered was also startling. In one year there might be a majority of boroughs increasing expenditure, in the next a majority decreasing, or they might be almost equally divided. This was due to the tendency, clear in the detailed statistics for individual boroughs, for expenditure to be increased at most for two years running. Long sequences of declines were slightly more common.

Detailed examination of the figures shows that with some exceptions the boroughs[1] followed one or other of four patterns of capital expenditure. There was a group of twenty-seven whose expenditure reached a peak not later than 1927/8 and then decreased, never

[1] Comparable statistics are not available for Doncaster, Barrow-in-Furness or Bootle. The analysis relates therefore to eighty out of the eighty-three county boroughs.

TABLE IX.—Patterns of County Borough Capital Expenditure on Housing under the Wheatley and Chamberlain Subsidies, 1925–6 to 1933–4.

I. 27 Boroughs with 1 cycle.		II. 25 Boroughs with 2 cycles.		
	Maximum Years.		Maximum Years.	
			1st.	2nd.
Home Counties.				
Canterbury	1926–7	E. Ham	1926–7	1931–2
Croydon	1926–7	Hastings	1926–7	1931–2
Eastbourne	1926–7	Reading	1926–7	1930–1
		W. Ham	1927–8	1931–2
Midlands.				
Burton-on-Trent	1926–8	Birmingham	1925–7	1929–31
Derby	1926–7	Northampton	1926–7	1931–2
Leicester	1926–7	Stoke-on-Trent	1926–8	1931–2
Wolverhampton	1926–7	Walsall	1927–8	1931–2
Textile Counties.				
Lancashire and Cheshire.				
Birkenhead	1927–8	Blackburn	1927–8	1931–2
Blackpool	1927–8	Bury	1927–8	1931–2
Liverpool	1926–8	Wallasey	1927–8	1930–1
Manchester	1927–8	Warrington	1927–8	1930–2
St. Helens	1927–8			
Southport	1926–7			
Wigan	1927–8			
West Riding, Yorks.				
Barnsley	1926–7	Rotherham	1925–6	1929–30
Bradford	1927–8	Sheffield	1925–7	1931–2
Dewsbury	1926–8	York	1926–8	1931–2
Halifax	1927–8			
Wakefield	1926–8			
North East.				
Darlington	1926–7	Gateshead	1926–7	1932–3
South Shields	1927–8	Newcastle	1926–8	1930–2
West Hartlepool	1925–6	Sunderland	1927–8	1930–1
South Wales.				
Merthyr Tydfil	1926–7	Swansea	1925–6	1930–1
Cardiff	1926–7			
Rest of England.				
Gloucester	1927–8	Bath	1927–8	1931–2
Plymouth	1925–6	Bournemouth	1926–7	1932–3
Yarmouth	1926–7	Bristol	1925–6	1931–2
		Exeter	1927–8	1932–3
		Hull	1926–8	1931–2
		Middlesbrough	1925–8	1930–4

III. 7 Boroughs with expansions up to 1929–30 or later.
Midlands.
Dudley.
Nottingham.
Smethwick.
W. Bromwich.
Lancashire and Cheshire.
Stockport.
West Riding.
Huddersfield.
Rest of England.
Southampton.

IV. 7 Boroughs with approx. constant expenditure to 1929–30.
Homes Counties.
Brighton.
Midlands.
Coventry.
Lancashire and Cheshire.
Burnley.
Rochdale.
Rest of England.
Carlisle.
Lincoln.

TABLE IX.—*continued*.

V.   10 Boroughs with erratic
          expenditure.
Home Counties.
   Southend.
Lancashire and Cheshire.
   Bolton.
   Chester.
   Oldham.
   Salford.
South Wales and Mons.
   Newport.
Rest of England.
   Grimsby.
   Ipswich.
   Oxford.
   Portsmouth.

VI.   4 Boroughs unclassified.

   Leeds.
   Norwich.
   Preston.
   Tynemouth.

again rising to more than 50 per cent. of the original peak.   Second in importance came a group of twenty-five, who, after going through an initial cycle expanding to a peak before 1927/8 and then declining, embarked on a second cycle of expansion with a peak between 1929/30 and 1932/3.   Only boroughs whose maximum expenditure in some years of the second cycle reached at least 50 per cent. of the original, have been included.   In most cases the second peak was nearly as high as or actually higher than the first. In practically every borough in the first group the greater part of the capital investment was made by 1927/8 or 1928/9; in contrast the expenditure of boroughs in the second group was in many cases greater in the second cycle than in the first.   The announcement in 1926 of the cut in subsidies the following year of course encouraged the boroughs to rush their programmes and thus helped to exaggerate the height of the peaks reached in 1927/8.   The third group consists of seven boroughs who increased their expenditure up to 1929/30 or later, without any major recession.   The fourth group also with seven boroughs showed only moderately small changes in any direction up to 1929/30.   Finally, there were ten boroughs whose expenditure can only be called highly erratic, and four whose expenditure continued to expand to 1928/9, or, followed some other individual pattern. The details are shown in Table IX.

It is evident that the boroughs in the first and second groups started out under the Wheatley and Chamberlain subsidies with certain definite programmes which culminated in peaks at different dates.   A small number passed their peaks in 1925/6, a very substantial number in 1926/7, and others in 1927/8, while in some cases the maximum lasted for two successive years. Among the twenty-five boroughs which embarked on a second cycle the second peak

H

was usually reached either in 1930/1 or the following year. Usually the gap between the two peaks was four years, three of decline and one of initial rise. The individual patterns of expenditure varied considerably, however, about this norm.

This variation of the patterns of expenditure of individual boroughs was, without doubt, influenced by the varying extent to which they bought land ahead of requirements and by the amount of preliminary development necessary. Expenditure of this type prevents exact correspondence between changes in expenditure and changes in the numbers of houses actually built. In the cases in which it has been possible to compare expenditure and actual building, however, the correspondence has been sufficiently close for it to be assumed that the timing of fluctuations in expenditure indicates broadly the fluctuations in building. These cases demonstrate that even if the capital investment in actual building could be separated from that in land, neither the fluctuations, nor their timing, would be changed significantly. The main cyclical arrangement of capital investment therefore cannot be ignored. It is obvious that in itself it is as undesirable as similar fluctuations in other types of investment. It tends inevitably to maximise the fluctuations in local employment in the building and related industries.

It is evident that the existence of the different types of capital expenditure and the variations within each group explain the curious features of Table VIII, which were commented on earlier. It may be assumed provisionally that the particular year in which the maximum of all housing investment occurred was partly the accidental result of the counteracting changes in the programmes of individual boroughs. If we can find out why particular boroughs came into particular groups, we shall have gone a long way to knowing why local authority investment and building receded so disastrously after 1927/8.

The Second Experiment worked out very differently in different areas, and the capital expenditure of the county boroughs corresponded broadly to their output of houses. It is not, therefore, surprising to find some relation between the patterns of capital expenditure and the extent to which the local authorities made large or small proportionate contributions to the housing requirements of the various counties in which county boroughs were important. For instance, in the three counties in which this proportion was over 40 per cent., Northumberland, the West Riding of Yorkshire and Staffordshire, the most important boroughs were in the second or third capital expenditure groups. In Northumberland, Newcastle, and in the West Riding, Sheffield, Rotherham, York, and Hudders-field were in these groups and, with the exception of Bradford, all the West Riding boroughs in the first group were small. In both these counties there were boroughs which came into none of the regular groups, Tynemouth and Leeds. Their building was spread out in considerable volume well beyond the first cycle. With the inclusion of Leeds, the West Riding boroughs not in the first expenditure group provided two-thirds of all the houses built by the West Riding county boroughs. The position in Staffordshire was similar, four of the boroughs were in the second and third groups, only two in the first. On the other hand in Durham and Lancashire and Cheshire, counties in which the local authorities provided only just over 30 per cent. of requirements, the distribution of boroughs between the capital expenditure groups was quite different. In the former, three boroughs came into the first and only one of the two in the second showed a really high peak of expenditure in the later cycle. In Lancashire and Cheshire the most important boroughs, including Manchester and Liverpool, were in the first group ; only four small ones came into the second, and the rest were unclassifiable, or came into the fourth and fifth groups. The boroughs in the first group provided two-thirds of all the houses built by the Lancashire and Cheshire county boroughs !

It is evident that in some areas at least the lack of building after the first early cycle cannot be explained on the ground that there was no shortage of houses. Indeed, the unsatisfied requirements in some of these towns were as great or greater than before the experiment started. This can easily be checked up from the population census of 1931. To take only one example—in Manchester, one of the biggest towns in the group, the deficiency of houses (measured approximately from the Census) was half as big again in 1931 as it had been in 1921. Sir Ernest Simon, writing in 1935, declared that the Manchester situation was worse then than at the Armistice of 1918. " There has been one overwhelming difficulty from the Armistice Day to to-day," he added " the shortage of houses, and unfortunately the increasing shortage of houses. . . ."[1] In some towns and in some counties undoubtedly the collapse of investment in housing had been the immediate explanation of the continued shortage of houses and, in some counties, of the low contribution of the local authorities in relation to requirements.

The mere existence of a second cycle of building activity or even continuous building did not necessarily solve the problem. In

[1] *The Rebuilding of Manchester*, by Sir E. D. Simon and J. Inman, p. 69.

Warwickshire and Worcestershire, for instance, the local authorities' contribution was only 35·9 per cent. of requirements. This county group was distinguished by the highest local authority rate of supply in the country, and by the dominance of boroughs either with pronounced second cycles or with more or less continuous building throughout the period. Against this it must be remembered that requirements were higher than in any county outside the Home Counties.[1] Naturally boroughs with two bursts of activity were likely, other things being equal, to produce more houses than those with only one, but it must be remembered that part of the potential production of houses was lost during the gap of low building between the first and second peak. This can be illustrated by the case of the London County Council, whose investment and output of houses formed two cycles. If there had been no gap in London building, if the level of output of the first peak had been maintained, and the second peak had been as high as the first, the number of houses built by the County Council in the nine years from 1923 to 1931 inclusive would have been increased by just over 40 per cent.[2] Thus the failure of some authorities to build effectively after their initial outburst and the waste of time during the low building gap in the case of the two cycle authorities, provide partial explanations of the general low average of building by local authorities and of some of the outstanding differences between counties.

This is a mere statement of facts. We still do not know why some boroughs behaved in one way and some in another. Undoubtedly, part of the explanation must be found in the particular problems of individual boroughs. Manchester may be cited again because its housing troubles have been described so clearly by Sir Ernest Simon. In 1925 it adopted an initial programme under the Wheatley Act of 10,000 houses. As any additional programme necessitated using land outside the city boundaries, the estate of Wythenshawe was actually bought in 1925. Obstruction by the rural authority in whose area it lay, however, prevented its incorporation within the city until 1930. Until then large scale development was impossible, because the rural authority was responsible for drainage but was incapable of carrying out the work on an adequate scale. In consequence building at Wythenshawe was negligible until 1933,[3] the year the Wheatley experiment was being shut down ! London

[1] See pp. 62–3 and Table VI p. 64 above.
[2] Calculated from data in *London Statistics*. The first peak in capital expenditure was reached in 1927/8 and the second in 1931/2. The first peak in building came in 1928 the second in 1931.
[3] *The Rebuilding of Manchester*. op. cit. Chapter VI.

provides another notorious example of the problems and delays of building on land within another authority's area.

Changes in the composition of the borough councils provide further reasons of an accidental type for delay in some areas. Programmes were in some cases slowed up, or changes which lead to delays introduced. The inclusion of a borough in one or another capital expenditure group, and its output of houses, was partly determined by such accidents which had nothing whatever to do with the requirements for additional working-class houses. The difference in the dates at which different boroughs reached peaks of expansion must also be attributed to these factors as well as to differences in the types of problems confronting various authorities.

Two apparent coincidences of a more general type suggest, however, that there were other underlying factors and explanations. First, the break in investment after 1926/8 coincided with the first cut in the subsidies. Second, the county boroughs in the most depressed and stagnating areas were predominantly in the capital expenditure groups least favourable to large outputs of houses, i.e. Groups I, IV, and V. The changes in the subsidies announced in 1926 presupposed that building costs would fall sufficiently to offset them. It was never explained to the local authorities how this would happen if the volume of building remained unchanged. In any case until the fall in costs actually occurred, the authorities were faced with the possibility of having to let new houses at rents higher by the amount of reduction in the subsidy. Hesitation about starting new programmes or even completing existing ones was natural. Many authorities would decide to finish off existing programmes as far as possible in time to qualify for the full subsidy and then use the breathing space to look round before starting new schemes. Whether an authority would adopt this course or not would naturally depend on the state of the current programme, on the local enthusiasm for dealing with the housing shortage, and on the estimates of the effect of a higher rent on the demand for houses. Thus, apart from any break which would have occurred automatically with the completion of the original programmes the change in subsidy must have led to hesitation and delay until the future of costs became clear. This interpretation of the collapse in the expenditure of so many boroughs after 1927/8 is supported by the fact that it was rare for serious new investment expansion to take place until 1929/30, that is, shortly after it had become obvious that the fall in costs had more than compensated for the cut in the subsidy.

The decisions, taken in 1928, to abolish the Chamberlain subsidy and to cut the Wheatley subsidy again naturally prolonged the period of uncertainty. Although in the end only the former decision was carried out,[1] this was a sufficient excuse, or reason, for the absence of a second cycle of expansion in some cases. While some boroughs had concentrated almost entirely on building with the Wheatley subsidy, and others had built with both to a considerable extent, there were a few which had concentrated almost entirely on the Chamberlain subsidy. Naturally it was the plans of this third group which were most disturbed by the abolition of the Chamberlain subsidy. Those that failed to change over to the Wheatley subsidy naturally showed little investment activity after 1929. This accounted for four boroughs with only one cycle and four whose investment was classified as erratic.[2]

The second coincidence referred to appears to explain, in part at least, the distribution of the other boroughs between the various investment groups. The economic depression of the areas dependent on export industries, and particularly on coal, had been causing concern before 1929, when the break in the boom made their depression still more obvious. Migration, particularly from the South Wales and Durham coal fields, had already taken place on a considerable scale.[3] The local authorities in these areas were faced with difficult questions. Was this likely to go on : if so, would not the shortage of houses solve itself? If not, was there any serious prospect of finding tenants who could afford to pay rents at the current levels even though below those of 1927? Unemployment among the skilled men in these districts was increasing; it was not certain how far employment would ever recover. In any case their capacity to pay the rents charged for local authority houses had fallen seriously as unemployment increased. In addition, rates in some areas were rising rapidly, increasing the total burden on restricted incomes of rent *plus* rates. Authorities in these areas might well hesitate and decide to do nothing definite until the economic blizzard was over. In the interval, which, in fact, lasted practically to the end of the Second Experiment, houses might be built only on a scale for which an adequate demand was certain. Such decisions would be reflected in very low or erratic capital expenditure.

[1] The Labour Government of 1929 cancelled the reduction of the Wheatley subsidy. See p. 45 above.
[2] Viz. Croydon, Birkenhead, Blackpool and Yarmouth in the former group, and Chester, Grimsby, Salford and Southend in the latter.
[3] *Report of the Royal Commission on the Distribution of the Industrial Population.* Cmd. 6153. 1940. Chapter IV.

In the face of these considerations it is surely no accident that the group, whose capital expenditure dwindled away or failed to recover after 1927/8, included the Durham boroughs of Darlington, South Shields and West Hartlepool ; in South Wales the boroughs of Merthyr Tydfil, Cardiff and Newport ; in Lancashire, Bolton, Burnley, Oldham, Preston, Rochdale, St. Helens, Salford and Wigan. On the other hand the boroughs whose expenditure recovered and expanded continuously included Birmingham, West Bromwich, Dudley, Nottingham and Smethwick in the Midlands, the most important West Riding boroughs and others like Bristol and Southampton. None of the latter had experienced the initial signs of depression and stagnation before the 1929 crash. The local councils could reasonably assume that prosperity would return. After 1928/9 both capital expenditure on houses and economic activity tended to move in the same direction in individual areas. The distinction between Inner and Outer Britain applied broadly to both local authority expenditure on houses and general economic conditions. Even in Outer Britain though there were considerable variations in the prosperity or depression of particular areas though real prosperity was at an end. In particular, the bigger towns in each area tended to suffer less acutely than the small. The big towns like Manchester[1] and Newcastle were less dependent on the staple industry of the district than the small ones. It was the smaller towns which collapsed most completely and lost population most rapidly. It is not surprising that erratic or declining character of capital expenditure on housing was apt to be most marked in the small towns.

Against this background of differing economic fortunes there is little difficulty in understanding why so many county boroughs failed to expand their building after the initial recession from the peak of 1927/8, despite the net fall in costs. It is probably legitimate to generalise these conclusions to small local authorities other than county boroughs, and it is worth remembering in this connection the tendency of small county boroughs to show the effects of depression more than the large ones. It must be repeated, nevertheless, that the part played by the individual peculiarities of individual authorities was also important. Further, although we now have explanations of some of the differences in the proportionate contributions towards having requirements of local authorities in the different industrial counties, we have not yet explained why these contribu-

---

[1] Manchester's inclusion in the one-cycle capital expenditure group was, as already explained, due to the difficulty over Wythenshawe.

tions were also low in some prosperous counties whose capital expenditure expanded in the later years.

It may be as well to take stock of our conclusions at this point. The course of capital expenditure on housing by the main urban authorities developed on a number of different lines. The way in which the expansions of expenditure took place depended on the nature of the local problems and the enthusiasm or lack of it of the individual authorities. There was a general tendency to finish off one programme before really starting another, and this produced rapid and undesirable fluctuations and waste of time. On the other hand it has become clear that the change in the subsidy in 1926/7 was responsible for exaggerating the delay between the winding up of first set of programmes and the start of effective work on others. This change took place just as the differences between the economic prospects of different parts of the country were emerging. These differences were increased by the break in the general trade boom of 1929 before new programmes had got started. This final cleavage between the economic prospects of Inner and Outer Britain accounts for many of the differences in policy about subsequent expansions in capital expenditure. The boroughs in prosperous districts tended to continue or re-expand their capital expenditure, while within the depressed or stagnant areas expenditure failed to revive ; the least depressed towns within the depressed districts showed more tendency to expand than the others. To some extent this explained the differences in the proportionate contributions made by local authorities noticed in Chapter IV. It does not explain, however, the failures of local authorities to build so much less than was needed in the prosperous areas and the outstanding failure of the Home Counties. The irregularity of capital expenditure shows that a great deal of building time was wasted even in prosperous areas between finishing and starting new programmes, but this cannot without further investigation be regarded as a final explanation.

Some things are clear, however. The fluctuations in local authority investment and its failure to revive after 1927/8 were the net result of the differing behaviour of different local authorities. This was partly the result of the individual reactions of the authorities to changes in government policy, and partly to differences in economic conditions for which housing policy made no provision, as well as to individual peculiarities of local authorities and their problems. The housing policy of the government was undeniably inadequate in the circumstances, but it must not be forgotten that the differences in timing of the initial expansion among all boroughs, and the differences among those which went on building, show that there were differences in energy and efficiency in carrying out housing policy. This means that if any attempt to maximise local authority building is to be attempted in the future far more control of individual authorities will be needed to make them plan and build efficiently. *A fortiori* far more control will be needed if local authority capital investment is to be fitted into any scheme for controlling the volume of employment. We have seen that the fluctuations in housing investment can be the determining factor in the total investment by local authorities.

III. THE RENT QUESTION

(a) The general level of rents.

In any discussion of housing policy and the behaviour of local authorities the questions of the best system for determining rents, the relation of costs to rents and other similar questions inevitably arise. So far we have referred to rents only in the most general terms; in this section we shall attempt to analyse the rent policies of local authorities during the second experiment. The data unfortunately are rather limited. The only comprehensive survey of local authority rents is provided by statistics published by the Ministry of Health in 1936.[1] These suffer from several weaknesses from our point of view. They show the rents actually charged by the local authorities in 1936 for nearly all the houses built under the Housing Acts between 1919 and 1936, that is, houses built during the first and second experiments and a number of houses built under slum clearance schemes. The rents are those of 1936 after the Ministry of Health had pressed for some form of differential renting for four or five years. They differ in some cases at least from those actually charged during the Second Experiment and the tables probably show a greater bias towards differential renting than statistics collected earlier would have done. Finally, figures for individual authorities are given only for the county boroughs and London, all the others are grouped together as urban or rural by counties. These features of the statistics are not quite so formidable as they appear, but it is well to keep them in mind.

The average rents of local authority houses will serve to give an outline of the rent question. These varied considerably according to the type of local authority; in 1937, they were from 1/- to 1/6,

---

[1] *Rents of Houses and Flats owned by Local Authorities (England and Wales)*, 1937. Cmd. 5527.

that is from 16 per cent. to 25 per cent. higher than those of the
controlled houses and were only slightly below those for de-controlled
houses.[1] It follows that the average rents of each type of local
authority were rather above the notional maximum assumed to be
appropriate for great numbers of working-class families. This
is confirmed by the detailed statistics published by the Ministry of
Health in 1936. More than half of the local authority houses in the
county boroughs and other urban districts outside Greater London,
and in the rural districts over two-thirds, were let at rents above the
appropriate notional maxima.[2] The averages thus give too rosy a
view of the situation.

TABLE Xa.—Median and average rents of Houses belonging to Local Authorities
in England and Wales, 1936–7.

Authority	Average rents[1]			Median rent Local Authority[2]
	Controlled	Decontrolled	Local Authority	
Greater London :				
London				10/7
County Boroughs	8/6 to 9/–	12/6 to 13/–	10/6	10/4
Other Urban Authorities				10/1
Rural Authorities				8/–
Other Authorities :				
County Boroughs	5/10 to 6/2	7/6 to 7/9	7/2	7/4
Other Urban Authorities	5/6 to 5/10	7/– to 7/4	6/11	6/11
Rural Authorities	4/6 to 4/10	5/9 to 6/–	6/–	6/–

[1] Ridley Report op. cit. page 17.
[2] Calculated from Table I of *Rents of Houses and Flats owned by Local Authorities 1936.*
Cmd. 5527. Includes all houses and flats included in the Housing Revenue Account.

Table Xa above shows the rents above which exactly half the
houses belonging to each type of authority were let, that is in statistical terms the median rents. Several things are obvious. The rents
charged by the London authorities conformed to tradition in that
they were above those of most of the county boroughs. The former
were naturally similar to those of the county boroughs within the
Greater London area, as many of the new houses belonging to the
London County Council were built in the areas of the other Greater
London authorities. Much more important, however, is the existence of considerable differences between the median rents among
the county boroughs. The rent picture was not one of very high
rents for local authority houses in the London area and low uniform
rents elsewhere. This is shown in the next table.

[1] *Ridley Report*, op. cit. See also Table Xa below.
[2] *Rents of Houses and Flats, etc.*, op. cit.

TABLE Xʙ.—Median Rents of Houses owned by County Boroughs, 1936.[1]

Under 6/- (1)	6/- and under 7/- (2)	7/- and under 8/- (3)	8/- and under 9/- (4)	9/- and over (5)
Barnsley	Bradford	Bath	Birkenhead	Blackpool
Canterbury	Blackburn	Birmingham	Bournemouth	Brighton
Halifax	Bury*	Bolton	Bristol	Burton-on-
Leeds*	Carlisle	Burnley	Derby	Trent
Norwich	Dewsbury	Cardiff	Gloucester	Chester*
Oldham	Dudley	Coventry	Grimsby	Croydon
Reading	Lincoln	Darlington*	Hastings	Eastbourne
S. Shields*	Middlesbrough	Exeter	Leicester	E. Ham
Walsall	Nottingham	Gateshead*	Liverpool	Southend
Warrington	Preston	Huddersfield	Plymouth	Yarmouth
W. Bromwich	Rotherham	Hull	Portsmouth	
	St. Helens	Ipswich	Salford	
	Sheffield	Manchester	Wallasey	
	Smethwick	Merthyr	West Ham*	
	Sunderland	Newport		
	Wakefield	(Mons.)		
	Wigan	Newcastle*		
	Wolverhampton	Northampton		
	Worcester	Oxford*		
	York	Rochdale		
		Southampton		
		Southport		
		Stoke-on-Trent*		
		Stockport		
		Swansea		
		Tynemouth*		
		W. Hartlepool		

[1] 11 boroughs had ranges of 3/- and over (cols. 4 and 5 of Table XI p. 123); these 11 boroughs are marked with an asterisk.

In twenty-three county boroughs the median rents were 8/- or over, in other words, in these boroughs half the local authority houses were let at 8/- or more ; in nine of these the medians were 9/- or more. Boroughs in this whole group, except those in Greater London, therefore were letting at least half their houses and probably more than half at rents too high for the mass market. We can conveniently call the whole group high-rent boroughs. In almost the same number of boroughs, twenty-six to be precise, the medians were between 7/- and 8/-. In these some of the houses at least must have been let at rents below or equal to the notional maximum, and it will be reasonable to call them moderate rent boroughs. In the rest of the boroughs the median rents were under 7/-, including eleven under 6/- ; in these the median rents corresponded with the notional maximum, and a large number of houses must have been let at rents below the maximum. They can fairly be called low rent boroughs. The division of the boroughs of England and Wales into three rent groups of nearly equal size with extreme sub-groups of exceptionally high or low rents demands explanation.

The collection of boroughs with exceptionally high rents is a little astonishing. Two were Greater London boroughs, Croydon and East Ham : four were seaside resorts, Blackpool, Brighton, Eastbourne and Southend ; finally, there were three strays, the fishing port of Yarmouth, the industrial town of Burton-on-Trent and Chester. Comparison with Table IX shows that during the Second Experiment all these boroughs, apart from East Ham and Brighton (strange bed-fellows, indeed), undertook the bulk of their capital expenditure on houses before 1928/9, that is, before the fall in costs. Their houses were therefore expensive. There is another feature of interest : Chester, Yarmouth, Croydon, Blackpool and Southend built almost exclusively with the Chamberlain subsidy, so that their rents were based on the smaller of the two subsidies available. It will be remembered that the rent statistics include the houses built with the original Addison subsidy ; in each of these boroughs these houses formed quite an important group, which was not offset by houses built under the special terms of the Greenwood slum clearance scheme, and also included in the statistics. They thus had a great preponderance of houses built during the years of high costs and/or with relatively small subsidies. In Blackpool, for instance, only ninety-eight houses were built with the Wheatley subsidy, but six hundred and sixty-six were built with the Chamberlain subsidy, and four hundred and thirty-six with the Addison subsidy. It was practically inevitable that such boroughs should have high rents, for they did not take advantage of subsidy or cost conditions favourable to low rents.

The rest of the high rent boroughs forms as odd a group as the one just described. There were three industrial towns : Derby, Leicester, and Salford ; two rather more residential towns, Birkenhead and Wallasey ; two seaside resorts, Bournemouth and Hastings ; five ports, Bristol, Liverpool, Plymouth and Portsmouth, the fishing port of Grimsby ; one Greater London borough West Ham, and one odd town, Gloucester. This group shows the same characteristics in a slightly less extreme form as the very high rent group. All but five of the boroughs did their main building before the fall in costs. The five exceptions were West Ham, Hastings, Bournemouth, Bristol, and Wallasey. West Ham as a Greater London borough needs perhaps no comment ; Hastings built more

than half its houses under the Addison and Chamberlain subsidies ;
incidentally, this applies to Grimsby, Birkenhead and Salford, too.
The high rents of the other three cannot be explained from the
information available.

In general then the high rent boroughs were characterised by a
high proportion of building during the high cost period and a low
proportion of building with the Wheatley subsidy, and three of them
it will be remembered were Greater London boroughs. It will not
have escaped notice that the boroughs in the group were of varied
sizes. The inclusion of small boroughs such as Chester and Yarmouth with really big ones, such as Liverpool and Bristol, suggests
that there was no obvious justification for the common belief that the
size of towns necessarily determined the level of rents of local
authority houses.

It will be convenient to look at the boroughs at the other end of
the scale. All the boroughs with the medians under 6/– were, it will
be noticed, industrial towns, except Canterbury and Norwich, and
perhaps Reading. Six of the group spread their investment under
the second experiment well into the period of low costs, and all of
them, except Leeds, built exclusively with the Wheatley subsidy in
this period ; even Leeds built relatively very little with the Chamberlain subsidy. As far as building during the Second Experiment was
concerned these boroughs took advantage of the most favourable
conditions for obtaining low rents. Finally, building with the
Addison subsidy was not sufficiently important in these boroughs to
affect the rent statistics.

In the five boroughs which did not conform to this pattern, South
Shields, Halifax, Oldham, Barnsley, and Canterbury, conditions
were rather different. Most of their capital investment took place
before the fall in costs. Although the first three built almost entirely
with the Wheatley subsidy during the Second Experiment, the
specially low rents need some explanation. In the cases of South
Shields and Halifax, it seems to be the inclusion of houses built with
the Greenwood slum clearance subsidy in the statistics ; if these
could be eliminated it is probable that the medians would have been
considerably higher. It is difficult to find any similar explanation
for Barnsley and Oldham. Canterbury, of course, is something
quite apart ; it is so small that its rents might be expected to conform
to those of the rural areas. On the whole the extreme low rent
group built under financial conditions almost exactly the opposite
of those under which the extremely high rent group built.

The rest of the low rent boroughs, those with medians between

6/– and 7/–, were, except for Carlisle and Lincoln, plain industrial towns, both large and small. The group included the rest of the West Riding Boroughs, except Huddersfield, six Midland boroughs, and six of the small Lancashire boroughs, and Sunderland and Middlesbrough. It is not surprising to find half of these boroughs spent capital on houses as much or more after the main fall in costs as before ; three others spread their building without interruption up to 1930. Only five definitely belonged to the category of boroughs which carried out the greater part of their expenditure before the fall in costs, and these five concentrated entirely on building with the Wheatley subsidy during the Second Experiment. In all this group of boroughs building under the Addison subsidy was too small to affect the rent statistics.

Thus low rent boroughs provide a contrast to the high rent boroughs in the combination of the timing of their capital expenditure with the extent to which they built under the Wheatley rather than the Chamberlain subsidy. Further, where the published rent figures are misleading, as far as the Second Experiment is concerned, it is in the inclusion of large numbers of slum-clearance houses in the case of the extremely low-rent boroughs, in contrast to the inclusion of Addison subsidy houses in the case of the high rent boroughs.

The financial circumstances of the building by the twenty-six boroughs with moderate rents were rather mixed. The most interesting feature of this group is the exceptionally large number of boroughs from the depressed or stagnant areas in it. There were all but two of the Northumberland and Durham boroughs, six from Lancashire, including Manchester, and all the South Wales boroughs ; against this large battalion there were only five, including Birmingham, from the Midlands and West Riding together, and a number of ports and semi-country towns like Exeter and Bath. Eleven in the group invested capital on about as large, or on a larger, scale after as before the fall in costs, but, in contrast to the low-rent boroughs, made a considerable amount of use of the Chamberlain subsidy. In the other fifteen boroughs building was concentrated in the high cost period, but the normal effect on rents was in part offset by concentration on building with the Wheatley subsidy. On the whole the influence on rents of the inclusion of houses built with the Addison subsidy was offset by the inclusion of considerable numbers of slum clearance houses.[1]

[1] Darlington and Tynemouth in the North-East and Merthyr Tydfil and Newport (Mons.) provide particularly striking examples.

In general, then, the characteristics of the moderate rent boroughs fit into the same general framework as those of the high and low rent boroughs. The financial circumstances under which they built were mixed, combining some of the features of both the high and low rent groups ; the rents came out in a sort of half-way position. There was one point on which the rent groups all resembled each other. They each contained boroughs of all sorts and sizes. We can conclude that (apart from the complications introduced into the statistics by the inclusion of the houses built under the subsidies belonging to the first and third experimentals) the variations in the timing of capital expenditure and in the relative importance of building activities under the Chamberlain and Wheatley subsidies, respectively, were among the most important factors determining rents. One of the more paradoxical results of this was the tendency for the rents of local authority houses in depressed and stagnant areas to have higher rents than those in the prosperous regions. There is little doubt that this was mainly due to the depressing influences exerted on local authority building by the deterioration of economic prospects.

It will naturally be suggested that there may have been other influences affecting rents. Some areas may have been traditionally high rent areas, and vice versa. The case of the high rents in London due to high site values can be quoted in support of the suggestion. It is difficult to test this possibility at all generally, for to do so we need information about rents in different towns before the Great War, and this is very scanty. The only figures available are those collected by the Board of Trade in 1912.[1] These are only partially suitable as a basis of comparison, for they include only fifty-three out of the eighty county boroughs we have been considering ; still more serious, the rents include rates.[2] The results of the comparison must, therefore, be treated with reserve, but they are of some interest. By 1936 thirty-four out of the fifty-three county boroughs included in the Board of Trade enquiry had changed their relative positions on the rent scale, if judged by the rents of the local authority houses

[1] *Board of Trade Inquiry into the Cost of Living, 1912.* Cd. 6955. The inquiry does not provide data for calculating medians or even averages. Instead the upper and lower limits of rents charged for houses of different sizes are given. In deciding whether to rank a borough as having low or high rents, etc., in 1912 compared with 1936, the rents of the apparently most common type of house have been used.

[2] It will be realised that under the system of rent control after the Great War, increases in the rents of old working-class houses could in general only be made according to definite and uniform rules. Except, therefore, where rates increased exceptionally fast between 1912 and 1936 the gross rents of old working-class houses ought to have increased by the same proportions in all towns, and the classification of towns as high or low-rented on this basis of old houses would have been similar in 1912 and 1936.

in 1936. For instance, seventeen had been low-rented boroughs
in 1912, but in nine cases their local authority houses did not come
into the low rent category in 1936. Four of those which had been in
the low rent group in 1912 were in the highest rent group in 1936,
and four others had gone through a similar transmigration in the
opposite directions.

The evidence, such as it is, does not suggest any close or inevitable connection between customary rents, as shown by the 1912
data, and the rents of local authority houses in 1936. It would be
unwise, therefore, to assume that the peculiarities of the rents of
local authority houses can be explained away under any obvious
omnibus heading of widespread underlying factors, permanently
tending towards relatively high or low rents. This conclusion is
consistent with the observations already made about the sizes of
towns and local authority rents in 1936, for high site values and
high rents are always popularly connected with large towns and
vice versa. Thus, though we cannot say that such factors played no
part in determining local authority rents, it is clear that if they were
important, the others that we have isolated were often sufficiently
weighty to counteract them. The net effect of the latter has been
that, in comparison to both pre-war rents and the sizes of towns,
the varying rents of local authority houses give the impression of a
rather violent game of general post.[1]

(b) Variation of Rents within Boroughs.

So far we have only used the median rents to get some idea of the
levels of rents in different places. The question of the extent to which
the actual rents charged for individual local authority houses differed
from these medians was raised at the beginning of the 'thirties when
rent policy came under discussion. It will be remembered that
local authorities were urged to let the houses built at the new lower
levels of costs at correspondingly lower rents than those built when
costs were higher. The introduction of differential rent schemes
was also suggested. It was argued that this was the key to the
problem of letting houses at rents within the reach of the majority

---

[1] It is possible that differences in local building costs have affected local authority
rents. There is no real information about this ; it can only be stated categorically that
the arrangement in the building industry by which wages-rates vary with the sizes of towns
obviously provides no general explanation, as towns of all sorts and sizes came into each
rent group. It is perhaps worth mentioning, however, that the Ministry of Health com-
plained as late as 1938 that some local authorities gave preference to local builders
and local building materials, despite additional costs sometimes incurred by doing so
(*Ministry of Health Annual Report*, 1938/9). Thus, varying degrees of economy in the choice
of builders and materials may have had some influence on rents.

of working-class families. The extent to which rents did vary from the medians and the factors on which this depended became and remained a matter of interest.

The arguments about varying rents with the costs of providing houses applied only to the houses built with the Wheatley subsidy after the abolition of the Chamberlain subsidy. As the rent statistics, however, cover houses built with the latter, as well as with the other subsidies available from time to time between 1919 and 1936, we shall have to go carefully in order not to mix up the effects of different rates of subsidy with those of changes in costs.[1] There is one other point to be borne in mind. The houses built by the local authorities differed considerably in size. Although the majority had three bed-rooms and no parlour, some had parlours, some had four bedrooms, some had three and some only two. The bigger houses, or those superior in amenities to the others, would naturally be let at higher rents than others, and vice versa. There is a danger of confusing differences in rents which reflected these differences in quality with differences in rents due to changes in costs. For instance, though in some individual county boroughs rents varied from less than 3/– a week to 12/– and over, and in the majority they varied from less than 5/– to over 10/–, we cannot jump to the conclusion that county boroughs did vary their rents in relation to decreases in build-ing costs.

As a first approach to disentangling and digesting the hot-potch of statistics it will be useful to ignore the houses at the extreme ends of the rents scales in each borough. These were likely to be houses exceptional in some way, either in size or in regard to the subsidy under which they were built. It is convenient for this pur-pose to isolate the central block of houses containing about half of those in each borough by setting aside the 25 per cent. of the houses which had the highest rents, and similarly those with the lowest rents. The difference between the highest and lowest rents at which this central group of houses were let we will call, for simplicity the range of rents.[2] It is important to realise from the

---

[1] It will be remembered that the net fall in average costs between 1927 and 1929 was equivalent to 1/4 off the rent, and between 1929 and 1932 to 1/3. As it was only after 1932 that the further fall of 1/6 took place, the complete decrease of about 3/– to 4/– would only affect the situation in those boroughs building on a considerable scale in 1933 and 1934 with the Wheatley subsidy. On the other hand, the difference between the Wheatley and the Chamberlain subsidies was equivalent to 3/1 or 2/–, after 1927, accord-ing to whether the local authorities paid their full contributions from the rates or not, up to 1929.

[2] Those readers who are familiar with statistical terms will no doubt prefer to think of the range as the difference betweeen the upper and lower quartiles. In fact, it has not

I

start that the ranges isolate the central group of houses irrespective of which particular subsidies they were built with ; the size of the range is not necessarily dependent, therefore, only on the rents charged for houses built with the Wheatley subsidy. In some boroughs, as we shall see, building with other subsidies was on a scale sufficient to affect the size of the range ; in others, building with the Wheatley subsidy was relatively on such a large scale that many of the houses must have been let at rents outside the range. Provided this warning is kept firmly in mind, the ranges provide a convenient way of classifying the boroughs.

They fall into five distinct groups. In twenty-two, the ranges were less than 1/-, in twenty-nine they varied from 1/- to just under 2/-, in eighteen from 2/- to just under 3/-, in seven from 3/- to just under 4/-, and in the other four they varied from 4/- upwards. Comparison of these ranges with the changes in costs suggest a few tentative generalisations. It seems obvious that there may have been good ground for the criticisms brought against local authorities that they averaged decreases in costs over all their houses, instead of letting the newer ones at rents corresponding to the lower levels of costs. It is on the face of it improbable that the twenty-two boroughs with ranges of less than 1/- can have let the houses built after 1929 at rents appropriate to the lower levels of costs. The twenty-nine boroughs with the ranges up to 2/- present a rather more hopeful picture, it is true ; but the thirty-five boroughs with ranges over 2/- raise suspicions about all the others, for they seem " more Royalist than the King." The details are shown in Table XI.

The four boroughs with the largest ranges of all are easily disposed of. They were South Shields, Gateshead, Newcastle and Chester. For the first three the explanation is the inclusion of slum clearance houses in the statistics. For Chester it is the relatively very large amount of building with the Chamberlain subsidy. This seems to have created a block of houses with rents of 9/- and over, while those built with Wheatley subsidy were in another block with rents between 5/- and 6/-; as very few houses were let at rents in between, the range includes part of both these main groups. Explanations of a similar type apply to the seven boroughs with the next largest ranges. In Oxford, for instance, the size of the range was apparently

been practicable to use the precise quartiles in all cases as the rent series of some of the boroughs are extremely erratic, with great concentrations within particular rent grades, overlapping the quartiles, and the actual statistical quartiles are quite imaginary. In some boroughs two-thirds to three-quarters of the houses come within the range for all practical purposes. The analysis is thus really based on the quartiles but modified where it seemed reasonable to do so.

TABLE XI.—Ranges of Rents of Houses belonging to County Boroughs, 1936.[1]

Under 1/- (1)	1— and under 2/- (2)	2/- and under 3/- (3)	3/- and under 4/- (4)	4/- and over (5)
Barnsley†	Bath	Birkenhead*	Bury†	Chester*
Blackburn†	Bolton	Blackpool*	Darlington	Gateshead
Birmingham	Burton-on-	Bournemouth*	Leeds†	Newcastle
Bradford†	Trent*	Brighton*,	Oxford	S. Shields†
Burnley	Canterbury†	Bristol*	Stoke-on-Trent	
Derby*	Carlisle†	Cardiff	Tynemouth	
Dudley†	Dewsbury†	Croydon*	West Ham*	
East Ham*	Coventry	Eastbourne*		
Exeter	Gloucester*	Hull		
Merthyr	Grimsby*	Ipswich		
Oldham†	Halifax†	Liverpool*		
Preston†	Hastings*	Middlesborough†		
Plymouth*	Huddersfield	Rochdale		
Reading†	Leicester*	Salford*		
St. Helens†	Lincoln†	Southend*		
Sheffield†	Manchester	Wallasey*		
Smethwick†	Newport	W. Bromwich†		
Swansea	(Mons.)	W. Hartlepool		
Wakefield†	Northampton			
Walsall†	Nottingham†			
Warrington†	Norwich†			
Yarmouth*	Portsmouth*			
	Rotherham†			
	Southampton			
	Southport			
	Stockport			
	Sunderland†			
	Wigan†			
	Wolverhampton†			
	Worcester†			
	York†			

* Boroughs with high rents, i.e. coming in columns 4 and 5 of Table XB.
† Boroughs with low rents, i.e. coming in columns 1 and 2 of Table XB.
[1] See Note 2 to Table XA, above.

due to the same cause as that of Chester. In Tynemouth, on the other hand, it was the houses built during the first experiment which led to a similar result. In others the houses built under slum-clearance schemes were mainly responsible for the extension of the range. Thus, practically all the cases of wide ranges are explained by exceptionally high building activity under the Addison, Chamberlain or Greenwood subsidies relatively to activity under the Wheatley subsidy, the one which all the fuss was about.[1]

The eighteen boroughs with ranges between two and three shillings provide a more varied picture. One of them, Blackpool,

[1] Leeds was the only exception; its inclusion in this group was due to its elaborate system of differential rents.

built no houses at all under the Wheatley subsidy, while Croydon's building under it was negligible. In most of the others it seems probable that building under the other subsidies were so important as to affect the range, the central blocks of houses including some built with them. In brief it is reasonably certain that, in all those boroughs with ranges of 2/– or over, the apparently high degree of variation in rents was primarily due to the differing proportions of houses built under different Acts with different subsidies. We must not jump to conclusions at this point. This does not mean that none of these boroughs let Wheatley subsidy houses built after 1929 at the lower rents which could correspond to the lower costs. All the statistics show is that the extent of building under the other subsidies were a factor of major importance in creating the wide ranges of rents, *a fortiori* in the case of the boroughs which built relatively little after 1929.[1] Observant readers will have already noticed that some of the boroughs with wide ranges were low-rent boroughs. Actually, the boroughs with ranges of 2/– and over included only thirteen out of the twenty-three high rent boroughs, and even of these all but two had ranges under 3/–. Wide variations in rent, therefore, acted only as a very partial palliative of high rents.

The groups of boroughs with ranges between 1/– and 2/– provide an illuminating contrast. With a few exceptions, such as Newport (Mons.), the size of the ranges cannot be explained by reference to the volume of building under subsidies other than the Wheatley. *Prima facie*, it might be assumed that these boroughs at least let their cheaper houses at appropriately lower rents, but even in this case there are grounds for suspicion. There were a few boroughs in this group who hardly did any building after the fall in costs. In these the existence of the range must be attributed to the existence of houses of different sizes and amenities built with the Wheatley subsidy, or to the introduction of differential rent schemes. If this explanation holds in some cases we cannot be sure that it does not apply to others.

We can regard any appearance of variations in rents corresponding to changes in costs only with scepticism, and it is natural to assume that boroughs with ranges under 1/– certainly did not carry out schemes of this sort. For a number of these boroughs the assumption is perfectly justified, as ten hardly built after 1929. Merthyr Tydfil is perhaps the outstanding example, but four of the smaller Lancashire boroughs were also in this category, three West Riding

---

[1] As for example, Salford and Blackpool in Lancashire, Darlington, South Shields, Tynemouth and West Hartlepool in the North-East.

boroughs, and Derby and Plymouth. The rest, however, must have decided quite deliberately not to follow the official advice; they continued to build right up to the end of the Second Experiment, often with more energy after than before the fall in costs. Birmingham is perhaps the most astonishing example. It had 23,038 houses with rents from 7/1 to 8/– out of a total of 39,937 built under the various Housing Acts.

In sum, then, this examination of county borough rent policy, imperfect though it is, shows up a number of things quite clearly. First, it is practically certain that differences in the terms of subsidies were more important factors in creating a dispersion of rents, than deliberate attempts to fix the rents of individual houses in relation to changes in costs, at least up to 1936. Second, there is no evidence that local authorities were willing to make such attempts. We may be permitted to wonder if they would have been so conservative if costs had been rising instead of falling.[1] Third, the wide ranges in rents were only very partial palliatives to high rents, as it was by no means general for county boroughs with high rents to have wide ranges. There is a subsidiary point which has also emerged; some local authorities could not reasonably make the attempt to vary rents of new Wheatley houses with decreases in costs simply because they did not build on a serious scale after 1929. The dependence of rents on costs was an essential part of the rent policy put forward by the Ministry of Health after 1930, but no steps were taken to see that local authorities in fact built after costs fell. Failure to tackle this problem reduced the policy to pious aspirations as far as a number of boroughs were concerned. Finally, it is well known that the local authorities did not adopt the suggestion made at the same time, that they should introduce differential rent schemes of some sort. Even in 1936 only 80 schemes were in existence and these were mainly confined to slum-clearance schemes.

The long and short of the whole matter is that a very large proportion of local authorities ignored the Ministry of Health's advice on the rent problem. For this the local authorities cannot altogether be blamed. The Ministry proffered it so late in the day that to follow it up thoroughly would have involved changing the rents of many firmly-established tenants, and it might reasonably be argued that this would cause more trouble than anything else. Moreover, the economy campaign and the first signs of winding up the Wheatley

---

[1] In this case they would have made a loss if they had applied the old rents to all the houses, and incurred unpopularity if they had raised the rents of old houses to average out the higher cost of the new.

subsidy followed quickly on the advice. Confronted with closing down building under the Second Experiment, it might seem hardly worth while introducing a new rent system, as there would not be the opportunity of following it out to its logical conclusion by building more ordinary houses for ordinary unskilled and semi-skilled working-class families. Inevitably, however, one is left with some suspicion about how far the Ministry of Health could have induced the local authorities to adopt the new policy even if the Wheatley subsidy had had a long life ahead of it.

RENT POLICY: CONCLUSIONS

We have emerged at last from the maze of statistics with results of considerable significance. We have succeeded in disentangling some of the influences which determined local authority rent policy in the past. The most important general conclusion we have reached is that the relation between the timing of building and changes in costs, and the choice of subsidy made by local authorities, as well as the actual size of the subsidies, were major factors in the determination of rents.

The interaction between these factors worked out in the following way. Rents were high in certain boroughs because they built large proportions of their houses under subsidy or cost conditions which were unfavourable for low-rent policies. The question of which subsidy they built under during the Second Experiment was a matter they decided for themselves. Those that preferred the Chamberlain to the Wheatley subsidy in fact chose to provide houses with rents higher than they need have been. In short, they more or less ignored the theory that houses should be provided at the lowest possible rents. Even after the abolition of the Chamberlain subsidy, many of them continued to be indifferent to the opportunities offered by the Wheatley subsidy.[1] This opportunity for freedom of choice between building houses to let at high or at low rents during the Second Experiment was the accidental result of the haphazard manner in which the Wheatley subsidy had been introduced on top of the Chamberlain subsidy. In effect this had meant that there was no clear definition of the object of housing policy in terms of the proportions of houses of various types needed.

Some boroughs, however, had moderately high rents because, although they made great use of the Wheatley subsidy, they failed to go on building on a large scale after 1929, following the fall in

---

[1] The effects of building under the Addison subsidy on rents were in general much less important than those of building with Chamberlain subsidy.

costs. These boroughs were on the whole in the depressed areas in which, as we have seen, economic circumstances were not favourable to building after 1929. On the other hand the very low rents occurred in boroughs which took heart under the Greenwood slum clearance subsidy, even though they were in some cases in depressed areas; it is quite possible that it was the further large fall in costs after 1932 which influenced their behaviour rather than the Greenwood subsidy, but we cannot settle this point.[1] The rest of the low-rent boroughs were in general boroughs which built as much or more after the fall in costs of 1929 as before, and which, relatively speaking, did not devote much attention to the Chamberlain subsidy. It was these low-rent boroughs which not only had opportunities for providing houses at relatively low rents, but took advantage of them.

These curious and disconcerting results sprang from the failure of those responsible for housing policy to appreciate the existence of three problems connected with the use of subsidies. First, as we have seen the purpose of the subsidies, in terms of the relative importance of providing houses to be let at various levels of rent, were not defined; instead, local authorities not particularly interested in housing questions were offered opportunities of evading their responsibility for providing houses at reasonably low rents. Second, no attempt was made to deal with the special difficulties caused by deterioration of the ability of prospective tenants to pay rents in depressed or stagnant areas. Third, rather vague decreases in costs were relied upon to bring the rents of new houses within the reach of the lower working-class income groups, but no attempt was made to work out some sort of plan of capital investment, in other words, building schemes, in relation to these expected changes. The important issue of what quantities of houses were built at various levels of costs was left to be settled by chance.

This brings us to another point of importance. We found that differences in the terms of subsidies had more apparent effect in creating wide ranges of rents than changes in costs. This was only partly due to the fact that the changes in costs, during the most important years of the Second Experiment, were small in comparison to differences in the terms of the subsidies available. It was also partly due to the fact that many local authorities were unwilling to fix the rents for new houses built after 1929 at rents corresponding to the decreased

[1] The Greenwood subsidy was very nearly the same as the Wheatley subsidy for families containing four people, so that in terms of finance the change in subsidy was less important than the change in costs after 1932 in so far as families were of this size, except in certain special cases. See p. 136 n. 1. below.

costs. In view of the inevitable uncertainty about the future course of costs and the vagaries of local authorities' reactions to such changes, it might well have been better to have tackled this question in a different way. For instance, some system of grading subsidies in relation to the variations of rents, and to the numbers of houses needed at each rent level, might have worked better; changes in costs either up or down could then have been dealt with by appropriate changes in the scale of subsidies. The policy of relying on decreases in costs to produce lower rents during the Second Experiment, but taking every opportunity to counteract the decreases by cutting the subsidies, was plainly stupid.

In the early 'thirties, however, it was argued that whatever the inherent weaknesses of the system of subsidies might be, they would not have mattered if the local authorities had followed the official advice on rent policy put forward in 1930. It is open to doubt whether even model behaviour in this respect would have made a great deal of difference in practice. The net fall in costs between 1929 and the decision to close down the whole Wheatley scheme in 1932/3 had only been equivalent to a decrease in rents of 1/6. This might have just tipped the scale and opened up big new markets in local authority houses in some areas. It represented a sum sufficiently large to make a perceptible difference to some family budgets. But there is little reason for thinking rents lower by that amount would have had much effect in areas suffering from serious unemployment, in which earnings in the basic industries were low and irregular. It certainly would be insufficient to induce families in which the chief wage-earner was unemployed, or expected to become unemployed, to take on a new house. A decrease of 1/6 was rather a poor carrot to dangle in front of hesitant tenants.

The other criticism of local authorities on the score of rents was that they did not introduce differential rent schemes. These were only 112 even in 1938, and many still covered only families rehoused under slum clearance schemes. It was undoubtedly true that many families on the local authority estates were enjoying subsidised rents, though they could have afforded to pay the full economic rents. The argument that if differential rents had been introduced the tenants could have been drawn from a wider range of income-groups, and that in consequence the effective demand for houses would have been greater, is obviously sensible. On the other hand, it is possible that even differential rents would have failed to solve the problems in many areas. Where a large proportion of tenants are poor the amount of subsidy that can be saved by letting houses at or near the economic rent is small because few tenants can afford it; in consequence, the number of houses which can be let at low rents with extra subsidies is also small. Moreover, in depressed areas there was always a danger that the relatively wealthy tenants might turn in to poor ones overnight, thereby upsetting the financial balance of the scheme. The experience of differential rent schemes under the Third Experiment provides a number of illustrations of these difficulties.[1]

But though differential rent schemes might not have solved all the problems, in some areas they would undoubtedly have been possible and useful. It is argued in defence of the local authorities for not introducing them that they were not told to do so until too late, and that their legal powers were uncertain. This is true. But it was not until after 1930 that they made any attempt to find out whether it was possible to introduce differential rents. They had not been sufficiently interested to bother, and they had failed to use either imagination or initiative. Their protests against cuts in subsidies, which they were apt to blame for all their difficulties, stand out in sharp contrast to their lack of energy in trying to help themselves. The preference of some authorities for the Chamberlain subsidy rather than the Wheatley was merely an extreme illustration of this inertia. The families who could afford these rents of Chamberlain houses were likely to be those with relatively secure incomes who could be relied upon to pay their rents regularly, and the authorities were not obliged to subsidise them from the rates.

There is really no doubt about how rent policy worked out in practice. The market for local authority houses was largely confined to a limited range of income groups, that is, in practice, the better-off families, the small clerks, the artisans, the better-off semi-skilled workers with small families and fairly safe jobs. Right up to the economy campaign of 1932, and even later, it was these families who absorbed most of the houses. The special enquiries as to the type of families on the estates of the larger authorities of Birmingham, the London County Council or elsewhere provided additional evidence.[2] The Ministry of Health admitted it. This was the reason why it was possible to argue that the market for ordinary local authority houses was satisfied by 1932. It was so, no doubt, in many areas, as far as the effective demand for houses at the prevailing rents were con-

[1] See Chapter VIII, Section III below.
[2] See for instance *When We Build Again*—Bournville Village Trust Research Publication, 1941, particularly Chapters IV and VIII, and *Becontree and Dagenham*, by Terence Young, 1934. Chap. 12.

cerned. In depressed areas the point of saturation had almost certainly been reached much earlier, probably at about the time the local authority expenditure tailed off between 1927 and 1928. Even those authorities who had built mainly with the Chamberlain subsidy might claim that the demand for their houses had been satisfied even by 1927, and that this justified the lack of active building between 1927 and 1929 in the last years of the subsidy's life. The fallacy of all these arguments is that demand is discussed as though it was something fixed and independent of rent.

Among the disastrous and inequitable consequences of the confusion over rent and subsidy policy were the effects on the incidence of the subsidies. The families who could afford local authority rents got new houses with the aid of the subsidy. They got them, that is, with the assistance of a subvention from the other members of the community. Even the families who themselves were unable to get new houses, usually because they could not afford the rents, contributed to the finance of the subsidy by paying rates and taxes. In effect, the working-class families who benefited most directly from the subsidies were the relatively small group of about half a million families who were among the best off. On any ordinary way of argument these were precisely the families who were least in need of financial aid of any sort. Those with incomes of £3 and upwards would have been better off even if they had paid the full economic rents (amounting, with rates to perhaps a total of fifteen shillings a week in 1928), than unskilled labourers' families with fifty shillings a week, out of which they had to pay rent, rates and everything else. In short, the direct effect of the subsidies was to enable the better-off to have the better houses without seriously reducing their ability to buy other things.

Of course, it can, and should, be argued that a much larger group than this benefited indirectly. The new houses, whoever got them, eased the pressure on the supply of houses. The families unable to get them had a better opportunity than they would have had otherwise, of getting houses to themselves, or getting larger shares of houses, or even better older houses. This benefit, however, also tended to be most pronounced for the relatively best-off of the inhabitants of old houses. For they in their turn had relatively the most financial resources with which to take advantage of the greater selection of old houses available. It must not be forgotten that the relief was very patchily distributed. Pressure was eased only in areas in which substantial numbers of families moved away into new houses, and there was little improvement in the highly congested central areas of the big towns. This uneven incidence even of the indirect benefits of the housing subsidies was reflected in the failure of the slums and of serious overcrowding to disappear, a failure which caused such public and official consternation in the early 'thirties.

This gloomy recital does not bring us quite to the end of the consequences of rent and subsidy policy. The incidence of the subsidy was inevitably inequitable between large areas as well as between families and income groups. Some districts, as we know, found it advisable to give up building long before others, they were able to take advantage of the subsidies to a much smaller extent in relation to their population than the more fortunate areas. For example, in Merthyr Tydvil and in West Hartlepool the Treasury contribution to the Chamberlain and Wheatley subsidies worked out at 6d. and 2/- respectively per head of population in 1931, but in Birmingham and Leeds it was 6/6 and 3/2½, respectively.

THE SECOND EXPERIMENT: EPILOGUE

The answer to the question of whether the Second Experiment was a success or a failure depends on how its purpose is defined. If this purpose was the encouragement by means of subsidies of an output of houses sufficient to overcome the shortage, it can be regarded in very general terms as a success. By the time the experiment was brought to a close, the acute shortage had been wiped out. If the results are examined more closely, however, the success is seen to be incomplete. Anything approaching complete success was only achieved on paper by counting every house in the country, irrespective of its suitability to the requirements of the families needing houses. It is only if matters of quality, size and location are ignored that there were nearly enough houses in 1934. If such simple assumptions are challenged by inquiring, for instance, whether the degree of success was uniform all over the country, the artificial character of the statement about the success of the experiment becomes obvious. For example, in 1931 over thirty per cent. of requirements were still outstanding in several counties, in others less than ten per cent., but the shortage in Middlesex had actually increased;[1] though by the end of the experiment the position in some counties had improved, it was still serious in others.

If the purpose of the policy of the Second Experiment is defined as the provision of a supply of working-class houses at rents within the reach of the majority of families on a scale sufficient, for instance, to permit the abolition of rent control, then the experiment must be regarded as a failure. In the same year as the Act bringing the Second Experiment to an end was passed, another Act was passed to prevent the continuation of even such piecemeal decontrol of working-class rents as had been taking place.

The contrast between the apparent success or failure of the experiment as judged by these two different, but equally plausible criteria, illustrates one of the major weaknesses of the whole housing policy of the years we have been considering: the absence of any clearly defined purpose or intention. The Second Experiment was based on two separate housing subsidies, provided by two different governments with quite different views about the housing problem. No attempt was ever made to ensure that these two subsidies were used in any sort of appropriate relationship to each other,

[1] See pp. 63 and 71 and Table VII p. 66 above.

until the matter was ultimately settled by the drastic method of abolishing one of them. This was not the only cause of confusion. The government was guilty of extraordinary vagaries about the relationship between changes in costs and changes in subsidies, and between both of these and rent policy. At one stage it was in a vague way hoped that as costs fell economic rents would be reduced, with the aid of the subsidies, to levels within the reach of the lower income groups. Yet the first time costs fell on a scale likely to bring this about one subsidy was abolished and an attempt made to cut the other. The second time costs fell substantially the remaining subsidy was abolished and the whole experiment brought to an end.

The self-evident failure of the Second Experiment as regards the provision of working-class houses was primarily due to the inadequate output of houses by the local authorities, and to the high rents charged for them. The most important causes of this failure can be summarised conveniently:

(*a*) The confusion over the major issues of subsidies, costs and rents;

(*b*) The absence of any defined rent policy until the experiment was drawing to an end and the failure to enforce it when it had been enunciated;

(*c*) The assumption that the gap between the rents people could pay and the costs of providing houses was uniform all over the country, irrespective of differences both in economic conditions determining the incomes of working-class families and in local conditions affecting the cost of providing houses. From this sprang the assumption that the need for assistance from the Treasury could be measured by the numbers of houses actually built in each district;

(*d*) The lack of central control over the activities of local authorities and the inertia and inefficiency of a considerable number of them.

We can put the whole matter shortly by saying that the unsatisfactory outcome of the Second Experiment with respect to working-class houses was due to the fact that the purpose of policy was not defined and that subsidies were offered to local authorities, and to private enterprise, without any clear instructions about how they were to be used, if at all.

Viewed against the broader background of the development of economic institutions the history of the Second Experiment appears as a transitional phase from one system of providing houses to another. Before the Great War the majority of small houses, both of working-class and superior types, were built by private enterprise and bought by investors in house property who let them to other people. The capital for the investment was mainly raised privately and locally. After the Great War during the Second Experiment this system was superseded. The investors in houses to let for the non-working class market was replaced by owner-occupiers financed by building societies. The building societies collected capital on a national instead of a local scale and pooled it for investment in mort-gages, repaid on the instalment system. The success of this system was limited only by the ability of people to become owner-occupiers on this basis. The supply of working-class houses became, on the other hand, dependent on state enterprise worked through the local authorities. This supply was also financed by capital borrowed nationally, either by the direct issue of local authority stock, or through the Local Loans Board. Though the advantages of borrow-ing on a national scale were as obvious in the case of working-class houses as in the case of the other group, the verdict on the success of the local authorities and on their suitability for performing the function of providing working-class houses was highly doubtful.

Chapter VII

THE THIRD EXPERIMENT

THE RETURN TO A SANITARY POLICY
1933/4 TO 1939

So far we have studiously ignored the whole question of slums.
For all practical purposes so had the British Government until 1930.
The reason for this was obvious. While efforts were being made to
catch up on the actual absolute shortage of houses, it seemed foolish
to tear down existing houses, however bad. Thus, while the powers
of local authorities to clear slums, and force recalcitrant landlords to
repair their property, install water closets, etc., were, in fact, slightly
strengthened, the subsidies were mainly intended to encourage the
building of additional houses. Consistently with this, local authorities
were subject to practically no pressure to clear slums, either from the
public or from the Ministry of Health. Up to 1930, about eleven
thousand slum houses had been pulled down and replaced.[1]

By 1929, however, the public conscience was beginning to stir,
and slum clearance programmes became planks in the General
Election programmes of that year. The new minority Labour Government decided to tackle the matter. Mr. Greenwood, as Minister of
Health, introduced a new policy, and a new subsidy specifically
for Slum Clearance, with the Housing Act of 1930.[2] Greenwood's
Act marked an important stage in slum clearance policy. The post-
war doctrine of solution by subsidy was applied to the slum problem
seriously for the first time.

Greenwood's scheme had a number of interesting features. The
subsidy paid from the Treasury to local authorities was variable.
Instead of being a fixed amount per house, it varied directly with the
numbers of people *displaced and rehoused*. This had two advantages.
It would discourage the pre-Great War custom of demolishing of
slums, leaving the ex-inhabitants to find what accommodation
they could. It would also make it easier for the local authorities to deal
with the large poor families, as, in practice, the subsidy increased

---

[1] See *Ministry of Health Annual Report*, 1931/2. The main subsidy for slum clearance
purposes before 1930 was that provided under the Chamberlain Act (Sect. 1 (3)); the
Treasury contributed half the annual loss on approved schemes.
[2] *Housing Act, 1930*, 20 and 21. Geo. V. Ch. 39.

with the size of the family rehoused. The subsidy also varied between agricultural and urban parishes, £2 10/- for 40 years per person rehoused in the former and £2 5/- in the latter[1]; in addition an extra £1 per house for 40 years was provided when agricultural workers were rehoused. Provision was also made for an additional subsidy in urban areas where the cost of acquiring and clearing sites was high and rehousing accommodation had to be provided in flats.[2] It was intended that local authorities should have no justification for avoiding the rehousing of large families or agricultural families, on the ground that they could not provide houses at sufficiently low rents. Nor was there to be any reason for shirking rebuilding in the centres of towns because land was expensive. Accordingly, the local authority's contribution from the rates was fixed at £3 15/- for forty years per house or flat, irrespective of the size of the Treasury contribution. The rents of the houses built under the scheme were left to the discretion of the local authorities. Provided that they were what the tenants " could reasonably be expected to pay," any local authority could adopt any scheme of rebates or differential renting it liked. The accounts, of course, had to balance, annual expenses were to equal the actual receipts from rents, plus the Treasury and the local authority contributions.[3]

The combination of a fixed maximum contribution per house by local authorities with a Treasury subsidy varying according to certain broad categories was new. It differed from the original 1919 Act subsidy in two important aspects. The cost to the local authorities would increase with the scale of their slum clearance; those local authorities with large slum areas would be involved in greater cost than those with small, whereas the 1919 Act had limited the cost to a local authority of any housing scheme in proportion to the yield of its rates. The new arrangement was thus no more favourable to poor areas than to rich, or to areas with large housing programmes than

[1] For families of four persons rehoused, the ordinary Greenwood subsidy worked out a £9 a house a year from the Treasury; this was, of course, the same as the original Wheatley subsidy for general building before the 1927 reduction. With the lower contribution from the local authorities, however, £3 15/- (instead of £4 10/- with the original Wheatley subsidy) the Greenwood subsidy was about 6d. a week more than the reduced Wheatley one. See Statistical Appendix Table 6, notes (d) and (e).
[2] This special subsidy, amounting to an additional £1 5/- for forty years per person rehoused in flats became available where the cost of acquiring and clearing sites exceeded £3,000 per acre.
[3] Housing Act, 1930. Parts III and IV. The local authorities were given power to make arrangements with housing associations to carry out the rehousing operations. They could not, however, hand over their powers of compulsory purchase so that associations could only work by agreement with the local authorities unless they were prepared to forego the financial advantage of compulsory acquisition of slum property.

to those with small ones ; in this regard it resembled the Wheatley subsidy scheme. On the other hand the Treasury subsidy varied to a limited extent with the differences in the ability of tenants to pay rent and difference in costs of providing new accommodation. Thus the new scheme was more generous than the Wheatley subsidy which, apart from a broad division between agricultural and urban parishes, made no allowance for differences in rent-paying capacity or costs. It was less generous than the 1919 Act, under which the Treasury subsidy varied without limit according to these factors and, also, in relation to the apparent financial resources of the local authorities and the differing sizes of their programmes.

When the Greenwood Act was passed, the Wheatley subsidy was still available for ordinary working-class houses built for general needs. It was no part of Greenwood's policy to repeal it. Taken together with the new slum clearance subsidies it formed part of a scale of housing subsidies graded roughly in accordance with the cost of providing new houses for, and the rent-paying capacity of, certain broad classes of the population. Viewed from another aspect this system was in part a system for providing additional houses, in part a system of replacing old houses. Ultimately, if sufficient additional houses were built with the Wheatley subsidy, a surplus would emerge, and some would become available for families who, though not living in slums, were living in old houses, unsatisfactory by modern standards. In short, *de facto* replacement of the nineteenth century houses above the slum level would begin. This would only be possible if Greenwood was successful in forcing local authorities to reduce the rents of new houses *pari passu* with reductions in building cost and interest rates *and* if differential rent schemes were introduced. The scheme might fail, however, even if everything else went according to plan, if the problem of the high costs of daily travel to work from new housing estates was not dealt with.[1] Apart from actual slums, no provision had been made for official demolition and rebuilding of old houses in the centre of big towns, and no additional subsidy was available to balance travelling costs for families moving into new houses on the outskirts of the big towns.

The Labour Government intended its housing policy to be taken seriously. Local authorities were to consider the needs of their areas for " further housing accommodation for the working classes " as often as occasion arises, or three months after the Ministry of Health had told them to. They were to prepare and submit to the Minister plans for the provision of new houses, distinguishing those built for

[1] On the question of travelling costs, see *When We Build Again*. op. cit.

K

rehousing in connection with slum clearance schemes. Moreover, no time was to be lost in making a start. Every local authority with a population of more than 20,000 was to produce a general statement of its plans for dealing with slum clearance and for the provision of more houses in the next five years. This procedure was to be repeated every five years. The idea of making local authorities work to a programme framed ahead for a definite and fairly long period was new. Not only might it be hoped that this would stimulate more rational arrangement of local building activity, but it would provide the Ministry of Health automatically with a time-table against which it could check the actions of the local authorities.[1]

If this Wheatley-Greenwood scheme had been tried out, the second housing experiment would have ended in 1930; the third would then have started that year, instead of in 1933/4, and would have been of a radically different character from that which was in fact put into practice. The causes which led to the repeal of the Wheatley subsidy by the Housing (Financial Provisions) Act of 1933 have already been described. The same economy campaign led also to postponement of effective action under the Greenwood Act.[2]

The Housing Act of 1933 turned Greenwood's slum clearance subsidy into the corner-stone of a new sanitary policy. The new era was explained unambiguously in the Report of the Departmental Committee on Housing of 1933. Slum clearance had hitherto made little progress. The Government's new housing policy was:

" to concentrate public effort and money on the clearance and improvement of slum conditions, and to rely in the main on competitive private enterprise to provide a new supply of accommodation for the working-classes—the provision by private enterprise to be supplemented where necessary by means of unsubsidised building by the Local Authorities."[3]

The concentration of public effort and money on slum clearance was to be achieved by a five years' demolition and rehousing programme carried out with the Greenwood subsidy by the local authorities. Complete programmes for the abolition of slums in five

---

[1] *Housing Act, 1930.* Sect. 25.
[2] As the Wheatley-Greenwood scheme was abortive, the new rent policy for houses built with the Wheatley subsidy became the final phase of the Second Experiment instead of part of the first phase of the Third. It was for this reason that it was included in the earlier chapter.
[3] Op. cit. *Cmd. 4397*, p. 4. This policy had been advocated in the famous *Report on Local Expenditure* in 1932. Op. cit. In that Report it had been argued that, owing to the fall in building costs and interest rates, a general housing subsidy was no longer necessary. Paragraphs 77 to 81. See p. 46 above.

years were to be made by all the local authorities immediately.[1]

This policy of concentration on slum clearance might, of course, be regarded as a *pis aller*. The experience of the preceding fourteen years had shown that local authorities preferred ordinary building to slum clearance and rehousing. It might be argued from this that, as long as local authorities had the opportunity of choice, slum clearance would be neglected. Such an argument, of course, can only be considered serious on the assumption that it was impossible to compel the local authorities to make double programmes, including both types of building, although it was possible to make them draw up and carry out slum clearance programmes. It will be noticed that the irregularity of building by local authorities discussed in the last chapter showed that lack of capacity to build on a scale sufficient to cover both types of building could not be deduced, except in one or two cases, from past experience. Justification on either of these grounds was not, however, really attempted. An essentially optimistic view was taken of the part to be played by private enterprise; it was explained that:

> " it is anticipated that, with the re-establishment of more normal conditions, economic forces, operating in a free field, will secure a large volume and variety of production at competitive rents, and that a great number of persons and organisations will play their part; private builders, housing companies, public utility companies, finance societies and private investors will, it is hoped, all take a share in the ownership of working-class houses."[2]

Borrowing from the building societies for investment in working-class houses to let was to be encouraged. The local authorities were given powers to guarantee the additional interest and capital involved, if building societies advanced 90 per cent. of the value of a new house, instead of the usual 70 per cent., and extended the period of repayment from the customary twenty years to thirty years. The guarantee was limited to houses suitable for working-class families, and intended for letting at rents within their reach. It was explained rather naïvely in a circular to the local authorities that this guarantee power had been given because the building societies were anxious to help.[3] At this time the building societies were finding it

---

[1] *Ministry of Health Circular to Housing Authorities, 1331.* April, 1933.
[2] *Ministry of Health Circular to Housing Authorities, 1334.* May, 1933.
[3] *Housing (Financial Provisions) Act, 1933.* 23 and 24. Geo. V. Chap 15. Section 2, and *Ministry of Health Circular, 1334,* op. cit. The rate of interest on advances was in these cases to be 1 per cent. below prevailing rates, subject to a minimum of 3 per cent.

so difficult to invest the capital that people of all sorts were trying to lend them that they had been forced not only to reduce the return they offered, but to limit the amount of individual deposits. Their public-spirited wish to exploit a new field of investment with a partial government guarantee was not surprising.

This optimistic policy would mean quite simply that those people who could not buy houses but could afford to pay either an economic, or a commercial, rent for new houses might get them, *if* they happened to live in areas where local authorities were particularly energetic, or private investors particularly enterprising. Those who could not pay even an economic rent for new houses would go without, unless they actually fell into the slum category. The Government had gone as near to rejecting responsibility for working-class housing as it could. The principles of 1923, unwillingly abandoned after the Wheatley Act, had at last triumphed. Practical responsibility for dealing with any but the very worst housing conditions had been abandoned. It was the pre-Great War sanitary policy in the modern dress of subsidies and the compulsory exercise of powers by local authorities. How limited the scope of the new policy would be was demonstrated by the programmes put forward by the local authorities for abolishing slums in five years. The London County Council only found 33 thousand houses requiring replacement out of the 749 thousand houses within its boundaries at the time of the 1931 Population Census; the City Council of Manchester found a mere 15 thousand out of its total number of 180 thousand; Newcastle only just over 2 thousand out of 61 thousand. The total number of houses in England and Wales included in the slum clearance programme accepted by the Ministry of Health was a quarter of a million out of the total of 9.4 million houses in the country in 1931.[1]

The introduction of a scheme to abolish overcrowding in 1935 did not alter the fundamental character of policy. By the 1935 Housing Act it was made the specific duty of local authorities to survey the extent of overcrowding in their areas, and to prepare plans for providing sufficient accommodation.[2] Overcrowding was to be abolished, it was announced, within the five years following the " five year programme " for abolishing the slums. Overcrowding was to become a legal offence, with penalties applied to both landlord and tenant, as the programme for abolishing overcrowding was completed in each area. Once this stage was reached the local

---

[1] *Slum Clearance Programmes of Local Authorities, England and Wales, 1933.* Cmd. 4535.
[2] *Housing Act, 1935.* 25 and 26. Geo. V. Chap. 10. Sect. (1).

authority would be responsible for preventing any recurrence by providing additional houses where required.[1] Subsidies would be available only in three special cases. First, if it was necessary to build flats, a subsidy graduated according to the cost of acquiring sites was offered; this was an extension of the 1930 principle of grading subsidies according to the height of land values. Second, a special subsidy not exceeding £5 a house p.a. was to be given to individual local authorities if, taking into account the scale and cost of the programme and the financial resources of the individual local authority, the burden imposed on the rates would be unreasonable. This was the first attempt since 1919 to provide a subsidy which would vary with the financial strength of local authorities. Third, in certain cases where new houses were provided in rural districts to decrease overcrowding among agricultural workers, subsidies equivalent to between £2 and £8 a house for forty years could be given. In these three cases, however, the local authorities were obliged to make contributions of varying amounts from the rates.[2]

The assumption that subsidies would only be necessary for the abolition of overcrowding in special cases, although a general subsidy, as well as special subsidies, was necessary for slum clearance, was, of course, quite untenable. There is unlimited evidence, as well as commonsense, to show that in fact people are obliged to live in overcrowded houses as well as in slums for the same reasons. People live in these sub-standard conditions as a general rule, either because they are unable to afford better accommodation, or because there is no alternative more suitable accommodation available. Nor is there real justification on grounds of cost for differentiating between subsidies for slum clearance and subsidies for de-crowding if new alternative accommodation has to be provided. Both slum families and overcrowded families can be equally well rehoused in individual houses, provided towns are small enough for people to be shifted to the outskirts; in these cases there is no cost peculiar to slum clearance as distinct from decrowding. Insanitary houses can be closed and the owner given no compensation, just as houses can be left empty because overcrowded families are moved out of them without compensation. If, however, more and/or better accommodation has to be provided on built-up sites, the costs of acquiring and clearing the land, including compensation, will be involved in both cases. Indeed, compensation may be more

[1] Ibid. Sect. 2 to 12.
[2] *Housing Act, 1935.* 25 and 26. Geo. V. Chap. 10, Sect. 31 to 35.

costly if houses have to be pulled down, not because they are unfit for human habitation, but because flats are needed in their place to increase the accommodation.

By 1938 the Ministry of Health had discovered these simple truths and remarked that the same problems arose both in slum clearance and the abatement of overcrowding.[1] The differences between the subsidies were abolished and a uniform scale established by the Housing Act of that year, with a subsidy of £5 10/- per annum per house for forty years irrespective of whether it was to be used for slum clearance or decrowding.[2] The principle already recognised of special subsidies in the three cases (rehousing in flats, rehousing agricultural workers, and rehousing programmes unduly costly in relation to financial resources) was maintained, though the actual rates of subsidy were altered.[3] In general local authorities were to contribute from the rates subsidies equal to half the Exchequer subsidies. The most important positive effects of the changes were to increase the attractiveness of decrowding compared to slum clearance, and to make more generous provision for building on expensive sites. Against this the new fixed subsidy for ordinary houses for replacement was much less generous than Greenwood's.[4]

In some respects the new policy of the Act of 1935 for abolishing overcrowding was revolutionary. For the first time overcrowding was to be defined and made a legal offence. The importance of the quantity as well as the quality of house-room received statutory recognition more definitely than ever before. The practical as distinct from the theoretical importance of this new policy turned, however, on the definition of overcrowding adopted. It might, or might not, be merely an attack on the very worst cases; it might be a serious attempt to provide modern standards or living space for all. Overcrowding was in fact defined in a way which limited

---

[1] *Ministry of Health Circular, No. 1696,* 1938.

[2] The local authority contribution was reduced from £3 15/- to £2 15/-.

[3] *Housing Act, 1938.* 1 and 2 Geo. VI. Chap. 16. Sect. 1–7. The special subsidy for rehousing in flats on expensive sites was more generous than previous ones, starting at £11 instead of £6, where the cost of developed sites exceeded £1,500. The special subsidy for rehousing agricultural workers was increased in certain cases. The third special subsidy given was less generous; it was only to be available for urban areas other than county boroughs, and was to be equivalent to an increase in the general subsidy from £5 10/- to £6 10/-, where the normal levels of rents were particularly low or the magnitude and cost of the programme particularly high.

[4] The cut in the Treasury subsidy was from £9 a year for a family of four rehoused to £5 10/-, that is, to about the equivalent of the original subsidy for rehousing two and a half persons. The parallel cut in the local authority subsidy per house was from £3 15/- to £2 15/-.

the scheme only to the worst conditions of individual families.[1]

It was defined, that is, without reference to the popular conviction that separate families in general required separate houses. It ignored questions of density of building or population in particular areas; these could only be dealt with by the slum clearance procedure for which no standard was defined.[2] Even the standard for individual houses taken was so low that the decrowding campaign would affect mainly families living in exceptionally small houses, and exceptionally large families living in ordinary houses.

The great majority of houses in England and Wales have at least four rooms, counting the kitchen, if it is usable as a dining-room, but great numbers of these, especially among the old houses, have only two bedrooms. Now overcrowding as defined depended on three things: size and number of rooms, including the kitchen if used as a dining or living room, and separation of sexes for sleeping. The size and number of rooms criteria worked out little higher than the Population Census standard of two or more persons per room. The separation of sexes standard was so worded as not to apply to any house with more than one room. This made nonsense of it, for people will not in fact divide up the family and accommodation so as to provide separate sleeping accommodation for the two sexes, if this involves sleeping in the parlour or the kitchen, merely because the children are over ten years of age. Moreover, no allowance at all was made for the existence, or non-existence, of separate domestic offices, closets, washing accommodation, kitchens, etc., for separate families.[3] On the basis of this standard only 3·8 per cent. of working-

---

[1] There were two separate tests of overcrowding. First, the test of separation of sexes for sleeping: if the number of rooms was such that two persons of opposite sex of ten years of age or more (not husband and wife) must sleep in the same room the house would be overcrowded. On this test only one-roomed houses would be overcrowded, for with two or more rooms it is always possible to separate the sexes. (Kitchens were counted as rooms if they could be used as living rooms.) Second, the test of the numbers of persons per room: Infants under a year old were not counted, and children between one and ten years were counted as half a unit for this purpose. The scale was as follows:

With 1 room the maximum number of persons permitted was 2,
  „ 2 rooms „   „   „   „   „   „   „ 3,
  „ 3   „   „   „   „   „   „   „   „ 5,
  „ 4   „   „   „   „   „   „   „   „ 7½,
  „ 5   „   „   „   „   „   „   „   „ 10,

with an additional 2 persons permitted for every room in excess of 5. These numbers were scaled down if any room was less than 110 square feet.

[2] Although the definition of overcrowding ignored these aspects, Sections 13 to 18 of the Act provided that in certain types of areas if at least one-third of the working-class houses were overcrowded or slums or were unduly congested, complete re-development of the area might be undertaken.

[3] Local authorities had had powers under the Housing Act of 1925 to enforce the provision of separate offices for separate families. The powers were, however, permissive, and they were not made compulsory under subsequent Acts.

class families were overcrowded, and of these 56·3 per cent. were exceptionally large families,[1] and 43·3 per cent. lived in exceptionally small houses.[2] The Registrar-General calculated that if a slightly higher standard had been used, 853 thousand families would have been overcrowded instead of 341 thousand.[3] The overcrowding policy was as limited as the slum clearance programme. Neither could remove the mass of decaying, crowded houses of the industrial areas, or provide opportunities for improvement in the general standard.

The change over to the limited liability sanitary policy was completed in 1936 by an attempt to rationalise the use of subsidised houses. For this purpose each local authority was to keep one housing account for all houses built under the Housing Acts from 1919 onwards. All the receipts, including subsidies,[4] and all the expenses were to be included. The local authorities were to regard the sum total of the subsidies as a pool out of which the rents of individual houses could be adjusted as seemed most suitable. It would thus be possible to determine an average or standard rent for all the houses, and adjust it to the capacity of tenants to pay out of the common pool of subsidies. Subsidies could be concentrated in this way on the tenants who needed them most. These new arrangements had a great advantage from the point of view of the new housing policy. They made it possible for local authorities to fill vacancies on their existing estates by poor families from slums or overcrowded houses. The possibility of concentrating subsidies would enable some of the houses built under the 1923 and 1924 Housing Acts to be used for *de facto* replacement. The extent to which this could be done was limited only by the necessity of preventing slum houses once emptied being reoccupied by families unable to find houses, and by the necessity of ultimately abolishing overcrowding as officially defined.

This new development in rent and subsidy policy derived, of course, from the recommendation of the famous 1932 Report on Local Expenditure in England and Wales, that housing subsidies should only be given to those who were unable to buy houses built

---

[1] An exceptionally large family is taken to mean here one containing more than five units, counting children between 1 and 10 years of age as half a unit and ignoring infants under 1 year. Such a family might consist, for example, of two adults, one child over ten, and five between one and ten years, and an infant under one year.

[2] *Report of the Overcrowding Survey, England and Wales, 1936*, pp. xiii and xiv.

[3] *Report of the Overcrowding Survey of England and Wales, 1936*, pp. xiii et seq. The higher standard used in this calculation excluded living rooms from use for sleeping purposes.

[4] *Housing Act, 1936*. For the first time it was made compulsory for local authorities both to contribute their full contribution under the Wheatley Act, and to make some contribution under the Chamberlain Act.

by private enterprise, or who were unable to pay the full economic rent for modern standard housing. Superficially this is obviously a reasonable attitude, provided there is an adequate supply of new houses to let. In the context of the sanitary policy of 1933 to 1939, however, it was not so reasonable. There was no guarantee whatever that an adequate supply of houses to let would be available. The pressure on the local authorities to build such houses was relaxed, and the bulk of new houses built by them were to be for direct replacement. If the additions already made to the supply of working-class houses between 1919 and 1934 were to be used as far as possible for replacement, instead of new houses being built, the effective supply of working-class houses would decrease. Of course, it is true that the use of the original local authority houses for abatement of overcrowding would not necessarily have this effect. Wherever the old houses from which overcrowded families were moved were large enough for other smaller families, all that this procedure involved was a redistribution of families and houses in order to make a better fit. Under the accepted official definition of overcrowding, however, this might involve a material decline in standards for some families, and might even involve them in sharing houses, in order that certain other families might live in conditions which did not infringe the new law. The policy might easily develop into one of robbing Peter to pay Paul, on the plea that Peter was just a little richer, or his needs a little smaller.

It is not fair to consider the change in rent policy solely in the context of the sanitary era. The simplification of accounts and pooling of subsidies had very real advantages. It provided a much needed elasticity in the use of houses. Prospective tenants could choose freely between vacant houses, and select those in the areas most convenient for them, irrespective of the original cost of building, for the subsidy could be adjusted to offset any differences in the theoretical economic rents of houses built at different dates. This element of elasticity was a real gain; the weakness of the whole system was the inexpansibility of the supply of houses to let, and the criticisms of the new accounting system turn entirely on the point that it tended to discourage new building.

Policy with regard to rent control reflected an official recognition of the continued shortage of working-class houses to let. Decontrol of houses with rateable values up to £13 (£20 in the Metropolitan Police area), on changes of tenancy was stopped by a new Rent Restriction Act in 1933. Houses above these limits which were still controlled automatically became decontrolled, as before, on changes of tenancy. Five years later, the year in fact in which the slums were supposed to have been abolished, it was decided to raise the limit below which houses would not become decontrolled on changes of tenancy from £13 rateable value to £20 (from £20 to £35 in the Metropolitan Police area). All other houses were to be decontrolled.[1] It was explained that decisions as to the removal of control for any particular type of house were " dependent on whether the shortage of houses in that class is at an end, or likely to end within a reasonable period."[2] This provides interesting comment on the effects of the policy of the Third Experiment.

[1] *Rent and Mortgage Interest Restriction Act, 1938.*
[2] *Government Policy on Rent Restriction, 1938.* Cmd. 5667, p. 2.

Chapter VIII

THE THIRD EXPERIMENT *(contd.)*

SANITARY POLICY IN PRACTICE

I. The Slum Clearance Campaign

(a) The National Programme to Abolish Slums.

The sanitary policy was decided upon in 1933; building for slum clearance under its auspices began seriously in 1934/5. Some attempts at slum clearance had, however, been made during the 'twenties, and between the passing of the Greenwood Act in 1930 and the inauguration of the new policy. It will be useful to summarise what had been done in the earlier years to provide some sort of basis of comparison for the achievements of the new policy.

Between 1919 and 1930 only 17,000 persons had been rehoused under slum clearance schemes. It had been assumed that while the general shortage of houses was so acute it would be a mistake to divert building resources to replacing slum property. The subsidy available threw half the cost at least of any scheme onto the local authorities, and before building costs fell such a share would be substantial.[1] In comparison the subsidies for ordinary building were more generous from the local authority point of view. Moreover, the provisions for acquiring and clearing slum sites were cumbersome and troublesome. It was not surprising that only a few local authorities ventured on slum clearance and that their efforts were confined to small and isolated patches of slum property. More progress had been made in reconditioning houses and in forcing landlords either to carry out repairs and alterations or to repay local authorities who did the work; about 300 thousand houses had been made fit for human habitation in this way each year.

In theory at least the Greenwood Act removed some of these obstacles to slum clearance and local authorities were officially encouraged to deal with their slums. There is no doubt, however, that up to 1933 the Greenwood Act appeared to be a failure. The programmes put forward by the main local authorities added up only to 76,524 houses to be demolished and replaced.[2] This was

[1] See p. 135, n. 1. above.
[2] i.e. 145 authorities, including the London authorities, county boroughs, and other boroughs, with populations over 50,000.

only a programme equal to about eighteen months' output of houses by all the local authorities of England and Wales. Up to December, 1933, only 11,796 houses had in fact been built with the Greenwood subsidy. This was a fantastically slow start, compared for instance with the 96,944 houses built for general purposes in the years 1919/21 with the Addison subsidy. In the early part of the 'thirties there was no shortage of building labour or of materials. Nor can it be argued that the slow start was due to the inherent difficulties of slum clearance. Practically every local authority had to start its slum clearance schemes by building ordinary cottage dwellings on its outskirts, so that slum properties could be emptied without making families homeless. For many authorities slum clearance would only involve this type of building; even later, between 1937/1939, flats only represented about one-eighth of all the dwellings for which tenders were approved by the Ministry.[1]

As a more serious explanation for this slow start it might be suggested that even the Greenwood subsidy was inadequate. It is suggested that it only became sufficient after the fall in the rate of interest had become effective during 1932/3; this, of course, was too late to affect local authority building before the new campaign was inaugurated. This argument is sufficiently important to justify a little investigation. It was explained in Chapter VII that the subsidy available under the Greenwood Act worked out at about 6d. a week more than the Wheatley subsidy for families for four persons rehoused in ordinary three-roomed cottages; it increased by nearly 1/– a week for each additional person in the rehoused family.[2] In 1931 the average rent at which new houses could be let with the Wheatley subsidy was about 6/– a week. If local authorities considered this to be too high for rehoused slum families, the slightly larger subsidy available under the Greenwood Act was unlikely to induce them to regard slum clearance as practicable, except perhaps in the case of large families. Even in the case of large families it could easily be argued that the slightly better financial conditions would not compensate for the additional trouble in selecting the families and keeping the houses in repair. It must be remembered that it was frequently assumed that the cost of management and repairs would be greater for houses used by large families brought out of the slums than for those used by ordinary families. If the stimulus to rehouse slum families in ordinary cottages was inadequate, the question of whether the special additional subsidy for building

---

[1] For numbers of flats approved, see *Ministry of Health Annual Reports*, 1935/6 to 1938/9.
[2] See pp. 135–6 above.

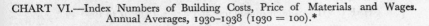

CHART VI.—Index Numbers of Building Costs, Price of Materials and Wages. Annual Averages, 1930–1938 (1930 = 100).*

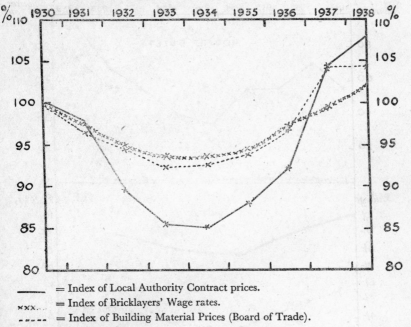

_____ = Index of Local Authority Contract prices.

×××.... = Index of Bricklayers' Wage rates.

- - - - - = Index of Building Material Prices (Board of Trade).

* See Statistical Appendix, Table 5.

flats was adequate might never be considered, for the difficulty of clearing sites without first moving families into cottages would obviously be considerable. A tendency to shelve the slum problem and to continue building ordinary additional houses under the Wheatley subsidy was under these circumstances perhaps natural, however much to be deplored.

There is another point. The bulk of the slums are concentrated in a relatively small number of large towns. A serious attack aiming at complete abolition would only be successful if these black patches were dealt with. To do so in any reasonably limited time might be beyond the organising capacity of the local authorities concerned, unless they gave up all other building. Serious slum clearance in such cases involved changing local housing policy to an extent which might prove politically impracticable in the absence of definite and unavoidable instructions from the Ministry of Health.

Thus, in the years 1931 and 1932, conditions were not entirely favourable for a great advance in slum clearance. They were highly

CHART VII.—Subsidised Building and Rents, 1930-31 to 1938-39.*

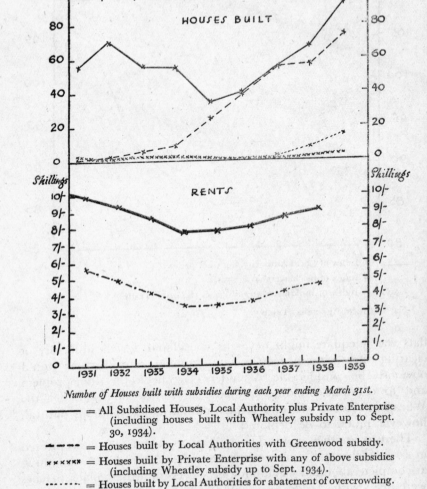

Number of Houses built with subsidies during each year ending March 31st.

———— = All Subsidised Houses, Local Authority plus Private Enterprise (including houses built with Wheatley subsidy up to Sept. 30, 1934).

——-—- = Houses built by Local Authorities with Greenwood subsidy.

×××××× = Houses built by Private Enterprise with any of above subsidies (including Wheatley subsidy up to Sept. 1934).

········ = Houses built by Local Authorities for abatement of overcrowding.

Annual Averages of possible rents for new Local Authority Houses.

—▬▬▬ = Economic rents per week.

—·—·— = Subsidised rents per week possible with Greenwood Subsidy for rehousing families of 4 persons in an ordinary type house by Local Authorities.

* See Statistical Appendix, Tables 2 and 6.

favourable on the other hand for local obstructionists, including those with vested interests in slum property. Changes in building costs after 1930 are shown in Chart VI and the numbers of subsidised houses built and subsidised economic rents in Chart VII.

By 1934 the situation was radically changed. The fall in the rate of interest, by between 1 per cent. and $1\frac{1}{2}$ per cent., and the continued fall in building costs had brought economic rents for new houses down by a total of between 2/- and 3/- a week since 1930.[1] Although this did not alter the relative financial merits of the Wheatley and Greenwood subsidies, it disposed of the argument that it would be impossible to build houses to let at rents within the reach of slum families. Finally, the temptation to continue building with Wheatley's subsidy instead of changing over to Greenwood's was disposed of in 1933 by the decision to abolish the former subsidy. The issue of instructions by the Ministry of Health to all housing authorities to produce plans for abolishing their slums within five years clinched the matter. The local authorities had no alternative. They had at least to make some show of intending to deal with their slums.

The new programmes produced at the end of 1933 by all the local authorities were on an entirely new scale. They involved the demolition, or closure, of just over a quarter of a million houses, and the rehousing of about one and a quarter million persons. In other words the programme was equivalent to replacing 2·7 per cent. of the houses in England and Wales in 1931, and rehousing about 3·1 per cent. of the population. Once the local authorities had really started on slum clearance they developed, it appeared, a certain enthusiasm. Successive upward revisions of the programme took place. By 1937/8 the original number of houses to be closed and demolished had been increased by 42 per cent. and by 1938/9 by 77 per cent. It must not be assumed, however, that this enthusiasm was disinterested or entirely genuine. The programme for the abolition of overcrowding envisaged by the Housing Act of 1935 forced the local authorities to face a prospect of building enough houses to abolish overcrowding in their area under a subsidy scheme in general much less favourable than that for slum clearance. In contrast to slums, overcrowding was defined unambiguously in arithmetical terms; there would be no escape from the necessity of producing and finally carrying out adequate programmes. If overcrowded families could be dealt with under the slum clearance programme by some reinterpretation of the local definition of what constituted a slum,

[1] See Statistical Appendix, Table 6.

larger subsidies would be obtained from the Treasury than if they were dealt with under the decrowding programme. There is not the slightest doubt, that where there was a possibility of choice as to the subsidy under which families could be rehoused they were included in the slum clearance schemes.

The plan for the abolition of the slums within five years was not however, entirely successful, even on the basis of the original programme submitted. By the time all the programmes were submitted and approved of course a considerable slice of the five-year period had been used up. Even if the opening date is taken as March, 1934, and the closing date is taken as March, 1939, instead of the official dates, the number of persons apparently rehoused was about 239 thousand short of the original number proposed. The numbers of houses closed or demolished similarly fell short by about 22 thousand, while the numbers of houses built in replacement exceeded those closed or demolished only by about 10 thousand. Altogether, by March, 1939, only about 245 thousand houses had been closed or demolished; just over half of the total of 472 thousand included in the revised programmes.[1] Thus of the houses officially admitted to be slums nearly half were still in use at the end of the campaign to abolish the slums. The Ministry of Health was not particularly disturbed by this result; in its annual report for 1938/9 it remarked in connection with the upward revisions of local authority programme that " slum clearance is a continuing process. Further reviews by the local authorities have revealed more houses which can only satisfactorily be dealt with by demolition. . . .The completion of the programme will keep local authorities occupied for some time yet."[2]

The fact that the original campaign had appeared approximately successful only as a result of serious under-statement of the size of the problem to be tackled, that is, by setting the goal too low, does not of course detract from the absolute magnitude of the achievement. More people living in slums had been rehoused in the five years ending in the spring of 1939 than under all the earlier official slum clearance scheme since 1890 altogether. This was not the only achievement. In the five years up to 1939 439 thousand houses had been repaired and rendered fit for human habitation. This brought the total since 1930 up to 751 thousand. On the other hand, the original under-statement of problem does raise several questions. Did it lead to unnecessary dilatoriness or complacency in carrying out schemes?

[1] See Table XII below.
[2] *Ministry of Health Annual Report, 1938/9*, p. 81.

TABLE XII.—Slum Clearance Programmes of Local Authorities, England and Wales, and Progress up to March, 1939.

A. Programmes all Local Authorities[1]

Date of Programmes	Nos. of Houses to be		Nos. of persons to be rehoused†	Average No. of persons to be rehoused per new House†
	Built for replacement	Closed or Demolished		
January, 1934	285,189	266,851	1,240,182	4·3
As revised—				
March, 1937	*	377,930	*	*
March, 1939	*	472,000	*	*

B. Progress all Local Authorities

Period	Nos. of Houses		Nos. of persons rehoused†	Average No. of persons rehoused per new House†
	Built for replacement[3]	Closed or Demolished		
1930 to March, 1934[2] ..	17,688	27,564	91,109	5·2
April, 1934 to March, 1939[2]	255,701	245,272	1,001,417	3·9
Total 1930 to 1939 ..	273,389	272,836	1,092,526	4·0
Deficit in progress 1934–9 cf. to—				
(a) 1934 programme ..	−29,488	−21,579	−238,765	−0·4
(b) 1939 revised programme	*	−266,728	*	*

* Not available.

† Strictly persons displaced and assumed to be rehoused.

[1] *Slum Clearance Programmes of Local Authorities, England and Wales*, March, 1934 and *Annual Reports* of the Ministry of Health, 1936–7 and 1938–9. The figures include programmes submitted even if not actually approved.

[2] Source, Ministry of Health six-monthly statement *Housing*, op. cit.

[3] Including houses built by private enterprise under the schemes.

Could more have been done if the programme had been larger from the beginning and more pressure had been brought to bear on individual authorities to carry out large programmes within the five-year period? In short, was the complacency of the Ministry of Health justified? It will be convenient to postpone final conclusions on this point until later and to consider certain of the obstacles in the way of the fulfilment of any serious programme to abolish the slums.

(b) Individual Programmes to Abolish the Slums and Individual Progress.

In examining progress under the earlier Housing Acts we discovered that subsidy schemes worked out quite differently in different places. We concluded that final judgment on the success or failure of housing schemes could only be reached by taking account of these

L

TABLE XIII.—Individual Authorities : Relative size of programmes for Slum Clearance, 1934, and estimated progress.[1]

Local Authority (1)	1934 Programmes			Maximum estimate of % deficit or surplus of houses built compared to houses to be demolished[2] (5)
	As % of total England and Wales		Persons to be rehoused as % of 1931 population (4)	
	Persons to be rehoused (2)	Houses to be demolished (3)		
The " big five "				
London	21·4	12·4	5	−17
Leeds	9·0	11·2	23	−66
Liverpool	4·8	4·5	7	−25
Manchester	5·1	5·6	8	−38
Sheffield	3·2	3·4	8	+44
Total	43·5	37·1	—	−31
Other County Boroughs with demolition programmes 2,000 and over				
Birmingham	1·6	1·7	2	+74
Bradford	0·7	1·0	3	−31
Bristol	1·2	1·1	4	+30
Hull	1·1	1·2	4	+17
Newcastle	1·7	0·9	7	+110
Norwich	0·6	0·9	6	+35
Nottingham	0·6	0·8	3	+70
Stoke-on-Trent.. ..	1·5	1·4	7	+ 5
Wolverhampton ..	0·9	0·9	8	+47
Yarmouth	0·7	0·8	14	−76
Total	10·6	10·7	—	+30
Other Urban Areas with populations over 50,000 ..	15·3*	16·0*	—	}+42
All Other Areas ..	30·6	36·2	—	
TOTAL .. .. England and Wales.	100·0	100·0	—	+14

* The county boroughs not shown separately are included in this group and accounted for 14% and 13·5% of houses to be demolished and persons to be rehoused, respectively. Excludes programmes submitted but not approved by Jan. 1, 1934. These are included with " All Other Areas."

[1] Calculated from *Slum Clearance Programmes of Local Authorities*, op. cit.

[2] Separate figures for individual areas of the numbers of houses built for replacement are not available for the years 1934–39. The percentages are based on the numbers built for this purpose from 1930 to 1942 (furnished by the Ministry of Health). For England and Wales as a whole inclusion of the years before 1934 and after March, 1939, adds on an amount equivalent to about ten per cent. of the whole number built. This exaggerates the progress made and in fact by March, 1939, the total of new houses built for replacement were less than those scheduled to be demolished (but not necessarily demolished) by about 4%. The figures in Column 5 cannot be taken as accurate for the period 1934–39 therefore, and will probably in all cases give too favourable a view of the progress made with the 1934 programmes ; as there is little reason to suppose that this error affects the different areas differently, broad comparisons appear

differences. We must consider the result of the slum clearance programme in individual areas too. It will be sufficient for this purpose to concentrate mainly on London and those county boroughs with large programmes.

In Table XIII the original programmes are set out for the various types of local authorities and for London and those county boroughs with demolition programmes including more than two thousand houses. It will be seen that the original programmes for London and all the county boroughs together included just over two-thirds of all the people to be rehoused and just under two-thirds of the houses to be demolished. This will occasion no surprise; it is common knowledge that the bulk of the slums are concentrated in the older industrial towns and London.

Under the earlier Housing Acts building for ordinary purposes had not conformed to the geographical pattern required under the new scheme. Only half the local authority houses had been built by the London authorities and the county boroughs under the slum clearance programme: at least two-thirds of the new houses and flats would have to be provided by them. Even within these groups of towns the slum clearance problem was not evenly spread. The programmes of five towns alone: London, Manchester, Leeds, Liverpool and Sheffield, included 37 per cent. of all the houses to be demolished, and 43 per cent. of the people to be rehoused. The Ministry of Health never for a moment believed that these towns could complete their programmes within the five-year period. The slum clearance campaign was, in fact, one for the abolition of slums in five years with important exceptions.[1] By the end of 1939 the unfulfilled programmes of the " big five " accounted for the greater part of the gap between original programmes and completed programmes. But the " big five " were not alone in their failure; at least ten other county boroughs failed to complete their programmes as well as some of the smaller towns and industrialised urban and rural areas. On the other hand a considerable number of authorities,

to be safe. A more serious difficulty of these percentages as a measure of progress is that they are based on comparisons with the numbers of houses to be demolished instead of those to be built according to programme; unfortunately information about the latter is not available. As in general there is a tendency for the number of new houses required to be more than those demolished, owing to the dual occupation of slum houses, the percentages give rather an optimistic picture of progress, for this reason as well as for that given above. It seems probable, however, that this over optimistic impression is mainly important from the point of view of London. The percentages in Column 5 must, however, be treated with care.

[1] *Ministry of Health Annual Report, 1936/7*, p. III. The Ministry included Birmingham as one of the big five but it had a much smaller programme in 1934 than Sheffield. See Table XIII above.

including a large number of county boroughs not only completed their programmes but started on enlarged schemes.[1] Thus the results of the slum clearance programme exhibited the variation to which we have become accustomed on examining the results of the earlier subsidies.

It will be useful to go back for a moment and look at the size of the slum clearance problem, as assessed by the local authorities, in those towns which originally proposed to demolish and close two thousand or more houses. Comparison of the numbers of people to be rehoused under the schemes with the total populations of the individual towns will help to put things in perspective. The problem was proportionately most serious in Leeds. The Leeds programme involved rehousing 23 per cent. of the population, and demolishing or closing 30,000 houses. The size of the programme was due to the fact that large numbers of back to back houses had survived in Leeds. These were all automatically counted as slums. In terms of the proportion of the population to be rehoused, Great Yarmouth came second only to Leeds, with 14 per cent.; but this only involved the demolition of 2,100 houses. An important group of towns proposed to rehouse from 7 to 8 per cent. of their populations. This group included Manchester, Liverpool, Newcastle, Sheffield, Stoke-on-Trent and Wolverhampton. The London proposals were on a relatively small scale covering only about 5 per cent. of the population, but this involved demolishing or closing 33,000 houses and replacing them by between 50 and 60 thousand new houses.[2] The programme of the other county boroughs intending to demolish or close more than 2,000 houses covered less than 5 per cent. of their respective populations.

It is a matter of some difficulty to decide how far these towns completed their programmes. The figures of building by individual authorities have been published only since September, 1934, and do not distinguish houses built under the slum clearance schemes from houses built for other purposes. It is, however, obvious that programmes were not completed where the total number of houses were built between September, 1934, and March, 1939, was less than the number included for demolition in the original programmes. None of the big five completed their programmes; this was not unexpected. But four other authorities also failed to complete their programmes,

---

[1] See the next paragraph but one *et seq.*

[2] The large excess of new houses required over those to be demolished in London was due to the fact that a large proportion of slum houses were occupied by more than one family. These details are taken from *Slum Clearance Programmes, etc.* op. cit. The percentages are shown in Table XIII above.

Bradford, Hull, Great Yarmouth, and Stoke-on-Trent, although in the whole period from the begining of the Greenwood Subsidy in 1930 up to 1942 Hull and Stoke built enough complete to them.

The Ministry of Health's conviction that the " big five " would be unable to complete their programmes in time was based on a variety of reasons, of which the absolute size of the programmes was no doubt one reason. Another was provided by the fact that, in so far as the authorities would be obliged to rehouse some of the people displaced from slums in flats, building might be delayed while sites were cleared, particularly where this involved rehousing people moved from such sites. The difficulties experienced in getting suitable sites in London was constantly pointed out by the Ministry.[1] The Ministry's doubts may also have been partly due to the increase of the scale of building required, if the slum clearance schemes were to be completed in five years, compared with that attained under the Wheatley and Chamberlain subsidies.[2] The failure of the other four towns to finish by 1939 could not be explained away easily on grounds of the absolute size of their programmes. These did not approach those of the " big five " and they were not by any means the biggest even of those based on the demolition of 2,000 or more houses. Similarly, except in the case of Yarmouth, the percentages of the population to be rehoused under the schemes were not particularly high. Both Hull and Bradford proposed to rehouse under 5 per cent. of theirs. Nor was the problem of rehousing in flats one of major importance. It is obviously worth looking into this question of the failure of individual boroughs.

It seems that almost every conceivable explanation may be applicable to Great Yarmouth. Its programme was large relatively to its population though absolutely it was the smallest of the four. In addition, to replace the houses to be demolished by an equal number of new ones would have required a six-fold increase in the rate of building over the average rate achieved under the Chamberlain and Wheatley subsidies. Moreover, this comparison understates the magnitude of the problem of expansion, for in 1932/3 Great Yarmouth's rate of building had dwindled to practically nothing. Finally, inefficiency in planning its building was displayed. It failed to maintain an even or increasing volume of building. In the twelve months ending September, 1937, for instance, only 52 houses were completed compared to 110 in the preceding year. The fact that even by 1938/9 it had failed to increase its annual rate of

---

[1] *Ministry of Health Annual Reports, 1933/4*, p. 161 *et seq.*, and *1935/6*, p. 95.
[2] See p. 155 above.

building to a reasonable level may be put down either to inefficiency or inertia, or both.[1]

The case of Hull provides an obvious contrast. It could have replaced the houses to be demolished if it had maintained the average rate of building achieved during the period of the Wheatley and Chamberlain subsidies, but it built more slowly than in those years. Nor had it started from a difficult position, for though its rate of building in 1932/3 was below its average, it was by no means negligible. Bradford comes into still another category. It could have replaced all the houses it intended to demolish before 1939 even with an average rate of building well below that achieved under the previous subsidies. (Stoke would have had to double its output to finish in 1939). Bradford may have been faced with difficulties of expansion, for it was rapidly closing down its housing expenditure between 1931 to 1933. This, however, is no adequate explanation of Bradford's failure to build more than 293 houses between September, 1934, and March, 1937. Newcastle provides a striking contrast to those four failures. It succeeded in increasing the rate of building from an average of 568 houses a year under the earlier subsidies to an average of 767 houses between September, 1934, and March, 1939.

Examination of the comparable figures for the " big five " and for those of the other local authorities reveals the same sort of variations. The difficulties facing the individual authorities differed widely, but it was not necessarily those authorities which were faced with the greatest difficulties which made the least headway with their schemes. Success or failure did not depend entirely on the size of the authorities, or on the magnitude of their slum programmes, or on the need to increase their scale of building or on the presence or absence of other difficulties. Some authorities faced with apparently immense tasks succeeded in building more than enough houses to replace all those included in the programmes, others failed to make any reasonable progress. There were some towns of the type of Newcastle, there were others like Great Yarmouth.

There is no doubt about the general conclusions to be drawn from this. Even under the conditions of the slum clearance scheme which provided an opportunity for pressure to be exerted by the Ministry of Health, there was still plenty of room for individual authorities to

[1] Since 1935 the Ministry of Health has published the number of houses built each six months by individual authorities, see six-monthly report, *Housing*. The Housing Department have also been kind enough to give me complete figures for each county borough, covering the earlier years as well. These conclusions are based on comparisons of their various sets of figures.

evade their duties without sufficient reason. There was also plenty of opportunity for local authorities to under-estimate the need for slum clearance in their areas as they were in fact mainly responsible for drawing up their own programmes. A determined local authority could defy both the Ministry of Health and the policy accepted by Parliament in two ways: by understating its problem, and by omitting to carry out its programme.

(c) Conclusions.

We are now in a position to answer the questions raised at the end of the last section. Although our examination of the success with which the slum clearance programme was carried out in different areas has been extremely cursory, it has been sufficient to show the persistence of serious variations in the behaviour of local authorities. The Ministry of Health did not, in practice, succeed in forcing authorities either to carry out their programmes or to prepare adequate programmes in the first instance. Recalcitrant authorities remained able to abstain from slum clearance. Although the total achievement under the five-year programme was a very real contribution to the health and welfare of a very large number of people, the achievement was the result of the more energetic or willing authorities.

It is impossible to escape the conclusion that the scheme of control of local authorities provided by the five-year programme was inefficient. If it had been more effective at all stages greater headway would have been made in the country as a whole. There is no need to labour the point that there was urgent need for this. Half of the slums were still uncleared in 1939 on the basis of the local authorities' own estimates. If a uniform standard equivalent to that adopted by the authorities which were most progressive in this matter had been adopted, the outstanding total would have been still greater. The conclusion of the Clement Davies Committee on Tuberculosis in Wales in 1938 provides an unanswerable criticism of the lack of adequate control of inactive local authorities and, incidentally, of the complacency of the Ministry of Health. The Committee expressed " regret that a number of local authorities in Wales have not taken advantage of their statutory powers and of the assistance available from the exchequer to improve the housing conditions in their areas, which, in the opinion of the Committee are bad."[1] In the Ministry of Health Annual Report for 1938/9 it was stated that the Ministry of Health was going to confer with the authorities

[1] Quoted in the *Ministry of Health Annual Report* for 1938/9, p. 93.

concerned. It is not, we think, irrelevant to point out that the original five-year period in which slums were to be abolished had ended in 1938!

II. ABATEMENT OF OVERCROWDING

The scheme for abolishing overcrowding was interrupted at an early stage by the outbreak of the war. It is not possible, therefore, to find out whether it would have been satisfactory in practice or not. It may, however, be useful if a very brief summary is given of what had been done.

By March, 1939, 23,651 houses had been built by local authorities specifically for rehousing overcrowded families.[1] This was not the sole contribution which had been made towards the solution of the problem. The process of slum clearance in itself tended to decrease overcrowding for some of the slum families were also overcrowded. The tendency of local authorities to include marginal cases in slum clearance schemes rather than in decrowding schemes has already been mentioned. Naturally it helped to increase the effect of the slum clearance schemes on overcrowding. The local authorities had also been able to decrease overcrowding by the judicious movement of overcrowded families on their own estates into larger houses as they happened to become available. As overcrowding was higher on the average in the local authority houses than among privately-owned houses it was possible to achieve a good deal in this way.[2]

The effects of all these factors, combined no doubt with the increase in the total number of houses due to private building, had been considerable. The Ministry of Health estimated that by March, 1937, the latest date of which information is available, the number of overcrowded families had been decreased by about one-quarter since the survey of overcrowding of 1936. The Ministry had by 1937 been able to fix the date in the majority of local authority areas,[3] after which increases in overcrowding became an offence for which both tenants and landlords could be prosecuted. It would be a mistake, however, to attach too much importance to this development, for the Ministry provided for very important exceptions. Increases in overcrowding would not be an offence if it were caused by the increase in the numbers of children in the family, or if it were due to children reaching ages at which separation of the sleep-

[1] Private enterprise had provided 264.
[2] *Registrar-General's Survey of Overcrowding in England and Wales*, op. cit., p. xx *et seq.*
[3] The date had been fixed for 1,464 out of the total of 1,536 areas of local housing authorities, in most cases as January 1st, 1937.

ing accommodation of boys and girls was legally required, or if children had graduated in the natural course of years from the counting as half a unit to a whole unit for housing purposes. In other cases increases in overcrowding could be made legal if a licence from the local authority were obtained. There has been insufficient experience of the effect of this system to enable any definite judgment on its merits to be formed. No doubt it has the advantage that in theory increases in overcrowding might be controlled. It is, however, a rather peculiar reflection on the success of housing policy that in 1937 it should be thought desirable to provide a means of controlling increases in ovecrowding. The system of exceptions also involved the danger that some local authorities would regard these concessions as equivalent to official toleration of standards lower than those laid down in the Housing Acts, that is, as an opportunity to procrastinate over building programmes. They contain an unpleasant flavour of compromise on the vital question of standards as well as a suggestion of indefinite toleration of the continued overcrowding.

III. Rents and Rent Policy

The average number of persons rehoused in each new house built under the Greenwood Act was four. The complete subsidy worked out, therefore, at an average of 4/4 a week per house. When the Act was passed in 1930 this subsidy should have enabled local authorities to let ordinary new houses built under the Act at an average rent of 6/1 ; by 1934 this dropped to 3/5, but by 1938 it had risen with the increase in building costs to 4/8. For the whole part of the Third Experiment these average subsidised rents were, therefore, below five shillings.[1] Average rents of this type were obviously favourable for moving people out of the slums. The slum clearance scheme was intended, however, to be based on the general principle that subsidies should be varied according to the capacity of tenants to pay. Those who could afford least rent for their new houses were to receive the largest subsidy through various forms of rent rebate schemes or differential rents. The local authorities were left free to decide whether to adopt this system or not.

By 1938 112 authorities had adopted either formal or informal schemes of adjusting rents to capacity of tenants to pay. Most of these had confined their schemes to houses for rehousing people displaced under the slum clearance or decrowding schemes. Only a few, such as Leeds, had attempted to bring all their houses and

[1] See Table 6, Statistical Appendix.

tenants into one scheme. In several towns the number of families actually in receipt of rebates was only a small proportion of the total number of families covered by the scheme. For example, in Barking less than 40 out of 466 tenants covered by the rebate scheme actually received rebates in April, 1935; in Wolverhampton in March, 1939, 748 tenants out of 2,963 received rebates.

Necessarily, any scheme of adjusting rents on the basis of ability to pay, involves some sort of means test for those claiming favourable treatment, unless an automatic standard such as the number of children per family is adopted. The local authorities left to their own devices, produced naturally a wide variety of schemes. The Fabian Society pamphlet on Rent Rebates[1] provides the only fairly comprehensive collection of data on the rent schemes available. In the survey on which the pamphlet is based it was found that, apart from rebates based solely on the number of children, there were at least six main types of schemes in use all depending on means tests of some sort. Maximum or standard rates were fixed by some authorities, e.g. Barking, for each income level, rebates being allowed in each group according to the number of children. Others, such as Birmingham, fixed a maximum rent and calculated all rebates from this on the basis of incomes. This system was the most widespread of all. Four authorities worked the rebate simply on a basis of income per head. Eight, including Leeds, used subsistence scales; income in excess of that necessary to maintain the scale being regarded as available in whole or part for rent. Still others calculated the rent as percentages of incomes.

There was a great variety in interpretation both of rent and of income. Some authorities worked on the basis of rent including rates, others added rates on afterwards. Some included all income coming into a house and all people living in it, irrespective of whether it was payment from lodgers or the income of earning members of the family or dependants. Others took into account only part of the income of members of the family other than the head of the household.

There was equally no generally accepted principle of the relation of housing subsidies to other types of income or subsidy provided by the state. In some cases no rebates were given where the chief earner was unemployed. It was argued that the function of the U.A.B. and P.A.C. was to provide incomes sufficient to pay rent, otherwise the housing funds would be used in practice to meet the

[1] *Fabian Society Research*, Series No. 28. *Rent Rebates*. By Geoffrey Wilson, 3rd edition, 1939. Most of the information in this section is taken from this extremely valuable pamphlet.

general obligations towards the unemployed undertaken by the state as a whole.

These sources of variation were due to the absence of definition of the principles on which needs and incomes should be calculated. The result was the development of a new group of means tests varying in different degrees from those already in existence for other purposes. Clearly this was unsatisfactory. Not only did it mean that state assistance for housing purposes was provided on no uniform principle, even for housing, but also it meant that in some cases tenants were subjected to two or three inquisitions into their incomes by two or three different organisations at frequent intervals. If means tests are to be the condition of State assistance, it seems self-evident first, that they should be applied on the same principle all over the country; second, that the money for housing subsidies, which is ultimately provided mainly by the general tax-payer, should be disbursed according to principles at least consistent, even if not necessarily identical, with those on which money is used for other types of subsidies.

Whatever the variation in principle adopted as the basis of individual rebate systems, it is usually possible in theory to construct approximately similar scales of actual rebates, or rents. In practice, however, the various local authorities had to calculate their scales so that their housing accounts would balance unless they intended to make increased contributions from the rates. This meant that the possibility of generous scales of rebates might vary from place to place with the type of tenant to be rehoused and the incidence of unemployment. In an area, such as Tyneside, in which unemployment was high, a very large proportion of tenants would qualify for the lowest rents and relatively few for the highest. In towns such as Leeds, on the other hand, a considerable proportion would need no rebates. In districts like Tyneside it would be impossible to provide as generous rebates for those far down the scale with places like Leeds. In others again it would be possible to let a considerable proportion of the Wheatley houses at economic rents setting free funds for assistance for the slum clearance schemes. The effectiveness of the rebate system would tend to be least in areas with serious poverty and vice versa. Apart from the possibility that the actual Treasury subsidy may have varied from area to area, according to variations in the sizes of families rehoused, there was no attempt to apply the principle that subsidies should be concentrated on those who needed them on a national basis.

IV. Subsidies and Costs

The peculiar features of the subsidy provisions relating to the slum clearance scheme have already been described at length. It is impossible to decide definitely how far these special provisions affected the ultimate results. They were all altered or abolished in 1938 in the interests of the economy campaign and of the plan for the fusion of subsidies for slum clearance with houses available for the abatement of overcrowding. At the time at least 48 per cent. of the houses officially considered to require demolition were still occupied. The programmes of the large towns most likely to require the subsidy for flats, London, Leeds, Liverpool, Manchester and Sheffield, were still a long way from completion. The experience gained provides an inadequate basis for final conclusions as to the effectiveness of the original provisions of the Greenwood subsidy.

The experience available suggests, however, that the provision whereby the Treasury subsidy varied with the number of persons rehoused, instead of with the numbers of houses built, had little effect in inducing local authorities to concentrate on the large families. The average number of persons rehoused per new house built was 4·0. This average is well above the average size of families in the population as a whole of 3·43. It is not, however, so spectacularly high compared to the average of 3·77 persons found for the urban insured population in the Ministry of Labour Cost of Living inquiry of 1937/8. Still more interesting, however, is the fact that the average size of families rehoused under the slum clearance schemes was less than that of families living in ordinary local authority houses in 1936. The average family in these houses consisted of just under 5 persons, and the housing schemes as a whole contained a larger proportion of families of more than four persons than the working-class population as a whole, 47 per cent. compared with 37 per cent.[1] The high proportion of large families in local authority houses as a whole in 1936 was due to the preference given by the authorities to tenants with young children and to families which might be expected to increase in size. Thus, on the basis of the comparison of averages, the calculation of the Treasury subsidy in terms of the numbers of persons rehoused had

---

[1] Based on figures in the *Overcrowding Survey of England and Wales, 1936*, op. cit. According to the Survey, the average number of " units " per house included in it was 3·20, but the average in local authority houses was higher, about 3·87 units. It was estimated that 3½ units were equivalent to four persons or four units to five persons. The families in the Survey as a whole thus averaged 4 persons, and those in the local authority houses between 4½ and 5 persons.

no obvious influence on the size of families dealt with by the local authorities.

These results are not, however, conclusive. It is possible that the slum clearance schemes of the big towns if completed would have included a larger number of big families. Even if this did not turn out to be the case, however, the variation of subsidy with numbers of persons rehoused might have had the useful result of increasing the Treasury contribution in certain areas. Since the average size of family differs quite considerably between the north and the south, as long as it appears to be generally true that large families with young children are less able to afford adequate rents than other families, there is a prima facie case for providing specially large subsidies for their rehousing. There was no other provision for these families. In view, therefore, of this the lack of uniformity in their geographical distribution, the variation of Treasury contribution in a way which in practice would provide most help to areas with the heaviest incidence of such families had some justification. To sum up, this variation of Treasury subsidy would do no harm, and might do some good.

It is equally impossible to reach definite conclusions about the effects of the other special features of the Greenwood subsidy. The effects of special provision for agricultural rehousing were hopelessly confused by changes in other Acts relating to rural housing. In the case of the extra subsidy for rehousing in flats the data are seriously incomplete. Between 1934/5 and 1937/8 only 8 per cent. of the tenders for houses to be built under either the Greenwood subsidy or the subsidy for the abatement of overcrowding were for flats. Up to 1938 the slum clearance scheme was in practice mainly a scheme for rehousing slum families in cottages. It is inevitable that rehousing in flats should come towards the end of a programme. The sites have to be cleared, and in many cases the original inhabitants rehoused elsewhere, before blocks of flats can be erected. Moreover, the need for rehousing in flats was confined to the largest cities, and it was these which were furthest from completion of their programmes. The statistics of tenders for flats do not, therefore, reflect the full intentions of the local authorities to make use of the special subsidy.

It is, however, arguable that the special subsidy was inadequate, and that this discouraged rehousing in flats unduly. On the basis of four persons to a flat, it worked out at only 6d. a week per flat more than the ordinary subsidy. The average cost of flats, even excluding the cost of sites, was 50 per cent. greater than that of ordinary three bedroomed cottages, and average economic rents were from 3/10 to 4/6 a week higher, excluding the cost of sites.[1] The Ministry of Health appears to have accepted this argument by the introduction of a higher subsidy for flat building under the later Acts. In the case of rehousing on expensive sites, variations in the cost of sites may be a more important factor in determining rent than variations in the ability of families to pay rent according to their size. The former is certainly a more important cost factor than the size of families in that the accommodation needs for families of different sizes, e.g. with two children or three or four children, can be satisfied by 3-bedroomed dwellings. The change introduced with the consolidation of the subsidies in 1938 was thus almost certainly an improvement and should have stimulated rehousing in flats for slum clearance purposes. The outbreak of the war prevented this being put to the test.

Our tentative conclusions on the effectiveness of the special features of the Greenwood subsidy may be summarised as follows. It is probable that the variation of the Treasury subsidy with the numbers of persons rehoused might ultimately have increased the proportion of large families rehoused. Up to the time of its abolition by the Housing Act of 1938, there is no evidence to show that it had had any special effect compared with the ordinary Wheatley subsidy. Indeed, up to that date the slum clearance scheme was mainly a scheme by which families, on the average containing four persons, were selected as tenants for new local authority houses on the ground of existing unsatisfactory accommodation. This provides its main point of contrast with earlier housing schemes under which tenants were selected for a wide range of reasons, including ability to pay rents. On the other hand this absence of positive results provided, as we have seen, no real reason for abolishing the new principle of variation. In the case of the special subsidy for rehousing in flats, it is possible to make out a case that it was too small in view of the high cost of flats. On the other hand we saw that other reasons could be found for explaining the low scale of flat construction. In any case *a priori* the changes introduced under the consolidation of this subsidy with that for rehousing overcrowded families in flats was almost certainly an improvement.

Before leaving the subject of the Greenwood subsidies it will be useful to consider the circumstances in which the subsidy for ordinary houses needed for slum clearance was cut in 1938. The general state

---

[1] Calculated from comparative figures of costs in *Ministry of Health Annual Reports 1934/5 to 1938/9.*

of public alarm and despondency and the preoccupation with international affairs prevented the matter receiving the attention it deserved. The circumstances differed from those in which other subsidies had been reduced or abolished. In these earlier cases it had been possible to argue that there were special reasons for the alteration. In 1921 and 1926 it had been maintained that the type of subsidy or its size was inflating costs. In 1933 there had been some ground for considerating that the general subsidy had been wasteful in practice, and that in the difficult financial circumstances prevailing public resources should be administered more carefully. In 1933 in any case an entirely new housing policy was introduced.

When the ordinary slum clearance subsidy was cut in 1938 none of these arguments applied. On the contrary, there were very strong arguments for maintaining the subsidy at its existing level. The programmes were not complete. If the subsidy had not been over-generous in 1934 and 1935, it was not over-generous in 1938 when building costs were rising. The rise in building costs was not attributed to the activities of the local authorities, but to the new demand for building resources for the re-armament programme. The purposes of the cut were twofold, economy and the reduction of the demand for building resources. Both could have been achieved more rationally in a different way. Reducing the subsidy not only reduced the average Treasury contribution per house, but also tended to reduce the numbers of houses built by making it more difficult for local authorities to build houses to let at rents within the reach of the poorest families. It was in this indirect way that the public purse and the pressure of demand for building resources was to be relieved, by limiting the extent to which local authorities improved the housing conditions of the poorest and to some extent at least the worst housed. The cut was quite sufficiently severe to achieve this purpose. It reduced the weekly subsidy calculated on the basis of four persons per house from 4/4 to 2/9. By 1938 the increase in building costs since 1935 was equivalent to an addition of 1/2 a week to the rent. The combined effect of the cut in subsidy and the increase in building costs was to raise the average subsidised rent by 2/9, an increase greater than that which would have been produced by an increase of interest rates from $3\frac{1}{2}$ per cent. to 5 per cent. if costs had remained at the 1935 level. In short, it more than wiped out the effect of the fall of interest rates since 1930 on rent of local authority houses built under the slum clearance schemes.[1]

Both the economies and the reduction in pressure on the building

[1] See Charts VI and VII above and Statistical Appendix Table 6.

industry could, however, have been realised without any cut in subsidy, by the simple device of postponing some of the slum clearance work. This would have made it possible to continue at the same level of rents apart from the rise in actual building costs. Moreover, it would have made possible a rational selection of schemes to be postponed or carried out according to their apparent urgency, and in relation to the demands for building resources in different localities. This method had been used in the year before the cut in subsidy, with, according to the Ministry of Health, satisfactory results. In view of the effect on rents of the 1938 cut, the opinion of the Ministry in 1937 and in 1938 is of some interest. In deciding that certain slum clearance schemes would have to be postponed, it explained that it was of the greatest importance to reduce the pressure on building resources so as to avoid any increase in building costs which would be reflected in rents.[1] It was only a year later that the subsidy was deliberately cut in a way that would increase rents materially for ordinary replacement houses.

The 1938 economy cut provides perhaps the outstanding and most obvious example of the habit of disrupting housing schemes by ill-judged and ill-conceived attempts to achieve economies. The lesson had not been learnt it seems, even in 1938, that by suitable direct control of local authorities their building schemes can be reduced as may be necessary. Reliance was still placed on the clumsy and indirect method of wholesale reductions of subsidies.[2]

[1] *Ministry of Health Annual Report, 1936/7*, p. 115 *et seq.*, *1937/8*, pp. 87–8.
[2] It is sometimes suggested that reductions in subsidies have a useful effect in preventing extravagance. This is no doubt sometimes the case. But where unduly high building costs are due to the insistence by local authorities on the use of local building contractors and materials, the most common complaint made by the Ministry of Health during the Third Experiment (*Annual Report, 1938/9*, p. 87 *et seq.*, for example) general subsidy cuts are more likely to reduce the volume of building than to bring about the change of practice. The solution of this particular problem appears to be a greater control over the acceptance of tenders by the central department.

Chapter IX

THE THIRD EXPERIMENT (*contd.*)

THE PRIVATE BUILDING BOOM

THE Second Experiment had failed to provide an adequate supply of new houses for one of the most important sections of the community. The imposition on the local authorities of the responsibility for providing sufficient new working-class houses had not fulfilled the hopes of the founders of the system. On the whole the local authorities had provided their houses for the upper part of the working-class market only ; they had failed to solve the problem of how to provide houses for the semi-skilled and unskilled workers. Even in the relatively simple field of the actual production of houses they had been unsuccessful compared to private enterprise. During the Third Experiment these responsibilities were transferred for all practical purposes from the local authorities to ordinary private enterprise. The success of the Third Experiment cannot be finally assessed without considering whether private enterprise was successful where the local authorities had partly or wholly failed.

From the point of view of the actual production of houses in large numbers there is no doubt about the success of private enterprise. The average number built per year from 1935/6 to 1938/9 was 263 thousand: compared to an average of 151 thousand in the four years up to March, 1934, and an average of 133 thousand during the Second Experiment as a whole. This increase more than made up for the withdrawal of the local authorities' annual average contribution of 53 thousand during the Second Experiment.[1]

Private enterprise thus proved itself capable of expanding its output of houses with extreme rapidity and in practice achieved a rate of building which more than made up for the withdrawal of the local authorities in this field. The volume of unsubsidised building and changes in the cost of buying houses are shown in Chart VIII, and the growth of building societies in Chart IX.

The expansion of building was, of course, dependent on the adequacy of the supplies of building materials and skilled labour.

[1] Excluding houses built for slum clearance purposes. See Table 2, Statistical Appendix.

CHART VIII.—Unsubsidised Building, Rents and Weekly Cost of Purchase, 1930–31—1938–9.*

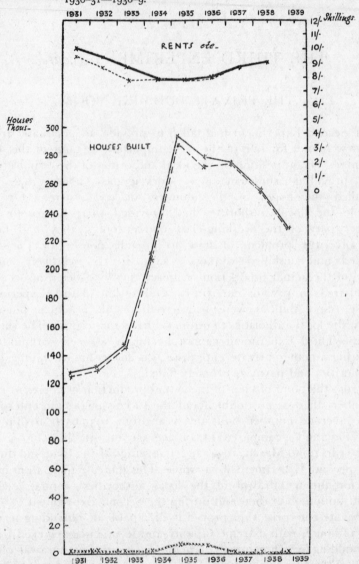

——— =Annual Averages of possible economic rents per week for new Local Authority Houses.
----------- =Annual Averages of minimum cost per week of buying a " Local Authority type " House.
Nos of Houses built without subsidies during each year ending March 31st.
——— =All unsubsidised houses—Local Authority† *plus* Private Enterprise.
— — — =Houses built by Private Enterprise.
xxxxxx =Houses built by Local Authorities.†

* See Statistical Appendix, Tables 2 and 6.
† Excluding 47 thousand houses built by local authorities between 1935 and 1939, of which details were not available in time. These houses are included in the Statistical Appendix, Table 2, column 8.

CHART IX.—The Growth of Building Societies, 1930–37.*   (Ratio Scale).

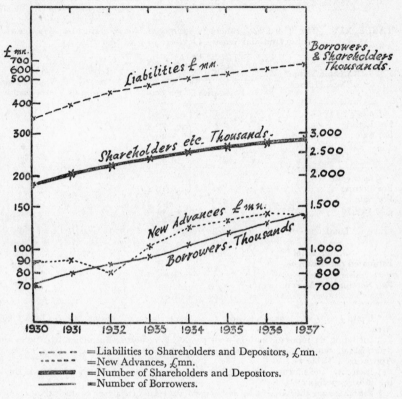

Statistical Appendix, Table 7A.

By 1936 it was clear that further expansion would be impossible unless these supplies increased or new methods of building were introduced. The additional demand for building resources, which was created by the re-armament programme, could not be met without reductions in the quantities available for other purposes; it led to increases both in the prices of materials and in wages. These developments are shown in Chart VI in the last chapter.

Those who had maintained that private enterprise was more than capable of providing the houses needed were justified by the event. Those who had gone further and maintained that private enterprise and private investors would succeed in solving the other part of the problem, the provision of houses to let at rents within the reach of ordinary working-class families were wrong. In the first place the majority of houses built were not of the ordinary working-class type. This is shown in Table XIV. 11·6 per cent. had rateable values

TABLE XIV.—The Third Experiment : Additional Houses built and Requirements (England and Wales), October, 1934 to March, 1939.

Rateable Value* of New Houses	Additional Houses		Require- ments Thousands	Surplus, March, 1939 Thousands
	Thousands	Per cent		
Up to £13 For Letting .. .. .. For Sale	258† 259	20·4 20·5		
Total	517	40·9	427‡	90
£14 to £26 For Letting .. .. .. For Sale .. .. .. £27 to £78	131 470 147	10·4 37·1 11·6		
Total	748	59·1	150	598
Grand Total .. Estimated net wastage§ ..	1265	100·0	577	688 103
Est. Net Surplus, March, 1939	—	—	—	585

* Up to £20, £21—£35, and £36—£105, respectively, in London Metropolitan Police Area.

† Including 84 thousand houses built by Local Authorities for general purposes and decrowding, but excluding houses built for slum clearance schemes. (See Statistical Appendix, Table 2).

‡ Including the shortage estimated at 127 thousand outstanding at the beginning of the third experiment.

§ Estimated on the same basis as between 1931 and 1934 (see Statistical Appendix, pp. 268–9 etc. for further details).

of £27 up to £78, 47·5 per cent. had rateable values from £14 to £26. Only 40·9 per cent. were typical working-class houses with rateable values up to £13; during the Second Experiment the proportion of these houses to the total built had been similar, 41·9 per cent.[1] As house building was on a larger scale during the Third Experiment, however, the average number of houses of this type built each year was larger, 104 thousand compared with 77 thousand, during the Second Experiment.[2]

There was, of course, a surplus of new houses in the highest category, houses with rateable values exceeding £26, over probable

[1] Between 1934 and 1939 the local authorities contributed 6·7 per cent. of the total of the new houses over and above those actually absorbed by replacement of slum houses.

[2] Even if the best years of local authority building during the Second Experiment are used as a basis of comparison, the average for the Third Experiment still comes out higher.

increases in the numbers of upper middle-class families. There is no information as to the changes of tenancies of houses in this class after 1933, but it can only be assumed that the very high rate of migration from old to new houses between 1931/33 continued and absorbed the surplus new houses. The gradual decline in the numbers of these large houses built each year indicates that the migration was slowing down. Similarly, the number of houses of the intermediate class was far in excess of the need for additional houses.

According to our estimates, about 150 thousand of the new houses with rateable values of £14 or over were needed to accommodate the current increases in the numbers of middle-class families. This left about 600 thousand to be absorbed either by manual workers, or by other families abandoning their old houses in favour of new ones. It is possible to make a rough guess at the relative importance of these factors. According to the estimates of the Ridley Committee in 1937 changes in tenancies of the old houses in this class averaged about 50 thousand a year.[1] It is fairly safe to assume that a very large proportion of these changes was due to migration out of the inconvenient pre-1914 houses into the new houses in modern suburbs. Common observation suggests that the migration continued after 1937. It is reasonable to assume a rate of migration averaging from 40 to 50 thousand for the whole period. This would account for another 200 to 250 thousand of the new houses, leaving 250 to 300 thousand over.

It has been pointed out already that the actual number of houses with rateable values up to £13 built each year was greater than before 1934. The total number built was more than sufficient to keep pace with increases in the numbers of working-class families between 1934 and 1939. The probable increase in the number of these was 300 thousand; the number of new houses of working-class type built between 1934 and 1939 was 517 thousand. There were thus sufficient new houses to make good the net deficit of between 100 and 200 thousand which was outstanding in 1934, even though all the cast-off houses of other types up to 1934 were counted as part of the supply. After 1934 all the cast-off houses of people moving into new houses were surplus; they were available for increasing the pool of vacants, for replacing old working-class houses or for decreasing the number of families sharing houses below that of 1911. By 1939 the shortage had disappeared, the total number of working-class houses built since 1919, i.e. one and a half million was one-third of a million less than the number required to balance

[1] *Ridley Report*, op. cit.

the increase in the number of families and make good the actual deficit outstanding in 1919. There was a surplus of houses of other types of about one and a quarter million which, if not demolished, could have been used to provide the balance of additional working-class houses required and to improve the standard of accommodation.

The excess of new houses built between 1919 and 1939 (including houses built for slum clearance purposes), over requirements for additional houses was equivalent to about 16·2 per cent. of all the houses existing before the Great War in 1911. During the whole of the twenty-eight years between 1911 and 1939, the old stock of houses could have been replaced only at an average rate of 0·6 per cent. of the original total, including the houses replaced under official slum clearance schemes. The extent to which different classes in the population had been able to get new houses in place of their old ones had varied considerably, as we have seen. The excess of houses of a non-working-class type over requirements for them was relatively much greater than in the case of working-class houses, even during the Third Experiment. A sufficient surplus had been built in the twenty years after 1919 to replace 51 per cent. of the houses of these superior types existing in 1911; the average rate of possible replacement worked out at about 1·8 per cent. a year between 1911 and 1939. In the five years before the outbreak of the present war this theoretical rate of replacement had been much higher, averaging 4·8 per cent. a year;[1] at this rate of progress completion of the replacement process would have taken only another ten years, even assuming that every pre-war house should be given up and demolished or made available for ordinary working-class families. Such an assumption is nonsensical. In consequence, by 1939 this particular field for replacement was becoming limited. The tendency for private enterprise to concentrate more and more on building the smaller houses in the years just before this war indicates that the impetus to migrate from old to new houses was wearing out among the better-off families.

The Third Experiment seems to have been satisfactory in that enough houses had been built in each main category to keep pace with current increases in the numbers of families in each; further, surpluses over these current needs emerged on a scale sufficient to make good the shortage of houses with which the period started. The replacement of old houses by migration into new ones had

---

[1] It has been necessary to ignore the relatively small number of houses built between 1911 and 1919 in making these calculations, as figures for that period show only net increases in the number of houses, not the number of houses built.

gone a very long way among the upper income groups, and there was some possibility of replacement even of working-class houses. Unfortunately these results cannot be regarded with unqualified satisfaction.

There are two serious criticisms to be considered. First, only 33 per cent. of the new houses of the intermediate type were for letting and barely 50 per cent. of those in the ordinary working-class groups.[1] Second, it has constantly been maintained that the new small houses, whether for letting or for sale, were out of reach of all but the best off working-class families.

There is no doubt at all about the first point. The Third Experiment was far less satisfactory than the Second as far as both the proportion and number of small houses to let was concerned. To some extent the comparison is misleading, however. During the Third Experiment the importance of the distinction between houses for owner-occupation and houses for letting diminished. The great obstacle in the way of many families who would have liked to buy their own houses through building societies had been, for many years, the initial payment of a lump sum equivalent to between a quarter and a third of the value of the house. Various attempts had been made to get over this difficulty, but it was not until the 'thirties that an arrangement by which this payment was reduced to 5 per cent. of the value of the house came into frequent use. The basis of the system was extremely simple. The building societies advanced as usual up to 75 per cent. of the value of the house against the personal security of the purchaser and the security of the house itself. In addition they made a further advance which might bring the total up to 95 per cent. by arrangement with the builder against sums deposited with them by the latter. The purchaser repaid the whole amount with interest in the usual way, and in the process the builder's collateral was redeemed. By 1938 this system or some variant was so widespread that possibly half the business of some large societies was transacted on this basis.[2] The development was due to the joint attempts of builders and building societies to maintain the demand for new houses. Both recognised the need to penetrate the market of potential customers who were unable to raise the capital for making the initial lump sum payment. The latter was no doubt relieved at being able to avoid stimulating building through the guarantee provisions of the 1933 Act, as this would have reduced their earnings. The new system provided a more profitable solution.

[1] See Table XIV p. 172 above.   [2] *Economist*, February 18/1939, p. 248.

Thus in the years immediately before this war, the problem of buying a small house had become similar to that of renting a new house; it turned almost entirely on whether the annual payments could be afforded. Clearly this development limited the market for new houses to let. Unless some means was evolved for providing new houses to let at rents substantially below the annual cost of buying through building societies there would be little demand for them. This possibility was very limited. To make investment in houses to let worth while, rents were needed which contained an element of profit as well as interest on the capital, and which would also provide for repairs and amortisation. The instalments paid by owner-occupiers to building societies included neither profits nor allowances for repairs. It is also doubtful whether the majority of purchasers made proper allowance for the cost of repairs in deciding whether to buy or not. Investors in houses to let would have, therefore, to realise considerable savings on capital charges if a large market was to be found. The opportunities were unfavourable. Direct investment in houses to let, no longer ranked as one of the safest methods of disposing of capital, even though, as far as probable changes in interest rates and building costs were concerned, the situation was more favourable than at any time since the Great War. The changes in building society practice had removed the fence between the market for houses to let and houses for owner-occupation. The existence of large numbers of subsidised local authorities' houses, and uncertainty as to their future use, added on another risk. Moreover, if a new Government altered housing policy and local authorities started building for general purposes again on a large scale, they would be able to undercut private owners as they could borrow more cheaply. The risks had greatly increased and at the same time opportunities for safe investment were greater than in the old days. There was a vast mass of Government and semi-Government stock, and there were the building societies themselves. In view of the additional risks involved in ordinary house mortgages and investment, it was difficult or impossible for borrowing to take place on more favourable terms than those provided by the building societies, taking into account both interest charged and terms of repayment. Both the opportunity and the incentive for large scale investment in houses to let was limited. Even the specially favourable terms offered under the guarantee system of the 1933 Housing Act did not produce more than 75 thousand houses to let.

There is some independent information about the social and economic incidence of owner-occupation in the late 'thirties. The collection of budgets made by the Ministry of Labour in 1937/38 showed that 17·8 per cent. of the families of insured workers living in urban areas were either buying or had bought their houses. Unfortunately, the families which had completed purchase were not separated from the others still involved in making weekly payments. The average weekly payment of 12/9, including rates, found in the sample thus under-estimated the average cost of buying a small house. In rural areas the prevalence of house-ownership was found to be less, only 4·4 per cent. of the sample. Agricultural workers were not separately distinguished from the rest in this section of the sample; presumably the low incidence of house purchase was due to the smaller proportion of artisan and clerical families in rural than in urban areas.[1] A sample of budgets of civil servants, local government officials and teachers in 1938/9 provides an illuminating contrast. 64·7 per cent. were found to have bought or to be buying their own houses, that is, a proportion more than three times as high as in the urban insured workers sample.[2] But the prevalence of owner-occupation showed only a slight upward trend with income; even in the lowest income group included (incomes of £250 to £350) the proportion of owner-occupiers was 63·3 per cent. It is of some interest to notice the average weekly payment, including rates, was 65 per cent. higher than in the case of the insured urban families. There is little doubt that on the whole teachers and civil servants were concerned with houses valued at over £13.

These budget inquiries made it perfectly obvious that house purchase was far more general among the professional or middle classes than among the ordinary working class, even when insured clerical workers are included with the latter. It cannot, therefore, be assumed without investigation that private enterprise had solved the housing problem merely by making it as easy for people to buy houses as to rent them. During the five years before this war the average weekly cost of buying a three-bedroomed non-parlour house of the local authority type was between 7/6 and 9/–.[3] This was more than the average net rent of a local authority house between

---

[1] Ministry of Labour Cost of Living Inquiry, 1937/8. In the *Ministry of Labour Gazette*, Dec. 1940 and Jan. 1941. The sample covered families insured against unemployment, i.e. manual workers generally and non-manual workers with salaries not exceeding £250 a year.

[2] Sample budget inquiry undertaken by the Civil Service Statistical and Research Bureau, 1938/9. See Paper by Philip Massey *The Expenditure of 1,360 British Middle-class Households in 1938/9*, read before the Royal Statistical Society, 1942.

[3] In addition to a minimum down payment of between £15 and £20—i.e. 5 per cent. of the capital cost of the house.

1925 and 1928 with the Wheatley subsidy. It will be remembered that it was constantly argued that this net rent was too high for the general run of working-class families. Private enterprise it seems had succeeded during the Third Experiment in providing houses for just the same sort of market as the local authorities had catered for earlier.

There has been a great deal of public confusion over the whole question of costs which it will be convenient to try to clear up here. It is often argued as though new houses, provided by local authorities or private enterprise without subsidies, must have been within the reach of the majority of families because building costs had fallen, and in particular the rate of interest had come down in 1932. It is forgotten that these were not the only changes of importance. In the first place, the Wheatley subsidy had been abolished by the Housing Act of 1933. It is not realised always that this more than offset the advantages that local authorities gained from those decrease in costs and interest rates. In 1931 the average minimum economic rent of new local authority houses was between 9/7 and 10/3. The Wheatley subsidy brought it down to between 5/9 and 6/5. The years in which interest and costs were at their lowest, after the fall in interest rates, were 1934 and 1935; in these the average minimum economic rent was about 7/9; by 1937/8 it had risen to 9/–.[1] In these years there was no subsidy. Thus, even if the local authorities had continued building for general purposes on a serious scale, the average rents of their new houses would have been above the subsidised rents of houses built before 1927.

In the second place, the shift of the main responsibility for building from the local authorities to private enterprise had the effect of wiping out the effect of the fall of interest rates on rents. After the fall in interest rates building societies lent money at between 4 and 5 per cent. instead of between 5 and 6 per cent. The new rate was about equal to the average rate of interest charged on capital used by local authorities for housing purposes before the fall in interest rates. The effect of changing horses in mid-stream was to lose the benefit of the changes in interest rates as far as building houses to let at lower rents were concerned. Now it was true of course that under the guarantee system of the 1933 Act it would have been possible for private investors to have got money on mortgage from the building societies at 3½ per cent. thus utilising the fall in rates. Quite apart, however, from the fact that this was not done on any large scale it would not have solved the problem, for such investors were in no

[1] See Charts VI and VIII and Statistical Appendix, Table 6.

better position than the local authorities without the Wheatley subsidy to provide houses cheaply.[1]

To sum up briefly—the economic rents of new houses did not fall after 1930 sufficient to compensate for the cancellation of the subsidy even if the full benefit of the change of interest rates had been realised. In 1930 subsidised rents were out of reach of a large section of the population, the higher unsubsidised rents available later were still further out of reach, a fortiori if the full advantages of the changes in interest rates were not secured. There was never at any time in the 'thirties a serious prospect of private enterprise being able to provide houses more cheaply than the local authorities had done in the 'twenties. It is true, of course, that real wages were rising over part of this period and that this should in theory at least have increased rent-paying capacity. It is improbable, however, that the increases were sufficient, particularly among the lower wage groups, to meet the new situation. It has certainly never been generally considered sufficient for the purpose. The continued failure to solve the rent problem was reflected in the decision reached in 1937 that the supply of houses to let at low rents did not warrant a general repeal of rent restriction.

Private enterprise then, it seemed, failed in just the same way as the local authorities. It did not provide houses any more cheaply in the years just before this war than local authorities had managed to do some time earlier. The private enterprise system, however, did better than the local authorities in one important respect. It provided so many more houses that with the aid of propaganda and easy purchase schemes it intensified the move of large numbers of families into new houses, leaving their old ones vacant for the less fortunate who were unable to afford new houses. The question outstanding in 1939 was, therefore, whether it was satisfactory that the supply of additional houses and replacement of old ones should depend for the mass of the working-class population on the haphazard emigration of better-off families into new houses.

---

[1] Actually, of course, private investors were in a worse position for the building society advances had to be amortised over 30 years. Local authorities could spread amortization over 60 years. Moreover, naturally private investors would want profit as well as interest on some of their own capital.

PART II

THE UNSETTLED QUESTIONS OF HOUSING POLICY

INTRODUCTION

In the first part of this book we have tried to show how state intervention in the field of housing worked during the period between the two world wars. We have concentrated mainly on the economic field, we have dealt with the needs for houses, the sorts of houses built, the effects of subsidies of different kinds, problems of rent and costs and some aspects of the activities of the local authorities. As we went along we tried to find out how far those economic matters affected both the course of policy and its results. The application of the conclusions we reached to problems of the present, or the near future, depends on the object of housing policy and on the extent to which the housing situation has been altered or modified by the present war. In the next two chapters we shall be concerned with rather more general questions than hitherto, the fundamental unsettled questions of housing policy, such as the possible alternative purposes of state intervention and of rent policy. Although the emphasis will still be on the economic aspects of these questions, we shall find it necessary to indicate the places where housing problems impinge on other social problems. In the last two chapters the effects of the war and the lessons derived from the experience of the three experiments will be taken up.

It is not the purpose of this book to lay down what housing policy should be. We explained earlier that all we hoped to do was to bring together and analyse such information of an economic nature as could be collected about the success, or failure, of state intervention in housing questions in this country. The purpose has been to provide some of the economic data which must be taken into account in deciding what sort of housing policy is practicable, and what conditions must be fulfilled if repetition of the mistakes made in the past is to be avoided.

Even in the fairly simple circumstances of 1939 there was little general agreement about the purpose of policy, and there was still less grasp of the implications of particular policies. The discussions going on to-day show that there is equally little agreement and still more confusion.

Dealing with outstanding unsettled issues of policy before the effects of the present war is not really putting the cart before the horse. The main questions of policy are the same to-day as they were in 1939. As we shall see, the war has only modified the housing situation, not fundamentally altered it; the housing system, the numbers and types of houses, the rent structure, the code of housing legislation existing to-day, in 1944, have been inherited from pre-war years. Even the " blitz " has only altered the situation piecemeal. It is much more satisfactory to discuss long-term principles and the structure of the housing system which we might decide we should like, before getting entangled in the new crop of emergency problems created by this war. When we have cleared the ground on these matters and have achieved some outline of the principles and commitments involved under alternative long-term policies, we shall be in a much better position to see how far the war has altered their desirability and practicability.

Looking back, it is obvious that what we have called the three experiments were the outcome of the varying influence of three groups of ideas about housing. First, there was the idea that state intervention and state responsibility for the supply of houses was necessitated by the shortage of houses at the end of the Great War. The state must intervene, it was argued, to increase the supply of working-class houses in order to remedy the shortage created by the lack of building during the war, and prevent excessive increases in rents. The natural deduction from this was that state intervention should be confined to the bare minimum needed to remedy these transitory difficulties as quickly as possible, and that a return to a free market should be made with all speed; public expenditure would be kept down to the level compatible with this object. Second, there was the rather vague idea, held by an important section of the community, that standards of working-class housing must be improved by state intervention. These two ideas combined produced the " Homes for Heroes " slogan, the First Experiment, and the Wheatley Act. The dominance of the first idea from 1923 to 1933 led to the Chamberlain Act, and the successive attempts to cut general housing subsidies and to relax the Rent Restriction Acts. The Second Experiment was the consequence of the incompatible marriage between this idea and the rather vague idea behind the Wheatley Act. The return of the minority Labour Government to power in 1929 brought about a brief revival in the influence of the latter and with it the abortive Greenwood policy.

Between 1923 and 1933 housing policy was therefore in practice dominated by the limited emergency theory. The attitude towards the whole complex of rent problems was inevitably based on the thesis that everything would get sorted out as soon as the period of emergency and state intervention was over. In consequence there was no real need to discuss them except in connection with fixing dates for the abolition or relaxation of rent control, or in connection with economising on the subsidies. No doubt it was inevitable that under the pressure of necessity serious discussion of the question of raising the general standard of working-class houses was shelved. There was, nevertheless, a great deal of confusion and political wishful thinking about this. The difference between establishing a new high standard for new houses built under the emergency schemes and of making that standard applicable to all, or to the bulk, of working-class houses was not kept clear. Naturally the abatement of the acute shortage improved housing conditions in comparison with the immediate post-war years, simply because there was more house-room to share out. Justifiable pride in some of the local authority estates developed into a self-satisfied assumption that the new houses were equivalent to a general improvement of working-class houses. It was forgotten that the majority of working-class families continued to live in the old houses which, with the passage of time, were deteriorating both absolutely and in relation to modern standards.

It only needed the general confusion of the great depression with its demand for public economy to bring the whole Second Experiment to an end. The worst of the shortage was obviously over, and therefore justification for state intervention disappeared, according to the supporters of the emergency idea. In the meantime the public conscience had begun to reassert itself on the matter of slums and the worst types of overcrowding; it was suddenly remembered that this old-fashioned housing problem had continued to flourish unchecked since the Great War. The belief that this question ought to be tackled was the third idea to influence housing policy. The evidence that the Wheatley subsidy was wastefully administered, that people who could afford economic rents were getting subsidies, provided an uncomfortably sharp contrast with the lack of help for those families whose housing conditions were undoubtedly deplorable socially, morally and on grounds of public health. In a period of financial stringency it was easy to argue that it would be much better to use such resources as were available to improve the worst housing conditions in the country. Thus, the Third Experiment, the modern sanitary policy, was an offspring of the union between the public conscience and the desire for public economy. The general questions of improving all working-class housing standards, and of attempting to solve the tangles of the rent system which had grown up, slipped still further into the background. The policy of attacking the slums and overcrowding, accepted during the economy crisis, continued to be regarded as all that was necessary, and by implication possible, even during prosperous years of the middle 'thirties. Necessity, it seems, is the mother, not of invention in housing matters, but of complacency.

This is not the place to discuss the forces which have gone to make up public opinion between the great depression and the present war. It is remarkable that the least ambitious housing experiment, the third, took place without widespread criticism during years of prosperity, of increases in real income, and of what was probably the greatest volume of private expenditure on middle class and semi-middle class houses in the history of the country. There is little doubt that the psychosis of the great depression numbed public interest and stultified serious discussion of housing policy long after economic recovery had taken place. The appeal of ambitious programmes in the years immediately after the Great War, the growing clamour for even more ambitious schemes to be introduced after this war, suggest that it needs the impact of war-time housing discomforts on the artisan and middle classes to evoke real interest in housing questions. Now, as twenty-four years ago, it is accepted both that there is a housing emergency which will demand State intervention, and that old-fashioned standards of housing are intolerable. This time there are to be homes for all; Britain, it seems popularly supposed, is to be rebuilt. Unless the major problems which went by default during the years of peace are settled, it is inevitable that housing policy will be even more confused after this war than after the last.

Chapter X

THE UNSETTLED QUESTIONS

THE PURPOSE OF HOUSING POLICY

In 1939 nobody was bothering about complications introduced into the housing situation by wars, past or future. The country appeared to have accepted the sanitary policy and held, rather vaguely, a belief that local authorities were responsible for providing such additional houses as might appear necessary, apart from the slum clearance and decrowding schemes. Apart from variants of the sanitary policy, the only serious alternative was that of a general scheme for replacing old houses and making improvements in standards of working-class housing in general.

I. The Purpose and Scope of Sanitary Policy

After the discussion of the sanitary policy during the Third Experiment in an earlier chapter, it is unnecessary to deal with it in detail again. Here we only need to emphasise the principles on which it was founded and to indicate the actual commitments by way of building and finance involved by it in 1939. A sanitary policy is based on a decision that particular types of housing conditions cannot be tolerated. It implies state, or social, responsibility for preventing any family living in houses involving these conditions. The special difference between the modern form and the nineteenth century form is the modern recognition that, in practice, this means that the state becomes responsible directly, or indirectly, for providing alternative accommodation at rents within the reach of the families concerned. Developments in other social services have been similar. It was long ago recognised that, if it was decided that no one ought to be allowed to die of starvation, food must be provided for those without means to buy it by some sort of poor law. Similarly, it was recognised that it was impossible to declare that every child was to receive an elementary education without providing the schools and free tuition. In such cases it has been decided in the general interest of the community at large that there is a certain absolute minimum below which people must not be allowed to fall. Thus reforms were made as much in the interest of the community as of

the individuals affected.   Begging is a public nuisance which
cannot be stopped if the beggars would otherwise starve.   Illiteracy
is a public inconvenience in a modern community.

The sanitary policy of the Third Experiment was the application
of this principle to housing.   Modern standards of building, however,
were not just above the minimum chosen as tolerable, they were a
long way above, and it was the intention that all new houses built
should conform to this standard.   The families whose housing conditions were below the minimum were to be rehoused, not at the
minimum level, but approximately according to this new high
standard.   About a million working-class families had achieved this
new standard with or without state assistance in the fourteen years
before the new policy was introduced.[1]   In between this group and
that affected by the sanitary policy were the majority of working-
class families still housed on an old-fashioned basis; for these no
responsibility was admitted.   The sanitary policy was limited only
to the black patches within a vast area of off-white or dark grey.
It would make the black patches white by providing housing conforming to modern ideas for the limited number, but it had no
concern with achieving this standard for all.

As interpreted between 1933 and 1939, the policy covered the
replacement of half a million houses and the provision of some
three hundred thousand additional houses under the scheme for
abolishing overcrowding.   At the outbreak of this war about half the
former programme had been completed and a start made with the
latter.   The financial obligations of the Treasury for subsiding rents
were running at the figure of about £2·2 million p.a.[2]   It was probable,
of course, that this liability would increase more than in proportion
to the number of houses as the programmes neared completion,
and flats built on expensive sites would become more important.
Both the commitments for actual building and the financial assistance
likely to be needed were those forseeable within fairly narrow limits.
Beyond these there might be in due course small additional liabilities
as local authorities decided that with the course of time more houses
had degenerated into the slum category, or that a recurrence of
overcrowding was threatening.   The Ministry of Health rather
optimistically declared that slum clearance was a " continuing
process," but unless some radical change in the interpretation of
the term " slum " or overcrowding were adopted " the continuing

[1] See Statistical Appendix Table 3A.   The number of working class houses built up
to 1934 was 1,032 thousand.

[2] *Ministry of Health Annual Report, 1938/9.*   Separate figures for the contributions of
local authorities are not available.

process " would dwindle to a mere trickle.[1] The supreme advantage of the sanitary policy was that for the first time a determined effort was made to deal with the worst housing conditions in the country. Moreover, as something like an official and serious definition of requirements were part of the policy, there was some method of checking up on the adequacy of local authority schemes. It was not ever claimed for the policy that it provided a long-term large-scale programme.

As far as housing policy was laid down in Acts of Parliament, the local authorities remained responsible for seeing that there were sufficient working-class houses in their areas, quite apart from the sanitary policy of the Third Experiment. There was, however, no official definition of sufficiency of working-class houses in this context, and there was no help available from the Treasury, except in terms of the abolition of slums and overcrowding. Indeed, it had been asserted by the Government that all house building outside slum clearance and decrowding should be left to private enterprise. In practice a number of local authorities did build houses not ranking for subsidy, so that in a highly erratic way the more rigid interpretation and most limited commitments of the sanitary policy were not adhered to.

This more liberal variant of the policy, as put into practice by some local authorities, implied a wider interpretation of state responsibility for working-class houses than the sanitary policy proposed. It is as well to look at its implications. The local authorities were permitted to build without subsidy for those whom they thought needed houses. This put part of the system for providing houses on to the same sort of basis as a trading service. Houses supplied in this way were only available for those families who could afford to pay the economic rents, unless the local authorities gave a subsidy out of the rates. Similarly, trading services which local authorities can provide if they like, such as gas, transport and markets, are available only to the extent that people can afford to pay for them.[2] Owing to the fact that even during the latter part of the peace the economic rents for local authority houses were out of the reach of a very large proportion of working-class families, the benefit of local authority

---

[1] See p. 152 above.
[2] The effect of providing houses on this basis is a little different from that of providing services, such as transport or gas. A family can only have a house if it can afford to pay for the whole of it (unless, of course, it gets permission to sub-let). Everyone in the area, however, can have some benefit from a bus or tram service, or from the provision of electricity or gas, though some may be able to afford more than others. The benefits are the more widespread than in the case of houses.

activities on these lines was limited to a relatively small section of the community. In so far as this was provision for families which private enterprise would not provide owing to general unwillingness to invest in houses to let, this appears as an unmixed advantage; something useful in itself cannot fairly be condemned because it helps some families and not others, provided it costs society nothing.

A quite different issue is raised if the authorities use their favourable position for raising capital cheaply to compete with, and undercut, private enterprise. This brings up the whole question of whether the credit of the state or of state organisations, should be used to provide something on particularly favourable terms although private enterprise is willing to provide it, and supersede the latter altogether. If it is reasonable in the case of houses, is there any reason why the same principle should not be extended to food or clothing? The answer to this depends on the answer to the much wider question of whether all the elementary needs of life should be provided in this way. Convinced socialists, and even others whose politics are of an uncertain shade of pink, would favour it; others would as naturally object. There seems no particular reason why this new principle should be introduced in the case of houses unless, and until, it is introduced for the whole range of basic needs.

This development of the provision of houses along the lines of a trading service raises another difficulty of a more practical nature. As long as the local authorities act in this matter only under what are effectively permissive powers there is, of course, little purpose in a central control of their activities, except perhaps to prevent them under-cutting private enterprise. Once, however, it is admitted that the development is desirable, it can be argued that it should be made compulsory for local authorities to provide houses without subsidy, wherever they are needed, on a trading service basis. The difficulty that arises is in the definition of need. Does it occur only where families would fall below the minimum standard set by the sanitary policy because of the shortage of houses, even though they could afford economic rents for new houses, or should it be defined in terms of the absence of sufficient houses to allow one house for each family? If both these interpretations of need are rejected, it is difficult to see where the line can be set, short of offering local authority houses to any family that can afford the economic rent; this interpretation would be tantamount to inviting any family who could afford it to move out of an old house into a new one. The intermediate interpretation suggests that every family of this type should demand a whole house for itself. The whole difficulty arises because it appears unreasonable for the state, on the one hand, to undertake financial responsibility only for preventing families falling below a low minimum standard, but, on the other, to undertake to enforce the provision of houses of a much higher standard for those, or for a section of those, who could afford to pay for it. Acceptance of the principle of housing activity by local authorities on the basis of a compulsory trading service is equivalent to an open admission that the minimum standard guaranteed is far below what is desirable, but that once that minimum is reached the state will only help those who can help themselves.

II. The Alternative—A General Replacement Policy

(a) *Principles Involved.*

In 1939 the only interesting alternative to the sanitary policy was of the type, shelved since 1923, of which the object would be to improve the housing conditions of working-class families in general, not only those of the families covered by the sanitary policy or of those able to afford economic or commercial rents. In 1939 such a policy would have been primarily concerned with replacing old working-class houses. The serious shortage of working-class houses which had led to the emergency policy had been made good; current requirements for additional houses to balance increases in the number of families was on the verge of a sharp decline with alterations in the rate of increase of the adult population. Replacement of old houses had become the main problem of interest; not only was the time opportune for an attempt to deal with it, but it was beginning to look as though the course of events would force its advantages into the foreground. It will be remembered that it was concluded that by the end of the Third Experiment there were signs that the force of the great building boom had spent itself. The impetus derived from the migration of families from old middle and upper working-class houses to modern ones was weakening as more and more of these families were rehoused. The possibility of a decline in private building held two threats to the maintenance of the policy of 1939. In the first place, the indirect opportunities for families unable to afford new houses to improve their housing conditions, by filtering into the rather better houses abandoned by the migrating families, would dwindle away. In the second, the dying down of the boom would cause severe unemployment in the building industry and its ancillary industries unless some state policy of building took its place. The limited nature of building commitments under the sanitary policy provided little prospect of this. An extended policy of replacement building might have been adopted in a hurry to avert such developments as part of a policy for maintaining full employment.

However desirable a policy intended to avert depression in the building industry might be, it implied a danger that the problems of a general replacement policy might be considered only from the angle of full employment. A large scale replacement policy would affect the health and domestic happiness of millions of families for years after its completion. It would involve social considerations of importance, and there are a number of fields in which problems of rebuilding the old houses must impinge on problems of social policy. It would be disastrous for a replacement policy to be considered on the same basis as digging holes in the ground in order to keep men employed. Undoubtedly the proper method of fitting fundamental problems of a housing policy of replacement into perspective with other social and economic problems is to consider the implications of housing policy first; then to find out where it impinges on other projects, including employment schemes.

The fundamental difference between a general policy of replacement and the sanitary policy derives from the intention of the former to bring *all* working-class housing up to the accepted modern standard. As the sanitary policy implies a guarantee that no one shall live below a certain low minimum housing standard, the more extended policy implies a guarantee that no one shall live below the modern standard. The object of policy thus becomes that bringing the new standard within the reach of all families instead of enforcing a certain minimum regarded as tolerable.

There are certain questions of scope which must be considered. First, should the new standard be compulsory for every family, whether they want it or not? Second, should the policy apply to all the population or should it be confined to the working-class population, and, if so, how is the working-class population to be defined? or, finally, should it be still further limited to the population in sub-standard houses? As the main purpose of the policy would be replacement, the new standard would probably have to be compulsory; at least in the towns rebuilding would have to be undertaken on a large scale, and it would be impracticable to leave isolated houses or groups of houses for those who were indifferent to modern ideas. To do so would wreck the opportunities for replanning the main towns and involve all sorts of administrative complications.

The second question is more difficult. The main purpose of the scheme would be to replace the large groups of houses falling below modern standards. These are, in fact, almost entirely old working-class houses or large houses come down in the world. The families actually living in these would obviously be the main group affected by the policy, for these are the families who would be removed from sub-standard conditions. The real difficulty arises with regard to new families, those for whom net additions to the supply of houses would be needed. Now it seems clear that those who were financially incapable of achieving the standard on their own would have to be provided for, otherwise they would form a new generation who would later have to be moved out of sub-standard conditions. The question of whether other families should be provided for is similar to that raised in connection with the extended variant of the sanitary policy. Should state responsibility be extended to pro-viding houses of the guaranteed standard to everyone wanting them? It was suggested in connection with the sanitary policy that such a policy appeared to be entirely beneficial provided the houses were not otherwise available.[1] A further possible extension would be provision through state agencies of houses rather above the standard as, for instance, parlour houses as well as non-parlour houses, if they were not made available for letting by private enterprise. Beyond such limits anyone who wanted anything different would have to find it for themselves. Acceptance of this limitation of state activity would provide a clear division between the field of private building and that of state building.

This arrangement would cut out all the troublesome questions of who were entitled to benefit from the guarantee. It would bring the struggling clerk and the small shopkeeper into the scheme, and all the miscellaneous families who might find the standard houses desirable. There seems little reason why the better-off families who, for some reason, are unwilling or unable, to obtain accommodation of a higher type should be obliged to do so, and it would solve local difficulties where there might be general shortages of houses to let. In practice demand from such families would probably not be of major importance, but it seems eminently desirable and certainly more democratic to provide accommodation of a certain type for all who need or want it. It would be, in this respect, the same as the provision of elementary education. The comparison with elementary

---

[1] The difficulty of this scheme in connection with a sanitary policy was that it implied the acceptance of two standards, and also that state help was in part only available to those who were in favourable financial circumstances.

education throws into sharp relief the question which is so constantly in people's mind about houses. Are rents to be subsidised? if so, how? It is the question of the financial terms on which standard houses should be available which crops up always and inconveniently; this subject, however, belongs to the next chapter.

(b) New Houses needed by the Policy.

This discussion of principles undoubtedly seems so much in the air and so general as to be completely divorced from reality. It will be useful to see what sort of magnitude in building commitments would be involved by these ambitious projects. The size of the commitments will depend of course on the way in which old houses are compared with new. There is little doubt that the new standard would be based on the houses already built by local authorities. There is, of course, a good deal of variation and some of the local authority houses might be regarded as needing improvements to bring them up to satisfactory levels, but a basic and usable standard could be based on the ordinary local authority non-parlour house. In making some estimate of the numbers of houses needed under the general policy just outlined, it will be sufficient to use this. It will be convenient to approach from several angles. First, there are the obviously sub-standard houses already included in the uncompleted slum clearance schemes at the outbreak of war in 1939, about a quarter of a million. Second, and almost equally obvious, are the houses which the inspectors of the sanitary authorities have since the 1930 Act had rendered fit for human habitation. We saw in the first part of this book that this bunch included houses just escaping inclusion in the slum clearance schemes, and it is safe to assume that the majority of them, even when rendered fit, were far below modern standards. It is uncertain how many existed in 1939, but as the number actually dealt with up to 1938/9 was 751 thousand, it is probably reasonable to accept this as the figure for the obvious pseudo-slums, for though some may have been destroyed, no doubt the inspectors missed some out. So far we have included just about a million out of the probable total of rather under five million typical pre-1914 working-class houses existing in 1939. There is no statistical evidence about the proportion of the remainder which are without modern facilities such as water-closets and bathrooms, and the total of slums and pseudo-slums may be taken as a minimum estimate.

To obtain an upper estimate, it will be necessary to work in another way. It is probably safe to assume that the great majority of the

3 and 4-roomed houses, except those built since 1919, were without bathrooms, if not without individual w.c.'s. These houses were built mainly in the nineteenth century. The older ones would certainly be without bathrooms, for fixed baths only became regarded as a conventional necessity for the middle classes towards the end of the century; the slightly newer houses of this size were generally houses built for the less well-to-do working-class families for whom baths would be regarded as quite unnecessary. When it is remembered that some of the philanthropic bodies putting up tenements in the last half of last century ignored baths and separate w.c.'s, and even water supplies laid on to the kitchens, the lowness of the standards of the pre-1914 houses becomes more obvious. It is safe to assume then that on this test of bathrooms between three and four million houses would fail to pass, and most of them are so crowded together that the addition of bathrooms would be impossible. We may be fairly confident that this is not an over-estimate, for we have ignored the larger working-class houses altogether. Many of these may be without bathrooms, but there is a greater chance that they could be added. This suggests another possible way of assessing the total scope of the replacement problem on more generous lines. If comparison with new standards is approached from the point of view of light and air, space and lay-out, it is probably that only a small fraction, certainly less than a quarter of all the pre-Great War houses below the £14 rateable value limit would pass a test. The replacement problem on this basis would amount to some total near four millions.

Approaching the problem from the angle of houses of ordinary working-class type has led to omission of the big houses come down in the world, and frequently occupied by more than one family without proper conversion. Some of these could undoubtedly be converted into quite reasonably satisfactory flats or maisonettes. Others have deteriorated too much to allow for work on improvements, and replacement of these and of unsatisfactory small houses above the rate compounding limit, may make it necessary to add on another couple of hundred thousand, bringing the maximum on these counts to rather over four million.

In considering the implications of any policy it is undoubtedly best to approach from the aspect of the maximum possible commitments involved. We have just considered the maximum number of houses which it might be necessary to pull down under a general replacement policy. It is important to realise that this is the maximum, however, for otherwise undue alarm might be felt. In practice the

number of houses to be destroyed might be smaller, for houses condemned in a large town might be regarded as tolerable in a small
one or in the country. On the other hand, it is equally important to
remember that the total number of houses needed for replacement
would exceed the number demolished, as a considerable number of
families were sharing houses, though, according to modern standards,
they should have had separate ones. This would probably be adequately allowed for if the total number of new houses needed for
replacement was put between four million and four and a half. Finally,
it must not be forgotten that the number of families is still increasing,
and the additional new families must be provided for. The additional
houses needed for this has been estimated conservatively at about
half a million in the six years, 1940/1945,[1] and another quarter of a
million might be needed for the years 1946/1950. Thus, in round
figures the number of new houses needed by 1950, if all the old
sub-standard houses are to be replaced and current needs catered
for, would be about five million.

This total is equivalent to between fourteen and fifteen years
building at the maximum rate ever achieved in this country of 350
thousand houses a year. On this basis it would have been possible
before the outbreak of the war to rebuild the sordid heritage of the
nineteenth century towns as far as houses were concerned within
about half a generation, relying on increased capacity of the building industry to deal with any additional families emerging after
1950. Success would have been a matter of finance and organisation.
Any increase in the size of the industry, any increase in the efficiency
of the industry, the development of pre-fabrication building on a
large scale, for instance, would have shortened the period, or,
made possible an allowance out of building resources for other types
of houses, or for bringing some of the early local authority houses
up to higher standards. The scheme need not be ruled out of court
because of its sheer size. It will be realised, of course, that in addition
to the houses a great deal of other building would be involved, for
schools, halls, public and social buildings. The provision of these
might mean that in practice a longer period would be needed to
complete the scheme. Finally, roads would have to be made, drains
laid, water supplies provided, and so on. But four million houses
were built despite these complications between 1919 and 1939, and
both the building and civil engineering industries were far below

---

[1] See Dr. Elsas's *Housing Before the War and After*, pp. 54 *et seq*. Dr. Elsas's actual figure
is 480 thousand reached on the basis of the same number of houses per adult as in 1939.
According to his estimate, the number of houses needed both in 1944 and 1945 (if there
had been no war) would have fallen to 55 thousand.

1938/39 levels for much of this period. Even these complications would not have made the plan unpracticable from the building aspect in 1939.

The question of finance belongs to the next section, and it will be more convenient to discuss problems of organisation in a later chapter. There are still a number of extremely important questions of principle to which we must pay some attention. Our first review has indicated that, if the war had not broken out in 1939, it would not have been beyond the bounds of possibility to provide enough houses for a complete replacement scheme in less than the time between the end of the Great War and the beginning of this one. But provision of houses within the scheme is not the only problem involved and the solution of the others of a more general, social and economic character, must affect any final decision as to whether a replacement policy is desirable.

(c) General Economic and Social Problems affecting Housing Policy.

The other problems are concerned mainly with wider issues which emerge where housing matters impinge on other fields, such as matters affecting the economic and social life of new communities, the responsibility for provision of public services and certain problems of local government. These are not entirely housing problems and cannot be settled solely in the interests of housing policy. Equally, since they affect housing, they ought not to be decided without reference to it. The intention of introducing them here is to show at what points housing questions become involved with other social and economic questions.

It will be simplest to approach from a rather practical angle. One of the difficulties which will occur to everyone about a general replacement scheme is that of the space which would be taken up by the new houses. Modern standards of housing require more space per family or per person than was thought necessary in the old days. While some of the houses could be rebuilt on the old sites either as houses or in blocks of flats, in nearly every part of the country some would have to be built on new land. The actual physical size of towns would inevitably be increased and the question is raised of whether this would be desirable in the public interest? Could a further sprawl of the big industrial towns be contemplated with equanimity? It would mean more and more people travelling in to daily work in congested buses and trains; it would create the opposite difficulty that people within the towns would be more than ever cut off from the country. Now to some people it seems clear that the answer is that this could not be tolerated. But it is easy to make a big bogey of it. It is a horrible thought that half a million people will have to be rehoused outside the boundaries of the County of London according to the L.C.C. plan for rebuilding it.[1]

Half a million people is equivalent to a town half the size of Birmingham or, to, say, Portsmouth and Nottingham rolled into one. It would seem fantastic that houses for so many people should be tacked on to the absurdly voluminous and tattered skirts of Greater London. But it must not be forgotten that London in this matter is the great black patch in the whole country. With a couple of exceptions even those towns which boast with misplaced pride of their size do not get up to over the million mark. We are apt to think of this country as so entirely industrialised that the bulk of the population live in large towns. We forget that most of the towns are quite small. The facts of the matter are quite simple. The County of London contained 4·4 million (Greater London, 8·2 million) people in 1931, the four next largest towns in England and Wales had populations over half-a-million each and totalled 3·1 million. If the whole of Greater London is counted as a densely-built up area of inconvenient size, 28 per cent. of the whole population lived in really large urban areas, or to allow for Greater Manchester, Liverpool, etc., say one-third. About another two and a half million people lived in eight towns varying in population from a quarter million to a half million, that is another 7 per cent. In all, in 1931, barely two-fifths of the whole population lived in towns which could be called really large.

Thus, though the problem is real, it applies only to certain of the towns or groups of towns, to only, in total, those containing barely fifteen per cent. of the population, as well as London. The fashionable solution for the difficulties of these towns is the building of new separate ones away from the old instead of suburbs. It is an attractive idea. It conjures up visions of new towns planned according to modern ideals, new settlements for emigrants from the old congested areas offering new opportunities for health and comfort. As far as the houses are concerned, the difficulty of providing them are matters of organising the appropriate supplies of labour. But the suggestion for new towns arouses far more complicated questions than this.

The fundamental problem is providing the inhabitants with opportunities of earning their livings and this involves persuading, or forcing, industry to go wherever it is planned to put the people. The experiment has been tried with some success already in this

[1] *County of London Plan*, pp. 32 *et seq.*

country. Letchworth and Welwyn Garden City show that it can be done at least on a fairly small scale. In both, however, it has been a slow and arduous business, and experience shows that if it is left to private initiative it could not be expected to fit into large-scale rebuilding schemes.

The question of government control of the location of industry has become a subject of popular discussion, since the Barlow Report suggested that the time had come to prevent a continuation of the drift of population south and a further increase in the size of London. The Report suggested that new firms and industries should be prevented from starting up in the congested region.[1] It did not go so far as to suggest the removal of existing firms into new districts. It would, of course, be possible to extend this suggestion for closing down Greater London to a large number of other towns. This would set up a negative type of pressure to locate new firms in particular places. The question of old firms obviously raises far greater difficulties. Another alternative would be the offer of positive inducements such as those provided by modern trading estates to get firms to new towns. It is not the function of this book to suggest what ought to be done about the location of industry; sufficient has been said to make it clear that new towns' schemes are involved with the question of the control of the location of industry.[2]

Hardly less important than the question of providing livelihoods for new towns are the whole group of sociological problems involved in building up a community and social life. It is well to remember that man cannot live by bread alone. Experience, even with building estates, has shown how difficult it is to transform into a society families strange to each other, and put into new places without tradition. They are apt to remain a large number of entirely isolated and separate families suffering from all the wretchedness, nostalgia, and frustration of exiles. In new towns cut off from their parent towns, people would be faced with new jobs, unable to return easily to their old haunts for amusement or business; these sociological problems might be specially acute. Possibly in this matter the lessons of experience have been grasped. At least the movement for the inclusion of public buildings and community centres in large local authority estates was developing before the war. From the point of view of building, of course, this need for public buildings must increase the pressure on the capacity of the building industry.

We must turn now to questions of a rather different character,

---

[1] *Report on the Distribution of the Industrial Population*, op. cit, pp. 206–7.
[2] See pp. 235 et seq. below on the effect of the present war on this question.

those connected with the ownership of houses in new towns, and their government and equipment with essential social services. It can scarcely be regarded as reasonable for new towns to be planned, built and owned by the old towns which are clearing out some of their population. It is quite conceivable that families from several old towns would have to be brought together into one new town. This would involve joint responsibility of all the exporting areas in planning, building houses, and owning the land and houses, and therefore in selecting tenants and fixing rents. Apart from the fact that the record of joint planning between local authorities is not encouraging, such a division of authority would inevitably lead to delays and inefficiency. There is undoubtedly a strong case for the creation of some new type of authority to fit together the needs of individual authorities for housing their surplus families and to plan and build the new town in relation to these needs.[1] This it will be noticed involves at any rate regional authorities whose relations to existing local authorities would need careful definition. On the other hand they would have to fit in with any national authority settling the broad issues of the location of industry just discussed.

There are other general arguments in favour of regional or national responsibility for new towns. New towns to be worth the name must have independent economic and political lives. This means they must be independent of old towns.   In any case it is hard to see what conceivable claim the London County Council, for instance, could have to determine the lines on which the lives of the families they export should run. The initial choice of location and the general building plan of the new town will, however, for many years have great influence in determining just these things. There is another, and perhaps final, point. If an old town plans and builds a new town, it would own the greater part of the land and buildings in it. It would be able to decide for ever what families should be able to rent houses there. Even after the original settlement of families, it could, if housing difficulties develop within its own boundaries, give preference to its own citizens to those of the new town. The housing needs and incidentally the social structure of the new town would remain subordinate to the interests of the old one indefinitely. A situation of this type is totally incompatible with the development of an independent civic life.

The arguments against planning, ownership and control of new

---

[1] An independent authority would also be in a better position to take into account the possibility that families from all parts of the country might, for the best of reasons, immigrate into the new towns.

towns by old ones are thus overwhelming. It must not be forgotten, however, that a new town would not come to life overnight fully equipped with Mayor and Aldermen and a civic sense, or even with public and social services. It would not be sufficient for the new towns to be planned and built by some national or regional authority, even if the problem of ownership is solved by vesting it in such an authority. Some responsible and powerful body would be needed after the new towns were built to guide them through their infancy and their teething troubles : a new type of authority capable of laying the foundations of the public and social services, and of running the young town on a trustee basis while its inhabitants move in, settle down, and get to know who they would like as Mayor and Aldermen. The exact form of such an authority, its relation to the planning and building authority, and the question of whether it should own the houses in trust for ultimate transference to the new town when it has achieved an independent corporate existence, are among the problems to be decided.

The suggestion that some of the difficulties involved by the amount of space which would be taken up by replacement building could be solved by the creation of new towns appears to raise a hornet's nest of problems; these include the location of industry, complex social questions, regional and national planning, and local government. Actually these are only particularly obvious illustrations of the problems which must arise under any housing policy which involves uprooting large, and somewhat miscellaneous, groups of families and depositing them in strange surroundings. The same type of problems would emerge even if all rehousing took the form of suburbs. Their relative importance is slightly changed and they will be easier to see after this discussion of the new town idea.

The questions associated with the establishment of new means of obtaining a livelihood would be of relatively minor importance, if the surplus families were merely moved from the inside to the outskirts of existing towns, for in general work in the old centre would remain available. The general issue of the control of the location of industry would, however, re-appear. The replacement policy would demand a great expenditure of effort, energy and of capital. It is questionable whether it is reasonable to inaugurate such a policy if the opportunities for employment are allowed to shift from a place, just rebuilt, to another place without surplus houses. Migrations of families in search of opportunities for earning their livings upset the balance between the demand and supply of houses. Would it, for instance, have been worth starting to rebuild the towns and villages of the depressed areas during the inter-war decades if the inhabitants were still left dependent on unemployment benefit, unemployment assistance and the poor law? Would it be tolerable that people should be encouraged, by the provision of new and attractive houses, to continue to make their homes where there is little or no prospect of earning a reasonable living? If the effort to rebuild the towns were made, it would only be consistent to make certain that industry and the houses would be in the same places. Rejection of the new towns idea thus would not abolish the problem of controlling the location of industry. On the contrary, it would make it essential to see that industry remained where it was and that new industries went to these old localities, however unsuitable. The possible loss of efficiency and of national wealth which might result from freezing the distribution of industry on the 1939 population pattern, cannot be calculated.

It is common knowledge that the next group of problems, the sociological ones, cannot be evaded by keeping to suburban development. They have already become familiar in various ways in connection with the large estates of the bigger local authorities built before 1939. It may perhaps be that they would be less acute as long as families were rehoused in suburbs, even outlying suburbs of big towns, than if new towns were built. All contact with established centres of civilisation would not be broken off, if only because the inhabitants would continue to be dependent on the original towns for earning their living. They would necessarily be going to and fro. This could apply, however, only to the mobile sections of the population, the housewives and children must be dependent for all their social contacts on the resources of the places they live in. Even the mobile sections will be partly dependent, for any sort of family participation in social life must depend on the place where the family lives.

The questions of planning, ownership, government and responsibility for public services would be still more closely connected with each other under a suburban rehousing policy than under a new town policy, but the issues would be less clear cut. Even before the war, the bigger housing authorities had difficulties in finding sufficient building land within their own boundaries. Some authorities succeeded in extending them sufficiently for their housing estates to remain an integral part of the main town. London in particular found this to be impossible. The extraordinary situation developed in the Greater London area in which one authority became an

o

important landlord within the area of another. The suburban development does not, it will be observed, evade the difficulty over the ownership question.

The questions of responsibility for providing social and public utility services also must occur whenever building takes place outside the boundaries of the building authority. These questions are likely to be even more important in the future and more widespread. Almost all the new house building under the replacement scheme would be for those classes entirely dependent on the public provision of health, education and other social services. Moreover, the volume of building in the twenty years up to 1939 pressed the capacity of the public utility services to the utmost. More building on a large scale would in many cases involve the provision of new sources of supply. If local authorities built across each other's boundaries on a large scale under a replacement scheme, it would be grossly unfair to push these new duties on to authorities who have had no effective say in the decision to build the houses. The latter might in fact hold up the actual building through unwillingness, or inability, to provide essential public works for which they were technically responsible. They might, after the houses were built, fail to provide the schools and other things needed. Even if these were provided they might well be of an inferior type since the receiving authorities would be bound to be rural or, at best, urban districts. The exporting authority could only secure the proper provision of these services by taking over responsibility. This can only be done if the boundaries are changed. Past experience of delays and difficulties indicate that either the extension of boundaries would have to be made easier or that some new authority would be needed to assume general responsibility for extra-territorial building.

We have reached the same result as before: the necessity for some new type of authority capable of resolving the conflicts of interest between local authorities, and of planning building schemes on a wider basis of interests than those of the local authority needing houses for its surplus population. We saw earlier that in certain circumstances there would be a need for some special body to take over the ownership and management of new houses. Looking back over the whole discussion, it is evident that the character of the general economic and social problems involved in a general replacement policy is much the same whether the policy is carried out by the creation of new towns, or depends on suburban development; only the relative importance of various aspects of the problems is altered.

III. Conclusions

We have deliberately left out any reference to two major topics which are relevant to any large scale building schemes. The first and most glaring omission is that of the questions connected with the control of the use of land and the acquisition of land for building: the second omission is that of the possible complications which might be introduced into housing policy by serious attemps to maintain full employment. Postponement of discussion of these subjects is due to the radical changes which have taken place in circumstances affecting them during the war. It would be a pure waste of paper to discuss the first group without taking into account the Uthwatt Report.[1] The recommendations of that report, if accepted, would entirely alter the problems. The report itself is a consequence of the war, for the Committee was set up to consider some of the complications connected with land brought about by the war. Similarly with the second group, the development of state control of economic life during the war has popularised the belief that state intervention to maintain full employment is possible and desirable. This change in public opinion, together with the complicated employment problems of the change back to a peace economy have fundamentally altered the issues involved.

Even with these omissions the discussion of this section has led to a number of conclusions which will be useful in the next two chapters. We have seen that a sanitary policy provides a prospect of dwindling state intervention in housing, of unemployment in the building industry (though, of course, the war affects this), and a slowing up of improvements in working-class housing conditions brought about indirectly through private building. We have seen too that a sanitary policy implies state responsibility only for maintaining a standard of housing far below that generally accepted as reasonable. The commitments of the policy, on the other hand, are limited and can be fairly confidently forecast.

Ambitious schemes for rebuilding the sub-standard houses as a whole undoubtedly present a far more difficult group of problems which clamour for settlement, than the limited sanitary type does. The reason is simple. A sanitary policy only commits the state to adding or replacing a relatively small number of houses. These numbers are too small in most places to affect major questions of economic or social policy; similarly they are too small for their usefulness to be

[1] *Report of the Expert Committee on Compensation and Betterment.* 1942. Cmd. 6386.

affected, however major issues are decided. The inter-dependence of
the decisions on the scope of state intervention in housing and other
fields, so obvious in the case of an ambitious housing policy, is
evaded by a sanitary policy.

This more ambitious replacement policy could logically be
interpreted as state responsibility for maintaining a modern standard
of housing for every family. We have seen that on the basis of the
pre-war capacity of the building industry the policy was not impracticable, but might take between fifteen and twenty years to
complete. We concluded, too, that the success of such a policy is
bound up with state control of the location of industry, with national
and regional planning authorities for house building and with
changes in local government. Incidentally, we have found that
the suggestion for building new towns gives rise to the same type of
problems of economic and social policy as a policy based on suburban
development.

Chapter XI

THE UNSETTLED QUESTIONS :—
THE RENT QUESTION

I. THE RENT SYSTEM IN 1939

MODERN housing policy in this country began with the excursion of the Government into the field of rent control with the passing of the Rent and Mortgage Restriction Act of 1915. The record of the three experiments has shown that the rent question has affected the scope of state intervention ever since. This, after all is natural, for the cost of state intervention partly depends on the rent policy adopted.

It may fairly be said that we embarked on the present war with a rent system that was acquired as haphazardly as the British Empire. In practice it confirmed to no set of consistent principles, economic, social or moral. We have traced in the earlier chapters the way in which the various elements in the system, or lack of system, turned up. During the Great War an attempt was made to base rent control on a rather vague conception of a fair price. Since then there has been little success in making it clearer. Initially, it was considered that the rents actually prevailing before the scarcity created by the Great War should be maintained as in some way fair. This in the first decade after the Armistice was perhaps not without some foundation. The ceiling on rents had originally been fixed as the rents existing on the day war was declared in 1914; it could be claimed these included no element of war profiteering—they were fair in the special context of those years. There were, of course, certain bad gaps in the system, rents for furnished accommodation and for sub-lets proved beyond effective control.

As long as the Great War shortage continued it could be argued that this ceiling formed the proper foundation for the rent system. The various amendments of the Rent and Mortgage Restriction Acts were made on this assumption. In theory the increases permitted were intended to cover increases in rates paid by the landlords, additions to landlords' costs for maintenance or improvements, and increases in the rates of interest payable on mortgages.

There was one serious deviation from this principle in the introduction, in 1923, of decontrol on changes of tenancy, irrespective of the fact that this would result in increases in the rents of houses becoming vacant. With this exception, however, decontrol was made dependent on restoration of normal conditions of supply for particular types of houses.

The effect of the system was extraordinarily odd. The whole basis of the rent structure for old houses in 1939 was still the particular rents charged for individual houses twenty-five years earlier. Now the rents of the 1914 were ordinary market rents. It is not usually claimed that these are necessarily fair rents in any ethical sense of the term. They are merely the rents resulting from the interaction of supply and demand. They have no necessary relation to the original costs of production of individual houses; indeed, these are often quite unknown. They have a rather loose connection with the cost of providing new houses of similar types, for if market rents exceed the annual yield which would make investment in building new houses to let profitable, new houses will be built, other things being equal. Other things are, however, often not equal because, owing to the absence of accessible unbuilt sites at suitable prices in and around big towns, these prospects may be for all practical purposes unrealisable. Some at least of the rents in 1914 can only be classified as semi-monopoly rents just because of the absence of competing new supplies of houses. They were, it is true, more or less free from the particular element of profit stigmatised as due to " war profiteering "; they were by no means necessarily free of other elements of profit stigmatised by the moralists as unfair. They formed a queer basis for the maximum rents ruling twenty-five years later on the eve of the present war and, it may be remarked, a still queerer and more irrational basis of rents for the second peace.

It will have been noticed that we qualified the statement that the 1914 rents were free from the war profiteering element. This was not necessarily true a few years later. Provision was made in the Acts amending the original restriction Act for increases in rents corresponding to structural improvements. No effective provision was made for the reduction of the permitted maximum in the converse case of deterioration. Yet the possibility of obtaining even the maximum permitted controlled rents for property deteriorating, absolutely and relatively, compared to modern standards, was dependent on the continued shortage of houses of particular types in particular places. In so far as such shortages were attributable to the Great War, there was, therefore, in the slavish devotion to individual rents of 1914 a loophole for a delayed type of profiteering.

It is clear that the rent control introduced as the result of an emergency had its ethical and popular justification only in the context of that emergency. The resulting system of rents a quarter of a century later could only very roughly be justified on those grounds. It can be argued quite convincingly that they were no longer seriously relevant, and it is difficult to see that there could be anything sacrosanct about the rents of individual houses. The price of something in 1914, a house or anything else, can be of little practical interest in 1939 or 1943. It is only if there were practical reasons for preferring the resulting scales of rents to any other scale that could be devised that there was any reason for keeping on the old system as late as 1939. To this point we will return. We must look first at the other groups of rents which we came across in earlier chapters, those of the new houses, for it was these that were bound up with the experiments in providing new houses.

The new houses can be divided into three main groups[1] for each of which the rents were based on different principles. Rents of the houses built by private enterprise for letting were determined by the ordinary market principles of supply and demand, with the exception of the small group provided by the public utility societies. They were market rents like the original rents of 1914. The rents of the new houses built by the local authorities introduced, as we saw, a diversity of principles. There was the large group of houses built during the Second Experiment for which the rents tended to approximate to the average costs of building less the subsidies. For this group neither ideas of fair rents nor genuine market principles had much importance in practice. Though the subsidies had been fixed with some idea of bringing their rents down to the levels of controlled rents, the actual controlled rents to which they were to be compared remained obscure to the end, and also the idea of a fair rent. Given the subsidy, it was the costs of original building, not of replacement, which were important. The costs of building as distinct from costs of replacement are normally irrelevant to economic market prices, so that an entirely new principle was introduced. It was based on the idea, it seems, that local authorities should not make losses greater than those laid down in the Acts, even if this meant freezing rents over a period of forty years or more while the houses were being amortised. The basis of these rents was as arbitrary in some ways as the basis of controlled rents.

Finally, there was the group of local authority houses for which rents were based on the principles introduced during the reaction from the idea of the general fixed subsidy in the early 'thirties. The main innovation was the introduction of various types of differential renting. Local authorities were entirely free to decide whether

---

[1] Excluding the relatively small group of houses built under the Addison Act.

they should have differential rent schemes, and on what principles
they should work out their schemes if they did. They were free to
introduce " means tests " and decide on the sort of tests. The result
was a very wide variety both of tests and rent scales. There was
thus a quite separate group of families whose rents were settled on
entirely different sets of principles to those of others.

A rent scale built up of these different elements could not be
expected to conform in practice to any principles, social, moral, or
economic. Each part reflected a different outlook on the problem
of how rents should be determined and how and why subsidies
should be provided. The problem had, in fact, been treated as a
series of isolated emergency problems. Each solution had been
produced in a hurry, more or less independently of what had gone
before. Before we are plunged into a new series of crises created by
the end of the present war, it would be well to try to separate out the
various underlying elements in the rent problem and the difficulties
they lead to.

II. The Ability to Pay Rents

In an earlier section of this book we have discussed with some care
the sort of gross rent which was too high for the mass working-class
market. The belief prevalent in the last ten years before the war
was that, except in special districts, a gross rent of 10/– was the
maximum that it was reasonable to expect a family dependent on
the earnings of an unskilled labourer to afford where there was
only one child. To meet the needs of families in still less favourable
financial conditions gross rents needed to be still lower. This belief
we saw received a good deal of support from the evidence of various
social surveys carried out during those years, and from attempts
made to calculate the lowest income per head compatible with health
and reasonable efficiency. Even during the four years, 1933/4 to
1936/7, when the cost of providing a local authority house was
lower than at any other time since the Great War, the gross rents
without subsidy remained in fact out of the reach of a great mass of
people who needed, or would have liked, local authority houses.

It was the persistence of this hiatus even during the period of low
building costs and interest that caused such bewilderment. It was
pointed out that housing subsidies used not to be necessary, and that
private enterprise in the good old days before the Great War was
quite capable of producing enough houses at least for most families.
It could be demonstrated that before the Great War the numbers
of houses on the whole increased as fast as the numbers of families

and, moreover, that the standard of working-class houses had improved gradually. This is all quite true. But in those days builders were free to vary the quality and size of working-class houses according to what they judged to be the demand, that is, according to the willingness and ability of people to pay for them. Since the Great War a different attitude has been taken, rightly or wrongly. A much higher minimum standard for new houses has been established, partly by law and partly by force of opinion.

Of course houses of a higher standard could still be built, but the new minimum was far above the old imposed by the building byelaws, and above that even of houses built for working-class families moderately well off. The quality of the houses could in consequence no longer be effectively adjusted downwards to the capacity of people to pay rents. This development would have caused no trouble, if there had been sufficient improvements in the efficiency of the building industry to counteract the greater costs of building houses conforming to the new standard instead of to the old. Technical progress was not adequate to achieve this, but the old proverb that " half a loaf is better than no bread " was placidly ignored.

III. The Problem of Local Rates

This was one element in the situation. There was another. Gross rent includes rent proper and rates. This for all practical purposes is the rent for houses which come under the compounding limit,[1] that is, ordinary working-class houses. For these houses the landlord is responsible for collecting the rates with the rent and handing the rates to the rating authority. Probably most families who pay their rates indirectly this way do not even know how much of the gross rent goes in rates. To them the gross rent is the sum they have to pay for living in a particular house. They do not worry about how much of it the landlord keeps and how much goes in rates. Rates, everyone knows, are a local tax levied on houses which are lived in, but it is not generally realised how important a part of the gross rents they form. The information collected by the Ministry of Labour, indicated that in 1914 rates accounted for approximately a quarter of the gross rents in urban areas.[2] Put round the other way, rates added about thirty-three per cent. to the cost of living in a house. This is a very important addition to any price or

---

[1] Houses with rateable values under £14 (£20 in the Metropolitan Police Area).

[2] This refers to working-class houses only. The relative importance of rates has probably increased since 1914, since the average level of rates increased by 71% between 1914 and 1937, while controlled rents increased only by 40%. See p. 209 below.

cost. It is obvious that if rates had not had to be paid a great part of the difficulty about the rents of houses built in the last ten years before the war would have disappeared. The economic rents for new local authority houses built in the most favourable years averaged between 7/9 and 8/8 without rates and without subsidy. If there had been no rates the economic rent would have been the same thing as the gross rent of these houses, which would have been, it will be realised, definitely below the 10/- generally accepted as the reasonable maximum gross rents.

Rates then, it seemed, might make a great difference to this question of whether new houses could be afforded, particularly as in many urban areas they were between three and four shillings a week and in some still higher on the houses built by local authorities.[1] The necessity for paying them altered the margin of income available for other things by an amount which might be expected to make a great deal of difference to the willingness, and reasonable ability, of families in the lower income groups to afford new houses. For instance, a family of man, wife and two children of school age with an income of 50/- would have had no margin at all over the requirements of Rowntree's *Human Needs* standard if they paid an economic rent of 6/6 and 3/- rates.[2] If there had been no rate payment, then there would have been a small though useful sum in hand each week for emergencies or for special items of expenditure, and to provide the much-needed relief from the counting of half-pence necessary to achieve the standard of nutrition included in the *Human Needs* standard. The importance of the rate burden can be illustrated by the various scales of allowances for children. The Unemployment Insurance Benefit scale provided 3/- a week for each child, for example, and Rowntree estimated that the first child cost 6/2 a week to keep, the second 3/1, and the third 2/5. The amount of rates due each week might well be regarded as equivalent to the cost of the second child in a family. Regarded in connection with housing subsidies the rates assume a special significance. They were for a local authority house frequently just about equal to the housing subsidy provided by the Wheatley Act after 1927, or just under the subsidy available under slum clearance schemes up to 1935 for a family of four rehoused in an ordinary local authority house. There is no possible doubt that the rate burden, though it varied from place to

---

[1] See p. 96 above. In Manchester the rates on ordinary local authority houses were 4/- a week. Manchester rates were, however, unusually high, and they may be estimated at between 3/- to 4/- for other towns. See *The Rebuilding of Manchester* op. cit. p. 168 and *Rent Rebates*, op. cit. pp. 17 *et seq.*

[2] See pp. 96–99 above.

place, was a very important element in making decent houses too expensive for a very large number of families.

It may be suggested that though these facts are impressive and show that rates were a heavy burden on families with small incomes, they do not show that rates had anything in particular to do with the difficulty of bringing rents, including rates of new houses, within the reach of such families in recent years. Rates after all existed long before the Great War and were levied on all occupied houses. To understand the problem we must go a little more deeply into the matter. The average level of rates increased from 6/8¾ in the pound in 1914 to 11/6 in the pound in 1937. This was an increase of 71 per cent., but the increase in the cost of living index number over the same period was only 54 per cent. Rates, then, had increased more than in proportion to the general rise in the cost of living since before the Great War,[1] thus helping to discourage or to make more difficult the purchase of housing accommodation compared to other necessities and conveniences. This, of course, was true whether people were trying to get old or new houses.

The effect on the relative cost of new houses for the poorer families was, however, particularly marked. As rates are levied at a fixed amount in the pound of the rateable value of each house, the total rate payment due from any tenant is proportionate to the rateable value of the house. In other words, it is approximately proportionate to rent. Whether a family with a small income pays as much in rates as a family with a larger income depends, therefore, on whether it is able to get a cheaper house to live in. Even before the Great War it was never in practice possible for families to vary their rent liabilities downwards in proportion to their incomes, and expenditure on rent was apt to absorb, just as the expenditure on other necessities, a higher proportion of the small incomes than of the larger incomes. The burden of rates tended, therefore, to use up a larger proportion of the incomes of the poor than of the rather less poor, and so on up the scale of income. The shortage of houses after the Great War, of course, increased the difficulty of adapting rent and therefore rate payments to incomes, because the range of choice of houses becoming vacant was more limited than usual. The establishment of the new high minimum standard for new houses aggravated the situation, for it cut off almost completely the possibility of adapting rent to income as far as new houses were concerned,[2] as the quality

[1] The actual increase in the rates payable on individual houses depended, of course, on whether their rateable value had altered.

[2] If rents were varied by variations in subsidy this, of course, affected the cost of rent proper; it did not, however, necessarily affect the amount of rates levied.

of new houses could not be adjusted at all to make their economic
rents fall with the incomes of those needing them. In consequence
there was no serious possibility of making the burden of rates vary
with incomes as far as the tenants of new houses were concerned.
Moving from an old relatively cheap house to a new local authority
house meant increasing not only rent payments in the absence of a
specially adjusted subsidy, but rate payments as well, irrespective
of incomes. The rate burden tended, therefore, to be even heavier
in proportion to income than before.

These developments can be described in rather more technical
language which it will be convenient to use. Rates were probably
once in effect a tax roughly proportionate to income. This meant
that they would tend to be *regressive*; that is, they would weigh
more heavily on small incomes than on large for, to take, say a third
of a small income away involves a bigger cut in necessities, or conveniences, than if a third is taken away from a larger income. Before
the war the regressiveness was intensified because in practice the
proportion of income absorbed by rent and, therefore, by rates was
greatest for families with small incomes. Since the war the lack of
freedom of choice of houses has aggravated the element of regressiveness; the shortage of houses has meant that it has been a matter of
luck whether a family looking for an old house has been able to find
one with a rent, and, therefore, with rate payments appropriate to
their means. In the case of new houses the fixity of standard, by
eliminating the possibility of effective choice still more, has made
rates especially regressive in the case of families trying to obtain new
houses.

A tax as heavy and regressive as rates may have some practical
justification for its continued existence; but it can be argued that even
before the Great War it was a hindrance to more rapid improvements
in the prevailing housing standards. Since then the level of rates
have increased disproportionately to the cost of living, and their
regressiveness has increased, particularly in the case of new houses.
The rate burden must be reckoned as an important factor in keeping
gross rents of new houses out of the reach of the less well-to-do
working-class families, even if only by a small margin. It can well be
argued that if improvements in the standard for new houses are
enforced, and if it is considered that the new standard should be
within the reach of the majority of working-class families, it is
ridiculous to retain a tax which has always been regressive and dis-
couraging to high standards of housing. In fact it has been allowed
to increase not merely absolutely but also relatively to other costs

of living, and to become particularly regressive in the case of families trying to live in the houses; this simply aggravates the paradox. Whether or not rates in their present form should be retained on practical grounds of convenience or not, or how they should be adjusted, is a problem of taxation. As long, however, as they remain at levels bound to reduce the ability of people to pay the gross rents of new houses, subsidies may be necessary to counteract them. Such subsidies are merely indirect subsidies to the social and public services financed out of rates; they are not subsidies for housing. Rates are not part of the cost of providing houses any more than the excise duty on whisky is part of the cost of providing whisky. In fact, the excise on whisky is levied partly to raise revenue to pay the costs of state services, partly because it is considered a good thing to restrict the consumption of whisky. Rates are levied in order to serve the same purpose locally by providing revenue to pay for local services; they also naturally act as a deterrent to the consumption of house-room both in quality and quantity. Since it has been a general object of public policy for some years to increase consumption of house-room in quality and quantity, the system of financing local expenditure on social services by means of rates is inconsistent with this policy.

We have got some way with disentangling the rent question. We have seen that the decision to raise the minimum standard of new buiding, in the absence of improvements in the efficiency of the building industry adequate to counteract the greater cost, introduced a new problem of the relation of economic rents to working-class incomes. We have also seen, however, that the rent question was in fact partly a taxation question, for it was mixed up with the problems of the level of local rates and their regressiveness. If the rate system is not altered, then the question of counteracting its effects on housing matters needs separate consideration. It is clear that the rent problem is the problem of economic rents in relation to capacity to pay them excluding rates.

IV. SPECIAL CIRCUMSTANCES AFFECTING THE ABILITY TO PAY RENT

The next step is to distinguish any special circumstances affecting the ability to pay economic rents for new houses. It is obvious that specially low incomes in relation to family needs came into this category. Social surveys since the Great War have made it clear that the problem occurs in two types of cases. There are the families with normal incomes but with exceptionally high requirements because they contain children below earning age. The difficulties

in maintaing even a minimum modern standard of life that frequently arises in these circumstances are, it has been found, exceptional both as a phase in the life history of individual families and in
comparison with the majority of families with similar incomes but
which have smaller liabilities.[1] Rowntree has described these alter-
nations between poverty and prosperity as the " poverty cycle."

The second main group of families unlikely to be able to afford
modern standards are those whose incomes are exceptionally small.
This group consists of families in which the main earner is unemployed, or for some reason or other unable to earn a full adult
male wage. This is the group containing the unemployed, those
temporarily or permanently unable to work owing to sickness or
accident, those unable to earn a full male adult wage even when
in work owing to physical or mental incapacity, and finally those
families in which the main earner is a woman. These groups are
dependent for all or part of their incomes on state-organised systems
for providing, or supplementing, income through the various social
insurances, and their extensions, and in the last resort, the Poor
Law. It is on the adequacy of these forms of state provision for
maintaining a modern minimum standard of living, including a
modern standard of housing as well as of nutrition, that the ability
to pay an economic rent depends. Normally these incomes have been
lower than those of unskilled labourers in relation to needs; thus
families dependent on them are apt to fall below the *Human Needs*
standard, and even below lower subsistence standards. The ability
or inability of these groups to afford the economic rent for a new
house has depended therefore in the past on the decision of Parliament, or local authorities, as to the size of their incomes.

Whether all these groups of families can or cannot afford new
houses depends on decisions about the responsibility of the state for
providing a remedy for the lack of elasticity of earned incomes with
the needs of growing families, and for providing incomes compatible
with modern ideas about minimum standards of living in general
for those dependent on the state for whole, or part, of their
incomes. The provision of course can be made either in cash or in
kind; food for children can be provided by free meals at school,
milk schemes, etc., which increase the real income of a family in
relation to the number of children; modern houses can be brought
within the reach of any family by means of rent rebates. The merits
of the two methods do not concern us here; the point of importance
is that, however they are organised, subsidies are given in aid of

[1] See p. 98 above.

incomes defective for some defined cause. Without such subsidies there may always be considerable groups of families unable to afford a new house, or adequate nutrition, although the economic cost of neither is beyond the reach of the majority of families in the country for the greater part of the life of healthy adults.

V. Local Variations in the Cost of Providing Houses

The existence of especially low incomes in relation to needs is only one of the types of special circumstances affecting the ability to pay economic rents. The other is of a different character. The cost of providing houses is particularly high in some places, low in others, so that the economic rents for new houses are not uniform either all over the country or even in different parts of the same district. The most generally recognised cause is the variation in the cost between the central and suburban districts of large towns, and the differences in the whole scale of land values between different towns. These variations automatically cause variations in the total cost of houses.

The use of expensive land can only be lessened by building blocks of flats on the expensive land or building on the cheaper land of the suburbs. Both lead to some saving of cost, but this is partially counteracted by other factors. Flats in practice are more expensive to build than ordinary houses,[1] while ordinary houses built in the suburbs involve additional expenditure on transport. The latter, though not normally reckoned as part of the cost of a house, is in fact a part of the cost of living in a particular house. From the point of view of the community at large, it is part of the cost of providing houses in congested districts just as much as the price of land.

Another factor affecting the cost of houses is the difference in the suitability of land for building; some land is easy to build on, other land is difficult—it may be on too steep a slope or it may be waterlogged. These are all cost factors connected with land, but there are others, connected with building materials. In some districts adequate and cheap supplies of building materials and labour are near at hand. In others, they may have to be brought from a distance involving an additional cost of transport.

To some extent the differences in building costs and in land values have become imbedded in the income structure of the country; thus wage rates tend to be higher in the large towns, particularly of course in London, than in the small ones, and in towns than in the country. These differences do not appear, however, to be reliable

[1] See pp. 165-166 above.

enough, or large enough, to bridge the whole gap between the difference in costs for houses or flats corresponding to the modern standard. Thus economic rents tend to vary more than incomes. Subsidies intended to meet these difficulties are obviously housing subsidies in any ordinary sense, since the difficulties are due to the special difficulties of actually providing houses.

VI. THE QUESTION OF GENERAL SUBSIDIES AND MINIMUM STANDARDS.

The rent question is complicated, as we have just seen, by a series of problems more or less loosely connected with the basic question of the relation of economic rent of new houses to the normal ability of families to pay. It is possible to argue that since the fall in the rate of interest became effective in 1933 there has been no general problem. The pressure of the re-armament programme on building resources imposed on the top of ordinary peace-time demands, it is true, drove up building costs and with them economic rents to an uncomfortable degree after 1937. This increase might, however, be regarded as abnormal, the prelude to war. If it had not been for the war and the rumours of war, no general problem at all would have emerged.[1] There was no serious reason to expect unfavourable developments in the cost of providing houses in a world at peace. There is obviously a great deal in this argument. Experts had freely forecast a long period of low-interest rates, and building costs were quite likely to fall for technical improvements were long overdue.

The whole argument rests, however, on the assumption that unskilled labourers and other groups with similar incomes could and would afford rents of 8/– *if* steps were taken to deal with rates and smooth out the poverty cycle. This is not intrinsically unreasonable, and those without an excessively pessimistic outlook will accept the thesis that, provided the complicating factors we have singled out were dealt with, the modern minimum standard did not inevitably involve a general housing subsidy. But it must be admitted that this conclusion is reached without much margin to spare for any other contingencies which might appear. It is not sufficiently firmly based to excuse us from considering some of the problems which arise if the minimum standard is so high that it cannot be generally realised without a subsidy.

Three alternative policies are possible. The standard can be

[1] The complications introduced into the rent question by changes in building costs and interest rates are describes in pp. 244 et. seq. below.

retained without a subsidy, it can be retained with an appropriate subsidy, or, finally, the standard can be abandoned and the problem of the subsidy entirely avoided. The consequences of the choice are far-reaching.

If the first alternative is adopted, new houses will, by hypothesis, be out of reach of a considerable group of families in perfectly normal financial circumstances. These will be penalised by the imposition of the standard. As they cannot afford the new houses they will be obliged to remain dependent on the supplies of old deteriorating houses. They are prevented from improving their condition by getting new houses rather better than the old ones but below the minimum standard for new houses. The state prevents them taking any step upwards at all because they cannot take a big enough one. It may be noticed in passing that if this policy is adopted state efforts to improve the adjustment of income to needs, or even to smooth out local differences in the costs of houses, are unlikely to be on a scale sufficient to bring new houses within the reach of the families affected by the special circumstances.

The choice of the first alternative is in effect a decision to refuse to sell a man half a loaf because he cannot afford a whole one. Such a decision ought not to be made light-heartedly. The question whether it would not be preferable to abandon the standard in favour of a lower one needs careful consideration. On grounds of general welfare it might so easily be better for everyone to have an opportunity of improving their housing conditions slightly, than for a fortunate few to improve theirs a great deal. In any case the acceptance of a lower standard would not necessarily prevent any families who could afford a much higher standard from achieving it. The more the matter is examined the less object there seems to be in setting a standard that can be reached only by the minority. Such a standard must be on the whole ineffective. Those who can afford it would afford it anyway;[1] those who cannot afford it are unaffected by it *in the sense that they have to continue to live in old houses which do not satisfy it.* It is only if there is serious reason for thinking that such a standard would, in the not distant future, come within the reach of the majority of families, that a case can be made for refusing to allow the country to be cluttered up with not quite so good houses.

We are forced to the conclusion that, except in special circumstances the establishment of a minimum standard for new houses by the state leads direct to acceptance of the responsibility for bringing it within everybody's reach, if it is not to do more harm than

[1] Unless difficulties of organising the supply of such houses occurs.

P

good. This is the case for the general housing subsidy. The community decides on a particular minimum standard of new houses out of reach of important sections of the community; that decision can only be useful if definite steps are taken to implement the new standard by making it generally accessible.

A decision to introduce a subsidy for new houses in general opens up the question of whether such a subsidy should be the same for all families, or not (on the assumption that the rate difficulty is resolved and the special cases are dealt with independently). The answer appears to depend entirely on practical convenience and this includes financial convenience. There appears to be no moral issue involved, and no general uniformity of practice as far as social services are concerned. Elementary education being free is financed entirely by subsidies; anyone, rich or poor, can send their children to an elementary school without paying fees. On the other hand the war-time National Milk scheme differentiates broadly between those who can afford to pay something, and those who can afford nothing. The case for a differential subsidy is, of course, that it is cheaper than a flat subsidy, for a flat subsidy has to be so large that every family can afford new houses, and in effect gets the maximum subsidy needed under a differential scheme. The importance of this consideration depends on whether the saving that could be achieved is worth the trouble and inconvenience of a differential scheme. It must be remembered that subsidies can always be partially recovered from people who do not need them by a suitably adjusted tax system. It is only when by force of circumstances the section of the community which pay taxes are separated from those who benefit from their expenditure, that this cannot be done.[1]

In any case the inconveniences and disadvantages of a general system of differentiation of a housing subsidy are formidable. Some sort of means test is inevitable, unless the people to benefit more from the differentiation of the subsidy can be separated from those who are to benefit less as clearly as the traditional sheep and goats. The greater the importance attached to degrees of differentiation of the subsidy, the greater the need and the greater the difficulty of distinguishing between one family and another; it is not so easy without the special training of a shepherd to distinguish one sheep from another as a sheep from a goat. Moreover, once the differential principle is adopted, there is no obvious limit to the degrees

[1] The extension of income tax to wages during the present war has blurred such division as existed in the past owing to the lack of flexibility of indirect taxation. Reform of the rating system would, of course, increase the flexibility of the tax structure as a whole, and in particular with regard to services provided by local authorities.

of fineness desirable. A rough and ready system not only is likely to be unfair as between individual families, but will fail in its purpose. It will either reduce the subsidy too rapidly and leave groups unable to afford new houses, or it will err in the opposite direction and fail in its purpose of saving money.

It appears extremely difficult to avoid these pitfalls without a comprehensive means test. Some sort of family means test seems inevitable, for it is natural that children more or less grown up and earning should contribute a share of the rent as long as they choose to live at home.[1] Indeed, the strongest argument in practice against a serious family means test as a basis for housing subsidies is the trend of popular opinion against the use of means tests in other connections. After the agitation and trouble over the application of the means test to claims for unemployment assistance in the ten years before this war, it seems to be seeking trouble gratuitously to introduce one at all generally for a housing subsidy.

VIII. The Importance of the Unsettled Questions of Rent

At the outbreak of this war there were two unsettled questions of principle connected with rent of great importance: First, whether the rent difficulties which arose from the existence of problems falling outside the field of housing policy proper, such as the difficulties caused by the "poverty cycle" and by the incidence of rates, were to be solved as part of the general social problems of the incidence of poverty and of taxation, or were to be left to be solved as well as possible by housing subsidies; second, how the choice between the alternatives of a general subsidy and a lowering of the minimum standard of new houses was to be decided.

As long as the extra-housing problems are in fact allowed to remain as part of the rent problem there can be no simple solution of the latter. The simple subsidies of the Second Experiment failed as we saw to provide one. They failed for various reasons. For the greater part of the period each local authority applied the subsidies on a uniform basis to each house and to each family. Used in this way even the unreduced Wheatley subsidy was not large enough to compensate for the specially small rent paying capacity of some families.

---

[1] The arguments that can be brought forward in support of some sort of family means test in the case of differential rent schemes provide a formidable obstacle in the way of basing the means test on assessments to income tax, since its extension to wages during this war. If differential subsidies for houses could be based on the incomes of man and wife alone, the size of their tax assessment could be used as a criterion for their need for a rent subsidy.

Probably by 1933 the economic rents for new houses had fallen sufficiently for the subsidy, used in this way, to overcome the difficulty at least in part; but of course it was just at this stage that the subsidy was abolished. The experience of the Third Experiment showed that differential rents did not provide a complete solution even at the relatively low level of costs prevailing. This was because the degree of differentiation possible varied from district to district, with variations in incomes and employment, *not* with the need for differentiation. A rather similar difficulty of lack of variation of subsidies had also, it will be remembered, emerged during the Second Experiment.

In short, the experience of the two experiments showed that the various elements determining the ability of families to pay gross rents lead to different relations between subsidised rents and capacity to pay in different districts. There were really two different problems which became merged: the problem of differences of capacity to pay between families within a single district on one hand, and the problem of differences in the general level, or average, capacity between areas on the other. It was because of the complications introduced by the latter that differential rent schemes drawn up within individual areas could not provide a complete solution. In consequence, neither the numbers of houses built, nor the numbers of persons or families rehoused, even with a special grading of subsidies varying with site values, etc., have in the past served as a reliable index of the amount of assistance needed by individual authorities.[1] In fact, it is fairly obvious that such indices were likely to work out the wrong way. The assistance needed is more likely to be indicated by the number of houses not built, or the numbers of persons not rehoused, than by the success realised by authorities. Fixed subsidies based on the conventional indices would only work if the average capacity to pay gross rents was in the same relation to gross rents in all areas. This was not so in the years between the Great War and the present war.

The original Addison subsidy of 1919 has so far been the only subsidy which has attempted to provide reasonable elasticity between areas. In the general denunciations of it this important feature has been constantly overlooked. It was undoubtedly both rather rough and ready and rather dangerous, and it is highly desirable that the necessary elasticity should be realised in a way both more accurate

[1] Need for subsidy is used in the sense of the amount required to enable local authorities to build appropriate numbers of houses, and to let them at appropriately low rents, without providing larger subsidies out of the rates than those stipulated in the various Housing Acts.

and less open to abuse. Provided that the rent problem is broken up into its component parts, this should not be impossible. There is no difficulty in drawing up a scale of rent rebates to give income subsidies in kind according to the number of children, or according to dependence on particular types of income known to be inadequate to maintain something like modern minimum standards. There seems to be no good reason why subsidies for these purposes should not be financed out of national funds rather than local. It has become more or less recognised that family allowances, when introduced, should be provided on a national basis, while responsibility for supporting the unemployed, for instance, has long been accepted as a national rather than a local matter. Provision of these subsidies out of central funds would, of course, give just that element of elasticity between areas that has been absent in the past. It was the two problems of unemployment and numbers of children, which led to differences in the capacity to pay rents between areas and to differences between families within areas.

The rate problem is rather more difficult. As long as the general principles determining the distribution of expenditure between the taxpayers in general and the ratepayers remain unchanged, it would be inconsistent to finance rate rebates out of central funds. The re-allocation of the local burden of rates would, it appears, be most appropriately achieved out of local funds. Nor would this be impossibly difficult. A local housing subsidy financed out of rates might be introduced and paid into a local rate rebate fund (this might also be used for dealing with cases of exceptional hardship). The use of the fund could be made dependent either on some automatic scale such as numbers of children, or on appeals from tenants. The question of which method should be used seems to be one which should be settled nationally.

Re-arrangement of the subsidies on these lines might be expected to remove some of the main difficulties arising from causes outside the field of housing policy proper. They would also have the advantage that subsidies to rents which may be needed to counteract these external factors would naturally be separated from those subsidies which are housing subsidies in the strict sense (that is subsidies required to reduce the cost of providing houses of the modern standard for families in normal circumstances).

These latter raise less difficult questions. The variation of subsidy with variations in the local costs of providing houses has already been accepted in principle in the case of site values. Extension to other cases of variations in local costs is only a matter, therefore, of need and practical convenience. Similarly, the issue of whether there is to be a general subsidy, if needed to make a particular standard of housing possible, or whether a lower standard is to be adopted is a clear cut housing problem. This does not in any way detract from its importance, or from the necessity of general appreciation of the issues at stake. Decision, however, does not raise all sorts of other questions which have nothing directly to do with housing.

The scheme of housing subsidies suggested raise some difficult problems of equity. Subsidies to income in kind, in the form of rent rebates, would automatically be limited to families living in modern houses, so would rate rebates. These families would, therefore, get preferential treatment. This, of course, would be no more inequitable than the results of housing subsidies have been in the past, but the inequity would perhaps be more obvious. If, on the other hand, the need for subsidies to family incomes in certain cases, or the reform of the rating system, were treated as part of the general social questions of poverty and taxation instead of as special aspects of the housing problem, the question of equity would not arise. The subsidies would be given irrespective of whether particular families were living in modern houses or not. The equity of a general subsidy depends on rather different grounds. In broad terms it may be said to depend on whether all families have approximately equal chances of benefiting from it by getting a modern house. This condition would clearly be more likely to be fulfilled if the extra-housing elements were treated satisfactorily separately from housing subsidies proper.

VIII. The Rent Question and the Scope of Housing Policy

It will be clear to everyone that there is a close connection between the solution of the complex of rent questions and the type of housing policy which is practicable. A scheme for building houses for working-class families in general came to grief in the past, as we have seen, partly because the rent question was not dealt with; for any such scheme must provide houses for families whose financial circumstances differ. The same necessity would arise in the case of a scheme for replacing old houses in general such as that discussed in the last chapter. A settlement of the main issues of rent policy must therefore be regarded as an essential preliminary to the adoption of any such policy. A sanitary policy, however, cuts right across these questions. It is concerned primarily with solving the rent question for a limited group of families whose financial circumstances probably vary less than those of families drawn from a wider field. The success or failure of a sanitary policy does not, therefore, depend to the same extent on a more or less scientific treatment of rent questions, provided some degree of variation in the subsidy between areas seriously dissimilar can be obtained.

These questions of rent have been discussed entirely in connection with new houses. It would clearly be desirable, however, that all housing subsidies should be made available on approximately the same principles, and that as far as rents are concerned, the local authority houses already built should be interchangeable with houses built in the future. This principle has already been adopted for the houses built between 1919 and 1939, with the pooling of all receipts, including subsidies, and all expenses. The rules on which the subsidies already pooled would be distributed in the future would have to be assimilated to the new policy. It would be necessary to calculate the expected cost of doing this, and of any other differential subsidies, before it would be possible to find out whether the amount left was sufficient to finance the general subsidy needed for the houses built at higher levels of costs. Some pools would be too large and others too small, and the position would vary from year to year with changes in unemployment, for instance. The difficulty of pools being too small would naturally be met by increased payments from the Treasury. The reverse case might be dealt with in the first instance through equalisation funds ; if the surplus was persistent, however, it might be used as under the present schemes partly to reduce the rate contribution, and partly to finance the subsidy required for new houses.

Rationalisation of the rest of the rent system and particularly of the controlled rents of old houses, presents far more difficulties and it would seem has fewer advantages. It may be doubted whether any attempt would be worth while. If a general building policy were again adopted with an appropriate subsidy and rent system, the need for the control of rents of old houses would gradually disappear as sufficient new houses at rents within the reach of most, if not all, families would mean that there would be sufficient alternative accommodation to prevent increases in the rents of old houses taking place when they were de-controlled. With a continuation of a sanitary policy, on the other hand, sufficient increases in the supply of houses at rents competing with those of old houses could not be expected, and straight de-control would probably be undesirable, or at least politically impossible. Nor, would there be much point in attempting a reform of the rent system as a whole, for there would be no body of principles on which to base the reform, and the result might be as chaotic as the present system.

The importance of solving the tangle of rent problems depends mainly on the type of housing policy adopted in the future, just as the practicability of any ambitious policy depends on the rationalisation of the principles by which rents for new houses are determined.

Chapter XII

THE WAR AND THE UNSETTLED QUESTIONS

I. THE NEW EMERGENCY

LOOKING back at the record of housing policy the Great War looms up as a gigantic watershed between nineteenth and twentieth century ideas. It is easy, however, to exaggerate the changes. A new housing problem was introduced by the Great War together with the belief in subsidies as a remedy for most things. But most of the ideas which have influenced housing policy since 1919 were in circulation before that date. The policy of establishing a minimum standard for new houses was introduced in the nineteenth century with the building bye-laws as a means of enforcement. This policy has persisted up to the present day though methods of achieving it have varied from time to time. Similarly the theory underlying the Third Experiment was a direct descendant of the sanitary outlook of the nineteenth century. Even the origin of the modern idea that the state should take active responsibility for bringing about general improvements in working-class housing conditions had little to do with the Great War. It emerged in the Report of the Royal Commission on Housing in Scotland, which was set up in 1912 and finished its report in 1917. That Commission was far less concerned with the effects of the Great War than with the generally intolerable state of housing in Scotland. Its recommendations went further and were far clearer than any put forward since.

The real significance of the Great War in the development of housing policy springs from the fact that it focussed public attention on the housing question and precipitated public intervention to provide houses. One thing led to another and not unnaturally the Government was still taking some active part twenty years later at the outbreak of the present war. The present war has created a new emergency problem. In the last chapters an attempt was made to sort out the major issues of a long-term character existing before the new war complicated the situation, and we must now see what these new complications are.

The most painfully obvious effect of the present war has been the creation of a new shortage of houses. First, the supply of new houses dried up. Building by the local authorities was brought to a standstill at the very beginning of the war, private building in 1940. Second, the blitz has destroyed large numbers of houses entirely, damaged others beyond repair and made still more uninhabitable unless repaired to a greater or less extent. In the meantime the arrears of ordinary repairs have mounted up. In the last war at least though arrears of building and repairs accumulated, the actual number of houses did not decrease; in fact, it increased, though less rapidly than the number of potential families.

There is certainly a new shortage of houses which is increasing with the duration of the war, but there is a tendency to exaggerate it. People are apt to think in terms of the present war-time difficulties. In some districts it is not only impossible to get houses, but practically impossible to get lodgings. It is natural for families faced by these difficulties to assume that they exist everywhere and will continue after the end of the war until millions of new houses are built. Since the Minister of Health blandly stated that three or four million houses will be needed after the war, the anxiety about the shortage has naturally been reinforced. It is often forgotten, however, that the war itself has created particular war-time shortages, and special demands for accommodation of all sorts which will disappear when it is over. There have been phenomenal shifts of population, irrespective of where the houses were available. The effect of the evacuation of individuals, government offices and private firms, was to pour vast numbers of people out of their usual homes into towns and villages believed to be outside the danger zones. Families were split up into two and even more parts and each might need separate accommodation in different places, and naturally these temporary families did not fit into rooms and houses left vacant by the general shuffle. As the war went on various counter currents set in. The south-east coast became dangerous and more people shifted round again. To avoid the blitz, factories were built in places where there were no houses. Just to add to the confusion, all sorts of new government and social and other organisations of a war-time character have sprung up overflowing existing possible office accommodation. Foreign governments and armies have come in, all needing more offices and more accommodation. Blocks of flats and houses have been commandeered as offices and billets.

In short, there is just the confusion that was to be expected as the whole nature of the demand for accommodation was revolutionised by the war, and the best had to be made of peace-time accommodation depleted by the blitz. Even if the blitz had not destroyed a single house or building there would have been some degree of chaos. Finally, the disappearance of domestic servants and the return of numbers of married women to work has concentrated middle-class demand on small modern houses and flats. In London the demand is all for new and preferably small flats which are easy to run. There were in 1943 still numbers of old-fashioned flats and houses empty which were perfectly usuable until 1939, but have become hideously inconvenient since. It is obvious that a great many of these troubles will sort themselves out automatically after the war. Families will get together again and the demand for lodgings will dwindle; the various government organisations will contract and give up their hotels and blocks of flats. Accommodation in the evacuated and restricted areas will be usable again. We shall be left with the problems of the damage done by the blitz, and the building arrears in general complicated by uncertainty as to where industry and population will try to settle down.

According to expert estimates, if there had been no war the number of families would have increased by about 425,000 in the five years, 1940 to 1944. Some of this increase may have been postponed temporarily for the duration of the war, but it must be expected to materialise rapidly at the end of the war and must be allowed for. Since the supply of privately built houses continued to increase in 1940, it is probably not far wrong to take 275,000 as an approximate figure for the growth of an excess of families over the supply of new houses attributable to the lack of building during the first five years of war.[1] The accumulated requirements for new houses by the end of the fifth year of war will therefore probably be considerably less than one year's output of houses of all sorts just before the war. Of course the war is still continuing, and so is the increase in the number of families: the houses needed for each year's addition to the number of families will increase the accumulation of requirements as long as the war lasts. Fortunately, since 1943 a sudden drop in the annual increase of families to about 55,000 a year is probable, so that about one-seventh of a year's pre-war output would be sufficient to balance each year's increase. Even if the war goes on the shortage will accumulate at a decreasing rate.

This expected decline in the annual additions to the numbers of families will be very important even if the war ends in 1945, for it

[1] See *Housing Before the War and After*, by Dr. M. J. Elsas. Chap. IV. There are no data on which to base estimates either of a possible increase in families due to a permanent inflow of foreign families, or of the effects of war casualties and epidemics on the number of families.

means that current needs for additional houses will be relatively small during the peace. It will be remembered that the continued high current requirements after the Great War added considerately to the difficulties of making up the war shortage : to meet it an expansion of the building industry beyond its 1914 capacity would have been needed even if there had been no Great War. When this war started on the other hand the capacity of the house building industry was far greater than the current needs for additional houses. A recovery of the house building industry to about half its 1939 capacity would be sufficient to deal in four years with the needs for additional houses, accumulated and current, up to 1950, excluding those needed to replace houses destroyed by air-raids, with some margin for arrears of repairs.

It must not be forgotten that, at the outbreak of this war, at least 225 thousand houses were needed to complete the slum clearance schemes outstanding, quite apart from houses which might be needed for replacement of those which might deteriorate into slums after 1939. Probably about 275 thousand were also needed to complete the decrowding schemes. Thus about half a million houses will be needed at the end of the war, before the interruption to these schemes caused by it is made good. The number of new houses needed to replace those totally destroyed, or irreparably damaged, by air-raids up to November 1944 was in comparison quite surprisingly small. According to the Minister of Home Security only 190 thousand houses had been destroyed or damaged beyond repair.[1] It will be observed that this number was considerably smaller than the number of houses which would have been demolished between 1939 and 1944 if the slum clearance schemes had been completed. To summarise : before the worst effects of the war on the housing position are counteracted 275 thousand houses will be needed to offset the increase in the number of families between 1939 and 1944; 500 thousand to complete slum clearance and de-crowding schemes, and 190 thousand to replace houses destroyed by air-raids up to November, 1944. The grand total of new houses needed is therefore 965 thousand, excluding any required to balance increases in the number of families after 1944. Since some of the houses destroyed by the raids were already included in the slum clearance schemes there is some duplication adding all these requirements together; against this, however, it is quite likely that

---

[1] Statement made in the House of Commons, February 8th, 1945. It is now clear that the total destruction of houses by flying bombs has been on a relatively small scale and the major problem created by the attacks is that of repairs. See note below.

rather more houses will be found to be in the end not worth repairing. In the present state of uncertainty it will be as well to accept the total without modification for these reasons.[1] The exact figure of requirements is perhaps less important than its composition. Less than a third of the houses needed immediately are for additional families, the rest are needed for some type of replacement or for decrowding.

The war then has not altered the fundamental housing problem —it has brought it into the foreground and focussed public attention on some of its aspects. The replacement problem new version overlaps both the old sanitary schemes and any general replacement plan. The blitz has destroyed some of the houses which were scheduled for destruction under the sanitary policy, and a further number of houses which would only have disappeared as part of a general replacement scheme: in addition, it has destroyed houses which would have remained under any policy. The effects of the blitz have been haphazard in other ways, for damage is not distributed evenly about the country. In some areas it has been negligible, in others it has been so extensive that complete replacement is inevitable.

It is most important, however, that this resemblance should not be forgotten, for it means that a far higher proportion of the new houses urgently needed are for working-class families than was the case after the Great War. Half a million working-class houses are needed to complete the slum clearance and decrowding schemes, and since private building continued for longer after the outbreak of this war than local authority building, it is probable that an abnormally high proportion of the houses for balancing the increase in families are needed for working-class families. What proportion of the blitzed houses are working-class appears to be one of the jealously guarded secrets of the Ministry of Health. Common sense suggests, however, that as so many of the well-known heavy raids have been concentrated on industrial areas, a dispropor-

[1] This is the picture as far as new houses are concerned with which we are concerned primarily in a discussion of housing policy. It does not give a complete picture with regard to the immediate pressure on the resources of the house building industry. Normal repairs to houses have been postponed during the war and arrears have thus accumulated of varying degrees of urgency. In addition there is the repair problem created by the air raids. By the beginning of 1944 about two and three-quarter million houses had received first-aid repairs, and nearly half of these had received more extensive repairs. This does not mean that there are not arrears of repairs to damaged houses to be completed before the pre-war standards are regained. During 1944 the flying-bomb attacks have added immensely to the urgent and immediate repair problem; how much of this damage will be outstanding at the end of the war, and how much more will have accumulated, cannot at present be stated.

tionate number of working-class houses have been destroyed. Instead, therefore, of assuming as in the past that working-class needs amount to about two-thirds of the total, it would be safer to assume that it would be sensible to take four-fifths for each of the last two groups of requirements. We know by now, or we ought to, that it would be a mistake to let predominantly middle and lower middle-class instead of working-class houses be built. Such a policy would obviously be absurd in places, such as the East End of London, where in any case the middle-class group in the population is only a small minority. We have seen, anyway, in the accounts of the Second and Third Experiments how unsatisfactory such a policy is even when the need is for additional houses. It means that the families at the lower end of the rent-paying scale gets houses only when the whole of the shortages higher up are satisfied. Even then it depends on the extent to which the better-off families decide to migrate to new houses from their old ones, and before the outbreak of war the tide of the migration appeared to be slacking.

There is no doubt that in the main working-class houses must be built rather than middle-class ones; what is uncertain is whether a greater or smaller proportion of working-class families will be able to afford to buy their own houses in the future than before. Families who have been paying income tax will have nest eggs due to them from the Treasury, and there has also been an accumulation of savings from the higher earnings of the war period; both might be used for house purchase. It should, perhaps, be pointed out that a general rush to realise these savings in order to buy houses may be very embarrassing to the Treasury. The strength of such a movement may well depend on the sense of security created, or not created, by reconstruction policy in other fields. In any case there are so many uncertainties surrounding this matter that it is probably unprofitable to speculate about it, and it would be rash to base housing policy on any assumption that the proportion of houses needed for letting will be smaller in the future than in the past.

The basic problem of housing policy in the future as in the past is the provision of working-class houses to let at rents which can be afforded by the great majority. The Government has so far given little indication of whether the satisfaction of requirements for new houses due to the war will be treated as an interlude to be followed by a return to the old sanitary policy or not. So far all that has been said is that it would be nice to have three or four million new houses. This is merely a platitude and has no significance until supported by a statement of who is going to build new houses and where, and on what terms they are going to be made available, and to whom.[1] In view of the general uncertainty surrounding the whole question, it will be as well to see how far the obvious urgent need immediately after the war for nearly a million houses, of which about ninety per cent. must be for working-class families, affects either of the two main alternative types of housing policy existing before the war.

II. THE WAR AND THE PRE-WAR QUESTIONS

The character and in some places the size of the problem will make it impossible to deal with the rent and subsidy question on the sort of basis adopted for the old sanitary policy. We saw in the last chapter that a fixed subsidy per new house, or per person re-housed, even with some flexibility in respect of site values, could not work out satisfactorily unless all the factors affecting both the gross rents of new houses and rent-paying capacity averaged out in much the same way in each part of the country. If this condition is not satisfied the subsidy turns out to be unnecessarily large in some districts or too small in other districts. The experience of the Second Experiment showed that the general condition for success was not satisfied, and that in consequence in some areas building came to an untimely end while in others never reached an adequate volume. Even though the system had a better chance of success in connection with the slum clearance and decrowding scheme of the Third Experiment, it was by no means entirely satisfactory. The supposition that rent-paying capacity of families living in slums, or of over-crowded families, would average out in the same sort of way wherever the slum and overcrowding occurred, turned out to be only partially justified in practice. It was open to question, too, whether the various subsidies of the Third Experiment solved the complex difficulties of transport and other costs of providing houses.

The immediate post-war problem of providing working-class houses for the population in general, amid all the uncertainties about costs, incomes and employment, is not likely to respond any more satisfactorily to treatment by a simple fixed subsidy. The intrusion of the replacement problem makes the prospect of success along these lines even less hopeful. The blitz has destroyed working-class houses of every kind so that replacement policy must cater for just as wide a range of incomes, ability to pay rent and costs of pro-viding houses as in the case of the provision of additional houses.

[1] Although since this was written the Government has announced its emergency housing policy, the obscurity about this point remains.

All these elements of the problem may vary from place to place. Nor is there any reason to assume without proof, either that economic prosperity will be the same in all districts or, that it will differ in the way it did during the peace. The nature of the post-war problem and the indeterminateness of economic prospects makes the prior need a subsidy system which will be highly flexible and sensitive to the needs of different areas.

It is because of the size and complexity of the immediate problem that the recommendations of the Uthwatt Committee are of particular importance. Though their report is of most obvious interest in connection with town planning problems, there are two groups of recommendations which are of direct importance in relation to housing. There are the measures intended to co-ordinate and strengthen the machinery for the general planning of towns and of larger areas which form single economic units. In addition there are the measures intended to facilitate the acquisition of land for building and for re-building on more favourable terms than hitherto.[1] If the first group of recommendations are adopted, planning machinery on a national basis would be set up with powers to deal, not only with houses and other buildings, but also with public services. This machinery might well be adapted to provide the organisation for the control of the location of industry and of new towns if it is decided to build them. It would also provide a means for settling the vexed questions of changes in boundaries of local authority areas, and of responsibility for the provision of public services if extra-territorial building by local authorities continues. Moreover, once the idea of a national supra-local authority and regional planning is accepted, there would be more hope of the housing requirements for regions as a whole being considered and taken into account.

The importance of the second group of recommendations is so obvious that there is no need for enlarging on them here. It is sufficient to say that they provide for the first time a reasonable basis for the acquisition of land, both for the purposes of carrying out a regional plan and for rebuilding existing built-up areas with less delay, obstruction and expense than is at present involved.

The number of working-class houses which will be needed to solve the emergency problem created by this war is nearly as great as the total built by the local authorities in the whole fifteen years

---

[1] *Uthwatt Report*, op. cit. Chaps. I and X and Chaps. IV (1)–(3), V and VI. These paragraphs were written before the introduction of the Town and Country Planning Bill in 1944.

of the first two experiments, between 1919 and 1939. Though these requirements are not much larger than those which were required by pre-war policy, their accumulation means that they must be provided far more quickly; this may cause the sort of difficulties over finance that arose during the old experiments. If post-war plans are to avoid frustration by sudden concentrations of economy campaigns on housing subsidies, the costs which are properly housing costs should be disentangled from those which are not. For the sake of financial clarity income subsidies in kind will need to be separated from housing subsidies proper, and the extent to which the subsidy or subsidies are in fact absorbed in off-setting rates must be kept clear.

Not less important is the question of the standard to be adopted for new houses. There is at present a widespread popular belief that it is only necessary to say that new houses should be much superior to those built before the war to make it possible for them to be so. All sorts of inquiries made both by associations and individuals are leading to demands for things which before the war were regarded as luxuries. Tiled bathrooms, permanent hot water, refrigerators, two lavatories, two sitting-rooms, and all sorts of other desirable things are being held out as necessities without which life will be intolerable. The Ministry of Agriculture, with supreme irresponsibility, has helped to set the pace by erecting, or rather trying with limited success to get erected, cottages for agricultural workers of a far higher standard than pre-war local authority houses. Now bigger and better equipped houses are undoubtedly desirable and would make the housewife's life far easier. The question, however, has not yet been asked as to whether ordinary families will be able to afford such palaces without a subsidy even when building costs have settled down to a new peace-time normal. The question of whether such further improvements in the minimum standard are worth subsidising, if they would require a subsidy to bring the houses within the reach of ordinary families, has yet to be considered by the enthusiasts. This is a heavily taxed community and money is needed urgently for improvements in a number of most important social services. It has not been made clear whether the realisation of the housing ideals which have become so popular recently would not, inevitably, be at the expense of some more essential improvement in, say, the maternity services, or in education. These improvements in housing standards suggested by all this propaganda may well lead to disaster, if they can only be realised with the aid of a permanent general subsidy and are included in a new minimum

Q

standard. Sooner or later the people who pay the rates and taxes but do not live in new houses will revolt, or the protagonists for the development of other social services will try to raid the housing subsidy. The subsidy would then be cut or reduced to levels which would keep the new standard houses within the reach only of the better-off working-class families. The same weary muddle of the inter-war years would repeat itself, and only a small minority of families would benefit from the new standards and the taxpayers' money. The rest would go without and be obliged to continue to live in the old houses, including the old squalid nineteenth century houses, getting older every year. It is essential that a decison should be reached on the question of changing the minimum standard for new houses only on the basis of a full realisation of the issues involved.

It will be noticed that the questions of principle connected with rent and subsidy policy which need to be decided are, to all intents and purposes, the same as those which would need to be decided if a general policy for replacing sub-standard houses were adopted as a long-term programme.

The war has thus brought to a head most of the questions connected with rents and subsidies which the sanitary policy evaded. Any housing policy after the war, if it is to have any serious chance of success, must take them into account, irrespective of whether a complete replacement policy is the ultimate goal or not. The war has, however, brought forth a notable contribution to their solution. The Beveridge Report includes, among other things, a scheme for improving the incomes of those groups whose inability to pay rents has caused so much trouble in the past. An official document, even though not fully endorsed by the present government, has laid down the principles of social security on the basis that a modern minimum standard should be ensured for every family. It has, moreover, enunciated the doctrine of central instead of local responsibility for this standard.[1] If it is put into practice, income subsidies, either in cash or kind, will be eliminated from the tangle of pseudo-housing subsidies. The proposals for family allowances are intended to abolish the old " poverty cycle " caused by the temporary inflation of needs due to the presence of non-earning children without parallel increases of incomes. The new plan for raising the school age from fourteen to fifteen and ultimately to sixteen has increased the import-

[1] This chapter was already in the press before the Government's White Papers on Social Insurance (Cmd. 6550 and 6551) and on Employment Policy (Cmd. 6527) appeared.

ance of this, for children will remain in the non-earning category for longer than they used to. The proposals for extended social insurance in general cover certainly most, if not all, of the other specific factors lowering incomes of particular families in relation to needs. Acceptance of the sections of the Beveridge Report covering these matters would open up the opportunity of obtaining new houses to sections of the population hitherto debarred on financial grounds unless they made undue sacrifices in expenditure on other necessities. The medley of differential rent schemes could be done away with, but it must not be forgotten that the questions connected with rates, with differences in costs of providing houses, and the minimum standard to be adopted would still remain.

The rent question was not the only unsettled question connected with housing policy before the war. There were a number of others overlapping into other fields of social and economic policy. It was pointed out, for instance, in the first chapter of this part that the sanitary policy evaded, while the large scale replacement policy necessitated, the most careful consideration of the problems of government control of the location of industry. A replacement policy based on the creation of new towns would, it was concluded, require active intervention, and even a replacement policy based on suburban development would make it highly desirable. The war has affected the issue indirectly. It has altered for the duration the location of industry and of the population. Shifts and counter-shifts have taken place; the traditional attitude both of people and firms about possible places to live and work have been shaken up. Already some new industrial centres have developed and some industries have gone into areas which badly needed this type of reinforcement. As a whole industry and population are in a state of flux. It is an extraordinarily favourable opportunity for intro-ducing some form of control. Even the blitz has made a contribu-tion. Factories, offices and public buildings of all sorts have been destroyed. As they will ultimately have to be replaced, there is an opportunity for getting them rebuilt in the most suitable places instead of in the old ones, if appropriate stimulation is provided. The question is still unsettled; no hint of an official decision has yet been wrung from the Government.[1] Unless something is decided soon, the opportunity will be lost for good. Local authorities are already making plans and buying housing sites. A delayed decision to introduce some sort of control of location of industry may hold some of the house building programmes up. In the blitzed areas, the

[1] See p. 234 n. 1 above.

immediate instalment of rebuilding necessary is in some cases large enough to make an immediate decision essential.

There is no need to re-open the other general questions which were discussed in the chapter before last. The war has had little or no effect on the sociological problems. The Uthwatt Report has, it has been pointed out earlier, rather improved the prospects of the creation of regional planning machinery on an *effective* basis, but its recommendations did not cover by any means all the problems of local government which require dealing with. Nothing has in case been settled in this field, and the war itself has not really altered anything, except that the scale of rebuilding necessitated by the war has brought these questions into the ranks of those requiring settlement if trouble and confusion are to be avoided.[1]

III. Conclusions

The new complications and problems, created by the war, have forced to the forefront all those questions of principle which needed settling before any policy of large scale replacement of sub-standard houses could be carried out, if there had been no war. Before the war they could be evaded by the adoption of a sanitary policy, but this immunity from discussion of fundamental principles which was the special advantage of this type of policy, has been destroyed by the war and the blitz. It does not, of course, follow automatically from this conclusion that the full replacement policy is now inevitable. Indeed, it is obvious that the destruction of all sorts of buildings and the creation of arrears of general building work, together with the depletion of the resources of the building industry during the war, must delay fulfilment of such a scheme if it were adopted. If, however, the unsettled questions are solved in order to deal with immediate problems, at least the first and essential condition for a full replacement policy will be provided.[2]

Such a policy does, however, appear in a rather new light as the result of the war. It has come out of the realms of pure speculation and now appears as the logical development of the solution of the

[1] The Government's scheme for temporary houses was announced after this chapter had gone to press and it has not been possible to include a discusssion of the scheme. It is clear, however, that the scheme for temporary houses, provided the houses are really treated as temporary to be replaced gradually, offers a breathing space for further consideration of the major problems connected with housing policy. The scheme it is obvious has it own particular difficulties related to rents, subsidies, and costs, and it has only a limited applicability in congested areas in which blocks of flats are needed. (See on this latter point, p. 240 below.)

[2] See pp. 219, et seq. above.

immediate difficulties. War damage is not evenly distributed over the country or even over individual towns. There is no real reason why some areas should be excluded indefinitely from enjoying the benefits of general rebuilding and replacement of their old houses. It seems absurd to decide that these advantages should for ever be confined to the particular places where bombs have fallen.

The recent growth of some general degree of acceptance of the thesis that the Government should take responsibility for the maintenance of something approaching full employment is of special importance in connection with this issue of the scope of housing policy. It is obvious that in order to cope with the immediate post-war need for houses and buildings generally, the utmost efforts must be made to increase the capacity of the building industry at least up to its pre-war level, and to hasten the introduction of all possible technical improvements now generally lumped together under the magic heading " pre-fabrication." These requirements give a special importance to plans for keeping up the demand for building resources over a long period; otherwise numbers of skilled men will be introduced into the building industry in the interests of the current emergency for whom there will be little prospect of long-period employment. (We saw that before the war the capacity of the building industry had reached a size beyond that which seemed likely to be required in the long run with a sanitary policy.) Similarly, a pre-fabrication industry may be built up at great expense of capital only to find the market has disappeared in a relatively short period. Judging by the experience of the difficulties of increasing the capacity of the building industry after the last war, the trade unions at least will be alive to the long-period danger of increasing the numbers of skilled men in the industry without some indication of a long-period building policy. They are likely to be particularly conscious, too, of the threat to their constituents of the development of a new competitor in the form of pre-fabrication. In these circumstances some preliminary decision in favour of a large-scale rebuilding policy may be an important factor in hastening the solution of the immediate problems.

From the more general point of view of the maintenance of full employment, not merely in the building industry and its ancillary industries, but in the economy as a whole, the scope of housing policy is of importance. The volume of investment in new houses by local authorities, on a scale approaching that realised during the Second Experiment, would provide openings for controlling employment in the interests of maintaining an even level over the building industry sector of the economy. The importance of this would depend on the scale of the house-building industry and the emphasis placed on building working-class houses. This in turn depends partly at least on the scope of housing policy. Provided the problems of housing policy are kept well in view, such control of the activities of the local authorities in the interest of maintaining the level of employment in the building and related industries directly, and in other industries indirectly, obviously has a great deal in its favour. The choice of a large-scale housing policy may be forced upon a government accepting responsibility of maintaining full employment in general.

Chapter XIII

THE WAR AND THE LESSONS OF THE PAST

THE most obvious effect of the present war has been to pile up urgent demands for building resources of all sorts for repair of blitz damage and for making up arrears both of new building and of ordinary repairs. Among other buildings urgently needed will be over three-quarters of a million working-class houses. The crux of immediate post-war problems will be the same as after the Great War, an overwhelming demand for building resources and an abnormally limited supply of them, together with uncertainty about the future of building costs, of the general level of prices and about interest rates. This time, however, we shall have the advantage of a good deal of experience if we bother to make use of it. It is with the application of this experience to the problems likely to appear after the present war that this chapter is concerned. It will be convenient to divide it into two parts : the lessons of an economic character relating to programmes, costs, subsidies, etc., and those relating to institutions, private enterprise, and local and central government organisations.

I. THE ECONOMIC LESSONS

(a) Costs, Programmes and Priorities in the Emergency Period.

Immediately after this war there is, we know, going to be an immense demand for building resources. In contrast to this accumulated and abnormal demand the resources of the building industry will be a good deal smaller than before the war. The supplies of skilled labour have been depleted by the disappearance of men into the fighting services; some of them have been killed or disabled, while it will take time to get the others out. Moreover, the natural wastage of the skilled labour force through retirement and death has not been replaced by boys and young men during the war years. This interruption in replacement will leave a gap which it will take several years to fill. Even if the Government's training scheme[1] is a success, there will be an interval before its first fruits, in the form of trained, or even partially trained, men will be available. Finally, there will be a shortage of materials, partly because the materials industries have been disorganised by the war, partly because some

---

[1] *Training for the Building Industry.* Cmd. 6428. 1943.

materials, timber, for instance, have to be imported and shipping may not be available or sources of supply in the exporting countries may be dislocated. There is some tendency to suggest that these shortages and difficulties will not matter much because it is now possible to use new methods of building which require relatively few skilled men and different types of materials. But even though technical progress has made great strides since the Great War and since the beginning of this, those advances have not yet been incorporated on any considerable scale into the building practice of this country. Nor can it be assumed that the development of the various systems of prefabrication, which are practicable in this country, has made sufficient progress to be used for building so-called permanent houses. It seems, moreover, at present that the new methods cannot be used for the construction of the multi-storey blocks of flats essential in congested areas for decrowding, and for the replacement of slums and blitzed dwellings on lines consistent with modern standards. At present, therefore, the new methods only offer a temporary and partial solution of the problem.

It is possible, however, that the prospects of success in making supply and demand for building resources of all sorts meet, are a little brighter than after the Great War. Then the best efforts of the first three years of peace failed to achieve an output of houses sufficient to satisfy the requirements for the current increase in the numbers of families, so that the shortage naturally got steadily worse. An output of houses of the same size in the first three years after this war would provide a contribution which would reduce the war shortage, by about 12 per cent., as the current increase in the numbers of families will be much smaller than last time. Such a glimmer of hope is not sufficient to excuse us from making efforts to do better this time, and to avoid the obvious mistakes of the past.

The problems arising from the pressure of demand on the capacity of the building industry were not dealt with satisfactorily after the Great War. No attempts were made to mitigate its effects and time, money and resources were wasted. The issues are so important that it will be useful to refresh our memories of the experience during the period of the First Experiment. After the last war the capacity of the building industry was at an exceptionally low level and demand at an exceptionally high level, for reasons similar to those which will create the difficulties after this war. The actual effectiveness of the remnant of the industry was further reduced by the chaotic situation in the transport industry and in the organisation of common services generally. To get the maximum results under these conditions it was necessary to adopt all sorts of expensive devices. Inefficient as well as efficient firms producing raw materials, and inefficient as well as efficient building firms and operatives, had to be employed to the limits of their capacity. Overtime had to be worked, involving payment for work at the high overtime rates. Every step taken to persuade people to work harder and longer than they were inclined to naturally had to be paid for. It was not only the scarcity of workmen that created bottlenecks; the employers also had to be cajoled into taking on work to which they were not accustomed, and for which in many cases they were unsuited, under the most difficult circumstances of scarcities of labour and materials and uncertainties about prices. Everyone of these difficulties added to the expense of building.

There were other factors of a rather different type tending to raise costs, which normally come into operation whenever the demand for anything outruns the supply. In 1919 and 1920 the immense competition for building resources pushed prices up to fantastic levels. Everybody who had postponed his demand for new houses or for new buildings of any sort, or who simply needed to make good arrears of repairs, tried to obtain resources for carrying out the work. The result was naturally increases in the prices of materials, in wages and in profits. The competition precipitated further increases in real costs by increasing the rate of labour turnover; most employers needed more men than they had and tried to obtain them by poaching from each other, and so the men shifted around and the work was interrupted. Work on all sorts of jobs was held up and workmen of one type often wasted, because their particular jobs could not be done until another type of workmen had completed the preliminary processes, or because the necessary materials had not arrived. These effects were of course simply the results of the ordinary competitive price machinery which runs wild when demand cannot be reduced effectively by increases in prices. Unless another type of mechanism for distributing resources is substituted this competitive struggle is the only method available, however unsatisfactory its results. During the First Experiment no attempt was made to introduce such new methods and the ordinary price mechanism was relied upon exclusively. Under these circumstances it was ludicrous for the Government of the day to be annoyed by the results. Houses were wanted, particularly working-class houses. The resources for building them could only be obtained if they were taken away from other work. In the absence of any administrative machinery this could only be done by competitive bidding in the open market.

The realisation that this was a costly process, driven home by the height of the contract prices accepted by local authorities, brought the First Experiment to a sudden and ignominious end.

The lesson was not learnt. It will be remembered that the main responsibility for the fiasco was imputed to the peculiarities of the Addison subsidy. It was not realised that any sort of subsidy offered to local authorities which enabled them to increase their demand for building resources effectively would be expensive. Nor was it realised that the rapid fall in contract prices in 1921 was primarily due to the collapse of the demand for building resources for other purposes.[1]

The importance of the influence of demand for resources for other purposes on their availability for house building, and on building costs, was illustrated again much later. It will be remembered that the greatly increased output of houses at the end of the 'twenties and during the 'thirties was not accompanied, until 1937, by serious increases in building costs. The recurrence of trouble in 1937 was in no way due directly to subsidies. This time it was admitted that the cause of the trouble was the sudden increase in demand for building resources precipitated by the rearmament programme on top of the boom in private building.

This insistence on the distinction between the direct cause of increases in costs, the expansion of demand, and indirect causes, such as subsidies, may appear to be pedantic. It is, however, of the utmost importance. Prices and costs are normally determined by demand and supply. Subsidies only affect the matter in so far as they increase or alter the demand. Subsidies can, therefore, be used either to increase the total demand in which case they are apt to be wasted in the form of increased prices; alternatively, they can be used to alter the sections of demand which are satisfied first, if this is managed so that total demand and costs are not increased. The key of the subsidy and cost question, therefore, lies in the control of demand. If, in the reverse case, in order to reduce demand subsidies are simply cut, the inevitable result is that though prices may fall, or cease to rise, the people who most needed the financial assistance in order to obtain houses get less than they would do otherwise. The reduction is imposed at the expense usually of the poorest section of the community. If, on the other hand, demand is altered or controlled by administrative measures, the building schemes which are to go forward can of course be selected on a basis of urgency, and the financial assistance available for individual schemes will not be curtailed by deliberate cuts in subsidies or wasted in increased prices.

[1] See Part I, Chap. II, Section II for a detailed account.

It was only in 1937, after eighteen years of experience, that the Ministry of Health showed any signs of realising this point. Then, owing to the limitations of the political situation, to put the matter politely, the Slum Clearance Schemes, or some of them, were held up; not the building of ordinary houses for ordinary people who were not living in slums. The Treasury, it appears, had not learnt the lesson, and a cut in the subsidy took place in 1938 in a final burst of economy.

The lesson should at any rate by now be clear; if houses are wanted they can be got either by competing for resources to build them, or by the introduction of administrative machinery for the allocation of resources, or for the control of demand, which works independently of the price system. Failure to realise this killed one housing programme and seriously hampered others between the Great War and this. Each time in the past the line has been taken, that this is all very unfortunate but that simple economic factors are very difficult to deal with. This has been made the excuse for what, in fact, has been the introduction of subsidies in circumstances in which they were bound to help inflate prices, or to retard their fall, except by some lucky accident. By blaming economic factors the sheer irresponsibility of this behaviour, and of the subsequent withdrawals and cuts in subsidies, has been concealed. There is no justification for the repetition of mistakes of this kind. The logical solution of the problem which arises when demand outruns supply, particularly if price is of little interest to some people trying to buy resources, is the adjustment by administrative measures of pro- grammes to the capacity of the building industry, reinforced by introduction of suitable priorities in the use of building resources. Anything else leads to waste of time and money and usually of the scarce resources themselves. In the absence of suitable controls of demand and supply price control is ineffective.

That these warnings are not without relevance to-day has been shown very recently. After three years of war a situation had developed in which any attempt to build houses would involve using building resources in a most expensive way. The summer of 1943 has become notorious in the history of housing for the fiasco over the three thousand new cottages to be built for agricultural labourers. The resources of the building industry had again become depleted in relation to requirements. To get any of the proposed three thousand cottages built involved considerable costs for the payment of overtime, travelling and subsistence. The employers once more displayed every sort of unwillingness to undertake the work under the difficult conditions of scarcities of men and materials. In consequence not only have the contract prices for the cottages been a severe shock to the general public, but there have been incredible delays in getting the work started, not entirely due to the division of control between several government departments. The Minister of Health had a hard time explaining away the delays to a critical House of Commons. The Minister of Works and Buildings has had to try and convince everyone that the ordinary indices of changes in wage rates, and of changes in the prices of materials, do not represent the changes in the cost of building since 1939. It is certain that some part of the extra increase in costs is due to increases in real costs due to overtime and so on; it is not at all certain, however, that some of it has not been caused by building contractors inflating the reward they demand for their trouble. What is clear is that demand has been allowed to press unduly heavily on resources.

(b) Costs, Rents, and Subsidies.

We have already dealt with questions of principle arising in connection with costs, rents, and subsidies, but there is a group of questions particularly relevant to post-war problems connected with changes in these factors which we have not considered. There are only three types of changes with which we need bother: erratic and violent changes in costs, long-term and relatively gradual changes to new levels of costs of providing houses and/or incomes, and finally minor fluctuations about a normal level.

The difficulties created by the first type of change are obvious, and are likely to be of great immediate importance. Apart from their generally disturbing and unsettling effects, they make it impossible to forecast the levels at which costs and economic rents will settle down. Hence the questions of whether general subsidies are needed and of what size they, or subsidiary subsidies, need to be in the long run cannot be decided; nor can the size of any current subsidies required. Now it is just this situation that is bound to arise after this war as it did after the last.

It will be convenient to summarise the factors which lead to these embarrassing changes in costs of providing houses. This will help to make it clear that the problem is bound to be of importance in the future. We know that there are three main causes of changes in costs: first, changes in the real cost of building; second, changes in prices and wages which may be due either to inflation of demand for building resources, or to monetary changes which affect the general price level and in the end percolate right through the system; finally, changes in interest rates. Immediately after the Great War the first two factors produced violent increases in building costs. This was followed by violent decreases due to changes in the other direction of these same two factors. We know that during the First Experiment the real costs of building actually started to fall as the building industry began to run more smoothly and the pressure on the industry relaxed while its capacity increased. The break in the industrial boom in 1920/21 decreased all sorts of demands for building resources for general and industrial purposes. It diminished thereby the competitive and inflationary element in prices and costs. The general deflation of the economic system after the boom also helped directly and indirectly to produce decreases. Amid these violent changes in building costs, prices and incomes in general, it was quite impossible to foresee at what level things would settle down and how far economic rents, plus rates, would be within the reach of working-class families. Consequently it was hopeless to try to introduce any fixed subsidy. The solution provided by the Addison Act to this dilemma is thus of particular interest. It was specially intended to resolve the problems arising from violent short-period changes in costs which occurred after the Great War and may be expected to occur again. The scheme provided quite definitely that rents should be determined independently of costs as long as costs remained at abnormally high levels. The detailed provisions of the scheme provided in effect for the writing-off of the inflated capital costs of the immediate post-war years, at the expense of the future. In this way a permanent block of high-rented houses could be avoided. As far as the experiment went, it worked. There was, broadly, no local authority problem in connection with the rents of the Addison houses. The problem was the problem of the Treasury which objected to the costs of the scheme. There were some reasons as we pointed out earlier for considering that the cost was unduly high, owing to the failure to control the building market. It is important, however, to remember that whatever the detailed defects of the scheme were, it provided a realistic approach to the problem which arose because economic rents were at least temporarily wildly out of reach of working-class families.

There seems no doubt that if costs after this war are of a type similar to those after the last war, some such attempt at writing-off or amortizing them as abnormal must be made. Any other decision would mean inevitably that there would always be an element in the rent system forcing rents up owing to the temporary conditions created by a major war. It is clear that somebody must take the loss resulting from the disruption of the house market by a war. The alternatives are the tenants, the local authorities or the Treasury. If the loss is imposed on the tenants, the houses built immediately after the war will either only be available for the best-off families, or if they are merged ultimately into the general supply of houses, they will result in unnecessarily high rents for the tenants of the newer houses built in more normal circumstances during the period of amortization.

We know already that some of the factors which made for instability immediately after the last war have already become important: we know that the reduction in the capacity of the building industry and the effects of pushing it to produce at the limit of that capacity, has already pushed building costs up by 100 per cent. or more. We know that there is an immense pressure of demand piling up, partly ordinary arrears of building, partly created by the blitz. We know that changes in the general price level have already been partly reflected in wage rates and labour costs, and in the prices of materials, in the building industry.[1]

On the other hand, we do not know what the future of these changes will be. Equally, the future of interest rates is uncertain. It is inevitable that even in the most favourable circumstances, the real cost factor will create instability in costs and conditions immediately after this war and will ultimately lead to a fall in costs. How the other factors will affect the situation is at present quite uncertain. It depends largely on Government policy. The rent problems which arose immediately after the last war are therefore bound to arise again.

We have already got sufficiently far to point out certain ways in which the price situation after the war can be mitigated. It should be possible to plan building programmes so as to avoid violent fluctuations in demand, and in particular extreme pressure on the capacity of the industry. It should, moreover, be possible to eliminate a great part of the inflationary element which was present in the cost increases immediately after the last war, by this planning. Some of the difficulties arising from the uncertainty about the future of interest rates could be avoided if borrowing for housing purposes is initially on short term. None of these suggestions, however, avoid the necessity of dealing with the essential question of how the abnormally high costs of building houses immediately after

---

[1] On changes in costs during this war, see two articles by S. Moos in the *Oxford Institute of Statistics Bulletin.* Vol. 5. Nos. 14 and 15.

the war can be prevented from upsetting the whole system of post-war rents, unless a special plan for amortization is introduced.

The Addison scheme envisaged a period of eight years ending in 1927, during which it would be impossible to fix a subsidy. By that date other difficulties were beginning to emerge. The period of violent fluctuations in costs was over, but a steady downward trend in the cost of providing houses developed, culminating with the fall of interest rates at the beginning of the 'thirties. The question then arose of the adjustment of rents and subsidies to what appeared to be a long-term change in the cost of providing houses. This was the pre-1939 version of the second type of cost problem distinguished at the beginning of this section.

Really there are two distinct problems included under the omnibus heading so far given; first, changes in costs of providing houses which merely reflect changes in the general level of prices and money incomes, or more shortly changes in the value of money; second, changes which are independent of the general level of prices but which alter the relation between economic rents and capacity to pay. We may well be faced with both types of changes, one after the other after this war. There is no reason to suppose that the general price and income level will return to the pre-war level, and there is reason to suppose that the overdue technical progress in the building industry will sooner or later materialise and reduce the cost of houses compared to other things.

In the former case the capacity to pay the economic rents of houses will be higher than before the war as well as those rents for new houses. There should be no case for attempting to reduce such rents to the level of those built before the war. To leave the rents of the old houses at the pre-war level would, however, have consequences both inconvenient and unfair. It would be inconvenient because it would divide the supply of houses quite arbitrarily into relatively cheap houses, those built before the outbreak of war, and relatively expensive houses, those built since the war. This would lead to great difficulties in the selection of tenants. The division would be unfair because those who happened to get the pre-war houses, or were already living in them, would merely, because of their individual luck, pay less than tenants with similar incomes for similar houses built since the war.

A solution which appears to have much to recommend it may be broadly outlined as follows. A standard rent would be adopted for each district, chosen as one within the capacity to pay of any family not eligible for the type of rebate suggested in the discussion on unsettled questions of rent, in chapter XI above. This would involve an increase in the rents of old houses. Once this rent had been fixed, the amount of subsidy needed to bridge the gap between it and the economic rents of the old houses and the new houses could be easily calculated. The gap between total receipts from standard rents of all houses, plus the old subsidies, on the old houses, and the total annual costs incurred on the provision of new and old houses would indicate the additional Treasury grant required for each area.[1] As more and more new houses were built increases in this additional grant each year would approximate more and more closely to the number of new houses built each year. In this way the profits realised from what would really be an appreciation in the value of the old houses would be used to finance in part the subsidy for the new houses. This would form a logical development of the system of pooling the housing accounts introduced in 1936.[2] It would obviously be necessary to any such scheme for subsidies for rent rebates, such as those discussed in earlier chapters, to be dealt with in a separate account.[3] (It might be suggested that such increases in the rents of old local authority houses might be used as a guide to the increases in rents allowed for the privately owned houses which are at present controlled, provided that they come up to reasonable standards of fitness. There can be no particular reason for freezing rents at their pre-war levels.)

The rent and subsidy problem raised by independent changes in costs can be dealt with more shortly. It has been pointed out that it is decreases in costs which are most probable and which caused confusion before this war. It is possible either to pass all reductions of costs on to the tenants of the new houses, to average them out over all houses, or to transfer them to the Treasury by means of reductions in the subsidies. It is essential to realise that any solution but the first would hamper any policy based on dependence on falls in costs to make houses available to people in the lower income groups. We know only too well that the failure to keep this in mind caused endless trouble during the Second Experiment. If, however, rent and

---

[1] Including additional subsidies in those districts where the cost of providing houses was particularly high.

[2] An attempt to apply the principle of increases in the rents of old houses in reduction of rent of new ones has already been made in Ashby de la Zouche in the case of the war-time agricultural cottages. This appears to be premature, as there is as yet no firm basis on which to assess future rent-paying capacity. Moreover, it has not removed the discrepancy between the rents of old houses and new, a discrepancy which may not be proportionate to the latter's superiority.

[3] Treasury grants for this purpose would be new and additional and would apply to tenants whether in new or old houses.

subsidy policy does not depend on this, then the choice between the other two alternatives appears to be merely a matter of the willingness of taxpayers to continue to pay for subsidies larger than those strictly needed, and no other principle appears to be involved.

The third problem of the relation between rents, subsidies, and costs, that of fluctuations in costs about a norm, has also caused trouble in the past. It will be remembered that from about 1936 onwards costs were rising under the pressure of demand for building resources, particularly on account of building for the rearmament programme. The solution adopted by local authorities varied, but with the pooling of the housing accounts and the creation of equalisation funds, it was obviously possible for this type of change, and changes in capacity to pay rent, to be equalised out over periods of years in which fluctuations may be expected to average out.

In general then, what appears to have been learnt in the past is that the rent, cost and subsidy question is simplified by a system of pooling receipts and outgoings for all the houses belonging to individual authorities. Extension of this system to cover houses built after this war, combined preferably with the adoption of the type of general rent policy outlined in earlier chapters, appears to provide the means of dealing with the most serious of the problems likely to arise from changes in costs or providing houses, and in general price and income levels after this war. It must be emphasised, however, that adoption of this policy during the intermediate period of unsettled costs and incomes and major fluctuations would be premature and lead to confusion. We have pointed out that there is a strong case for introducing a special scheme for amortizing the high capital costs of houses built in that stage; if this is done then there would be no real difficulty in bringing these houses into the general pool once the unsettled period is over. In the meantime existing rents should be frozen temporarily, while the whole new rent scheme is planned.

(c) Discontinuities in Housing Policy.

The failure to relate the grant of subsidies to the capacity of the building industry and the absence of any adequate solution to the problem of the relation between rents and changes in costs, were among the influences which produced sudden changes in housing policy in the inter-war period. The changes in policy had unfortunately, quite disproportionate effects on the output of houses. The three experiments did not dovetail into each other neatly. The main purpose of each experiment was the provision of working-class houses. During each experiment, in fact, approximately the same type of houses were built by local authorities, yet each major change of policy involved interruption of building.

Two years elapsed between the decision to abolish the Addison subsidy and the introduction of the Chamberlain subsidy in 1923. Nearly all the houses permitted under the Addison scheme had been completed six months before the first of the new subsidies was introduced, and the number of houses completed by the local authorities in the interval was only 17,350 compared to 40,185 in the half-year ending September, 1922. The Second Experiment started extraordinarily slowly. In the two years from March, 1923 to March, 1925, hardly as many houses were built as in the six months ending in September, 1921. The effect of the failure to make the experiments overlap is shown still more clearly perhaps by the fact that in the last year before the decline of building under the Addison subsidy, that is, the year ending September, 1922, just over 85,000 houses were completed by local authorities. In the next three years altogether the total built was barely 72,000. The housing shortage in September, 1925, was in fact worse than it had been in 1919. If building had been maintained at even two-thirds of the 1921/22 level, about another hundred thousand houses would have been built.

This interruption in building was not the only disadvantage of the change in policy. By 1921 an agreement with the building industry to increase the numbers of skilled men was approaching completion. With the decision to abolish the Addison subsidy the whole scheme was abandoned. Until Wheatley made his " gentleman's agreement " with the Building Unions in 1924, no active steps were taken by the Government to increase the capacity of the building industry. The possibility of overcoming the housing shortage by increasing the output of the industry was thus delayed.

The interruption to building at the time of the transition from the Second to the Third Experiment was not so disastrous. At least the Government made some attempt to avoid a repetition of the delay of the 'twenties. The inauguration of the five-year slum clearance programme and the abolition of the Wheatley subsidy were both announced early in March, 1933. There was no actual gap during which there was no policy for building some working-class houses. The subsidy for slum clearance was already available, and in theory local authorities were already dealing with their slums. In practice, of course, the replacement of slum houses was negligible at this time, and an hiatus between the two experiments developed. The old experiment was wound up more rapidly than the new one started. In the year up to March, 1933, when the change in policy was announced, the local authorities built 54,500 houses with subsidies. In the year ending March, 1935, however, which included the last six months of the Wheatley subsidy and the first six months without it, the subsidised houses built by local authorities dropped to 34,500, that is, by 37 per cent. This was the worst year, the total increased to 39,100 in the next one. This transition was obviously much better managed than that between the First and Second Experiments; the recession in building in these three years was equivalent, however, to the loss of six months' output at the rate of building in 1932/3.[1]

It seems clear that the hiatus was due at least partly to the fact that the local authorities were told, on the one hand, that the Wheatley subsidy would be available only for houses for which plans had already been approved by December, 1932, provided they were completed by September, 1934. On the other hand, they were also told to survey the need for houses for replacing slums and submit schemes for providing them during 1933. This meant that building under the slum clearance campaign could not start seriously until 1934, and by this time the building under the Wheatley subsidy had dwindled into insignificant proportions. A gap was inevitable. The authorities were not told, as they might have been, to carry on submitting plans and building houses continuously, and that houses not completed by September, 1934, would be ranked for slum clearance schemes. In the meantime the local authorities could have prepared their comprehensive plans for dealing with their slums. No doubt such a procedure would have involved some accounting difficulties, but as the first houses under any slum clearance scheme nearly everywhere were bound to be ordinary three-bedroomed houses, and as nearly every authority had slums to deal with it was in no way impracticable. The method of selecting the new tenant was all that had to be altered in the first instance.

The interruptions in building caused by the fundamental changes in housing policy were not the only vagaries of the Government which upset the output of houses. During the Second Experiment two changes were made in the subsidies. In September, 1927 and 1929 the alterations were reflected in violent fluctuations in output.

There will be little disagreement about the undesirability of fluctuations in building activity precipitated by changes in policy, or in rates of subsidy, such as took place during the twenty years

[1] The recession for all local authority building, i.e., unsubsidised as well as subsidised was smaller, i.e., 28 per cent. less in 1934/5 than in 1932/3, and the recovery more rapid. See Statistical Appendix, Table 2.

between the wars. In so far as they led to waste of precious building time they were inconsistent with the basic aim of a policy to increase the numbers of houses. Other disadvantages of the sudden changes have been pointed out in earlier chapters. For instance, they inevitably increased the element of risk and uncertainty in the building industry and its ancillary industries. They may produce, moreover, violent fluctuations in employment in the building industry and under some circumstances lead to exaggerated fluctuations in building costs.

Changes of this type in the past have been due to some extent to changes in governments and political outlook. In so far as it is impossible for one government to bind its successor such changes are unavoidable. But in each case in the past financial reasons have been made the final excuse for the alterations. The Treasury has lent its powerful support. The argument in favour of public economy at particular times has provided the opportunities for changes desired by different governments. It has been too easy in the past to maintain that housing policy has turned out more expensively than was intended, that increases in building costs have been precipitated, that the subsidies have been wasted and extravagantly administered, and that the wrong people have benefited from them. If the disturbing effect on the output of houses due to changes in policy are to be avoided in the future it is clear not only that actual transitions from one policy to another must be made more carefully than in the past, but also that financial and other pretexts for sudden changes should be eliminated. Far more careful planning of building programmes, far more appreciation in advance of the effect of subsidies, their costs and their incidence are necessary. If housing policy is to proceed smoothly without undue interruptions, policies internally consistent financially and economically are essential. Appreciation of mistakes is no doubt all very well, but hasty attempts to remedy them are apt to lead to a waste of time and resources.

II. The Institutions

The success or failure of housing policy have not in the past depended entirely on its freedom from obvious defects of an economic character. Policy has to be put into practice by institutions of one sort or another. In the past these have been the Ministry of Health, the local authorities, and that rather undefined entity known as private enterprise. At the time of writing it appears that housing policy after the present war will continue to operate through them. The detailed examination of the three housing experiments between the Great War and the present one have thrown a good deal of light upon their behaviour and reliability. From the point of view of the future it is the defects and weaknesses which have been shown in the past that are primarily important. It is these that need remedying if greater success is to be achieved than in the past. It will be convenient to group our conclusions about the weaknesses of institutions into two parts under the general headings of the limitations of private enterprise and the limitations of local authorities.

(a) The Limitations of Private Enterprise.

The dangers of relying on private enterprise to provide additional houses do not arise primarily on the ground of inability or unwillingness to build large numbers of houses. It has been perfectly clear throughout the three experiments that private enterprise working mainly in the form of small speculative builders has an immense capacity for expansion in relation to demand. The satisfaction of the demand for new houses, by people who could afford them, was dependent only on the number of building operatives and the quantities of building materials available. This is in no way surprising; it is a normal experience of private enterprise in all industries. Perhaps still more important than this normal phenomenon has been the development of attempts to increase the effective demand for houses by the building societies and the builders. The former have organised the collection and investment of capital for house mortgages on a national scale, a matter which has been of crucial importance in enabling people without capital of their own to buy new houses. As soon as demand showed signs of falling off, the builders joined in with the building societies in the development of this system to a point at which, as far as the provision of capital was concerned, it became almost as easy to buy a house as to rent one.

The limitations of private enterprise as far as solving shortages of working-class houses is concerned arise fundamentally from the nature of private enterprise itself. Private builders and private investors naturally only provide houses for people who can pay for them. The field of supply is limited by the effective money demand. This inescapable condition of the functioning of private enterprise has certain natural results. In the period of high building costs immediately after the Great War the privately built houses were for the well-to-do, for the middle and upper middle classes. It was only as building costs and interest rates fell that new houses came within the reach of lower income groups. Successive stratas of demand became effective and new markets opened up. It is natural that, if private enterprise is left to function independently, the people who can pay most for houses in times of housing shortages will get them first. This is precisely what happened during the 1920's. The situation can, of course, be modified by helping particular types of families to obtain houses by means of subsidies. The whole set of subsidies of the 'twenties were intended to do this. In particular the additional subsidy provided for small houses built by private enterprise in 1919, and the Chamberlain subsidy was used to increase the demand for small houses built by private enterprise. There is no doubt that to some extent both these subsidies achieved their purpose.

The experience of the experiments shows that private enterprise may have still more serious and permanent weaknesses. During the whole of the interlude of peace, building costs and interests rates never fell sufficiently to enable private enterprise to supply the great bulk of ordinary working-class families with new houses. This was equally true for houses for owner-occupation and for houses to let. Doubtless if housing standards had been relaxed, if the 19th century standards of cramped houses with two bedrooms and without bathrooms had been permitted, it would have been possible for private enterprise to have provided houses at prices within the reach of a very large proportion of families. The new high standard, however, had to be paid for. Both the cost of buying on the instalment system and the economic rents of new privately-owned houses fell outside the range of payments which the ordinary working-class family was willing, or able, to afford. It is only if popular ideas about what rent should be paid alter, or incomes rise, or costs and interest rates fall perceptibly, that this difficulty of costs could be overcome without subsidies.

The limitations of private enterprise are definite and fundamental in this respect. It is too often forgotten that it can provide houses less cheaply than the state bodies such as the local authorities who can raise their capital more cheaply than anyone else. This difference in the cost of capital may be equivalent to as much as 25 per cent. of the capital charges on a new house. Thus, despite the highly organised system of building society finance private enterprise can not do as well as the local authorities in providing cheap houses.

These considerations of costs apply both to the provision of houses to let and the provision of houses for owner-occupation. The question immediately arises, however, as to whether if this difficulty could be overcome by means of subsidies private enterprise could succeed in supplying the whole market. There seems little doubt that this might be true in the case of houses for owner-occupation.

There is little reason to suppose, however, that it would solve the problem of houses to let. In the twenty years of peace the collapse of investment by private individuals in houses to let was fairly general. It was not confined entirely to the provision of working-class houses. During the 'twenties in particular, building to let was rare even for the intermediate and upper class markets. The general uncertainty about future course of costs, and the belief that they would in any case fall sooner or later, created, as has been explained earlier, conditions highly unfavourable to the investment of capital in new houses to let. The alternative method of obtaining houses by instalment purchase was able, however, to flourish. The system by which the owner-occupier took any risks of capital loss was peculiarly suitable to the period in which the risk of such losses was so great and so obvious. As has been pointed out, the risks for the owner-occupier was of a different character for those of the investing owner, and much less. If similar conditions with regard to costs develop after the present war, and it is practically inevitable that they will, there will be no reason for expecting private investors to be any more willing to put their capital into houses to let than they have been in the past.

Even the long run prospects of revivals in private investment in houses to let are not promising. The trend of developments in the last years before this war has shown that, even when costs and interest rates were more or less stable, private investment of this type had not revived on a serious scale. The general tendencies since the Great War in the investment market have, as we have seen, been unfavourable. The desire for liquidity of investments, the habit of indirect investment through trusts, the growth of insurance funds, and the much greater opportunities for investment in gilt-edged securities have all contributed to alter the apparent desirability of investment by individuals in houses to let. Potential private mort-gagees had other things to do with their money than to lend it to private individuals on long-term to enable them to purchase houses to let. It must be admitted, however, that there have not been many signs of private individuals trying to raise such money. The desir-ability of becoming the equity owner of houses to let has not been very startling in comparison with other opportunities for tradi-tionally safe investments. Moreover, even if there had been people willing to invest in this field, either in the equity or in the mortgage, it is highly improbable that it could have taken place on a sufficiently large scale to provide a real contribution to the situation. The old-fashioned methods of raising capital for investing in houses are out of date and unsuitable for operations covering the whole country. Developments in institutions leading to the formation of a national market in this type of investment have not taken place. A long-term revival, therefore, is dependent in the future on the development of new institutions.

There is another matter of importance in connection with the limitations of private enterprise. Between the two wars the demand for new houses which could be provided by private enterprise was composed of two elements. The demand for additional houses by the middle and upper classes was the most important up to the beginning of the 'thirties. After this date, however, the demand for new houses for replacement of old houses to enable people to move into new and convenient suburbs became a predominating influence. It was this part of the demand which resulted in so many old houses becoming vacant and contributed thus indirectly to the solution of the shortage of working-class houses. By the time the present war broke out, however, this process of replacement was within sight of its end, it has already penetrated right down into the upper working-class market. Further developments were dependent on such major changes in cost conditions that private enterprise would have been able to supply houses for ordinary working-class families. There seems, therefore, little possibility of private enterprise making such large contributions to the general supply of houses in the future. It must be remembered that a large proportion of middle-class families now own their own houses ; they will be far less likely to abandon them merely for the sake of a little additional convenience, for still more modern houses, if such flitting would involve them in loss. The earlier migrations have been mainly from houses owned by other people, the person who moved did not stand to lose money. The contribution of private enterprise to the relief of the housing shortage is far more likely to be confined to the relief of the shortage of houses for the people who can afford to buy houses than to be general and indirect.

(b) The Limitations of Local Authorities.

The most disturbing feature of building by local authorities in the inter-war years was undoubtedly the widespread tendency for them to build less in relation to requirements than private enterprise. The extraordinary variations in the behaviour of different authorities made it perfectly clear that this feature could not be attributed entirely to the weaknesses of housing policy in general, as formulated by successive governments.

The local authorities naturally argued as a rule that they had not done this or that, because they had not had enough powers or enough financial assistance. Thus it was argued that the absence of differential rent schemes during the Second Experiment was due to uncertainty about the powers to introduce them. It was noticeable, however, that no serious attempt was made either to find out what the powers were until late in the life of the experiment, or to obtain definite powers. Even when the matter was cleared up there was little enthusiasm for carrying out the policy. Similarly, authorities have argued that they were not able to let houses at lower rents than they did because the Treasury subsidy was not high enough. What they omitted to add was that they were not prepared to increase the subsidy out of the rates.

Probably the most serious criticism that must be made of the local authorities as housing authorities is their preference for the line of least resistance. Not only has this been marked by the acceptance of the apparent defects of central policy, of which examples have just been given, but when there has been a choice between the terms on which they could provide houses, they have tended to choose the easiest for themselves. This was not true of all authorities, but it was true of a sufficient number to be disturbing. There were those authorities, for instance, who built almost exclusively with the Chamberlain subsidy instead of building a substantial proportion of houses under the Wheatley subsidy; it was the latter which was the most suitable for ordinary working-class houses. There were those who avoided doing anything under the Slum Clearance Act as long as they could; even when obliged to do something, there were some who understated their requirements and dallied over the execution of their schemes. There was throughout the three experiments a general tendency to deal with the families who were easiest to deal with, to postpone tackling the problems of the least well-to-do and of the families in slums and overcrowded families.

The local authorities have shown in practice that they are incapable of improving on central housing policy, however defective; on the contrary they tend themselves to exaggerate its defects. Where the official subsidy policy has appeared to favour the well-to-do, the authorities have tended to exaggerate this favouritism. When there has been delay and indecision at the centre there has been still more on the part of the authorities. The slow start of building under the Wheatley and Chamberlain Acts illustrated this, and again the delays after the cuts in the subsidies. Even though in the latter case there was some excuse, it was not a sufficient excuse in view of the known tendency of authorities to build in short spasms, and to omit to dovetail their programmes into each other so as to avoid violent fluctuations. The experience of the five year programme to abolish the slums showed some improvement in this matter. Five-year schemes were produced and in many cases fulfilled, but fluctuations in individual areas still occurred. The slum clearance schemes, however, showed that authorities were not competent to estimate their own needs and that if it seemed profitable to underestimate them they would. It was no accident that the slum clearance programmes were increased, after the survey of overcrowding in 1936 made it clear that there were considerable numbers of families who would have to be dealt with either by slum clearance, or under the Decrowding Act.

The experience of the Second and Third Experiments showed, in short, that the local authorities have been given powers which they are only partially willing to exercise, and duties many of which they are in fact unwilling to perform. In the absence of any effective central control, the local authorities can flout policies approved by Parliament, and the local councils can, and do, in practice, re-legislate as to the extent to which they will carry out, or accept, a national policy. It must be added that some authorities are more or less immune from these criticisms, but there is too much evidence of unwillingness and incompetence in the past for complacency to be justified. It has not been found possible in this book to generalise as to what type of authority is most immune from the criticisms. There has been little conclusive evidence that the large authorities do better than the small, or that the really big boroughs have been able to overcome their special problems.

There is no doubt that the organisation of the provision of working-class houses through the local authorities has not been satisfactory. Although there has in practice been little attempt to control their activities, there is no evidence at all that the Ministry of Health would be competent to do so. It is clear that if the authorities are to remain housing authorities they must be provided with a cut-and-dried policy about which there can be no misunderstanding; moreover, their attempts to carry out these programmes must be supervised and controlled. There must be some authority *who can and will* oblige local authorities to perform duties laid on them by Parliament or supersede them altogether. This much is essential if the maximum number of houses is to be provided for the families needing them, and also in the interests of the general control of public investment. The war has brought no improvements in this matter of control; it has worsened it by creating two more central authorities. In addition to the Ministry of Health there are now the Ministry of Works and Buildings controlling the building industry, and the Ministry of Town and Country Planning. How these Ministries fit in together is an unsolved mystery. That the division of functions may provide still further excuses for delay and lack of control has already been illustrated by the extraordinary confusion over the notorious three thousand agricultural cottages.

The question must indeed be raised as to whether the local authorities are in any way suitable bodies for undertaking the general provision of working-class houses. The practical experience of the past is most disquieting however the lack of consistent and clear central policy is blamed and however much responsibility is attributed to the inertia of the Ministry of Health. It must be remembered that these duties were placed on the local authorities in a hurry in the crisis following the Great War. At that time a nation-wide organisation was needed for the provision of houses with financial assistance from the Treasury. The local authorities already had housing duties of a limited type as part of their responsibilities as sanitary authorities. In the emergency they were turned into actual general providers of houses, a duty of an entirely different type. There was nothing extraordinary about this; local authorities have a tendency to accumulate powers and duties for which they have no particular qualifications, except their existence.

In some respects the authorities have made a good job of the new function. They have, on the whole, provided houses better built, designed and laid out than private enterprise has done, even for a more expensive market. Certain of the smaller authorities have not done so well in this matter, but on the whole the standard of quality has been satisfactory. Moreover, apart from the early mistakes during the First Experiment, there have been few if any examples of gross incompetency in placing contracts. Where the system has broken down is in the lack of initiative and imagination displayed by the authorities in assessing requirements and making plans. They have endeavoured to achieve the minimum instead of the maximum, and there has been no outside authority to force them to do otherwise. In view of the great urgency of the building problems immediately after this war this deficiency is alarming. It is possible that the whole difficulty is just an illustration of the inferiority of state organisations in matters of initiative and imagination by comparison with private enterprise. On the other hand there are one or two considerations which suggest that the local authorities are a peculiarly unsuitable form of state organisation for housing purposes. In the first place, there is no defined standard in housing matters to which they must conform. In education, for instance, there is at least a definition in that free elementary education must be provided for all, and the schools and teaching are subject to inspection by the independent inspectors of the Board of Education. In the second place, there are in each district large groups of rate-payers whose interests are definitely contrary to those of a progressive housing policy. It is clearly not in the interest of the owners of slum houses that they should be cleared away; it is not in the interest of landlords in general that there should be rigid limits placed on the number of persons who can live in a particular house; finally, it is not in the interest of property owners as a whole that the supply of houses should be increased! This is a formidable list of opposing interests rivalled perhaps only in the case of town planning. It might finally be added that it is not in the interests of speculative builders that local authorities' building activity should expand, for the small speculative builders are not particularly well suited to working on contract for local authorities particularly where building schemes are large; they have neither the capital, nor the organisation, nor the experience suitable. All these groups of interests have a maximum opportunity for obstruction of the building plans and programmes on the local councils which have the duty of making and carrying them out. It is noticeable that it is only when the housing shortage has been so acute that the demand for houses has become a political factor of first-class importance that local authorities have shown real energy and enthusiasm. This occurred during the period immediately after the last war when the shortage closely and painfully touched the interests of the organised and vocal groups, both among the middle-class and among the great trade unions. It may be no accident that the authorities' building activities have worked more in favour of the skilled workman, who is used to declaring what he wants, than to the advantage of the more humble sections of the community.

It is obviously no good, however, merely because of the defects, political and organisational, of the system of providing houses through local authorities, throwing it all over and declaring for a return to dependence on private enterprise. There has been too much experience of the disabilities of private enterprise as providers of working-class houses, and the evidence tends to show that there is unlikely to be an improvement in the future. The solution must be in an improved state organisation. Some suggestions for such improvements have been made in earlier chapters.

APPENDIX I
SCOTTISH HOUSING PROBLEMS

It was explained in the Preface that this Appendix is not intended to be a treatise on Scottish housing problems. It has been included simply to show the more important differences between Scottish and English housing problems, and to indicate whether these differences may need to be taken into account in the determination of post-war policy.

Two years before the outbreak of the Great War a Royal Commission was appointed to investigate working-class housing conditions in Scotland. Its Report, published in 1917, provided a thorough description and analysis of Scottish housing problems and contained plans for their solution. The Commission showed that working-class housing in Scotland was deplorable and intolerable, that everywhere standards were lower than those south of the Border, and that a special building programme was needed immediately. The Commission did not mince its words, and its own summary of conditions will provide the best background to our discussion of housing policy after the Great War.

" These are the broad results of our survey : " it was stated in the Report, " unsatisfactory sites of houses and villages, insufficient supplies of water, unsatisfactory provision for drainage, grossly inadequate provision for the removal of refuse, widespread absence of decent sanitary conveniences, the persistence of the unspeakably filthy privy-midden in many of the mining areas, badly constructed, incurably damp labourer's cottages on farms, whole townships unfit for human occupation in the crofting counties and islands, primitive and casual provision for many of the seasonal workers, gross overcrowding and huddling of the sexes together in the congested industrial villages and towns, occupation of one-room houses by large families, groups of lightless and unventilated houses in the older burghs, clotted masses of slums in the great cities. To these, add the special problems symbolised by the farmed-out houses, the model lodging houses, congested backlands and ancient closes. To these, again, add the cottages a hundred years old in some of the rural villages, ramshackle brick survivals of the mining outbursts of seventy years ago in the mining fields, monotonous miners' rows flung down without a vestige of town plan or any effort to secure modern conditions of sanitation, ill-planned houses that must become slums in a few years, old houses converted without the necessary sanitary appliances and proper adaptation into tenements for many families, thus intensifying existing evils, streets of new tenements in the towns developed with the minimum regard for amenity."[1]

It was not only, however, that the houses were insanitary, badly built and falling into disrepair, they were also far too small for the families which had to live in them. In 1911, 12·8 per cent. of the houses in Scotland had only one room, 40·4 per cent. had only two, 20·3 per cent. had three and only 26·5 per cent. had more than three. This meant in practice that 73 per cent. of the population lived in houses with three rooms or less, including 47·7 per cent. in houses with only one or two rooms. The contrast with England and Wales is startling; even in 1911 only 3·2 per cent. of the houses had only one room and only 8·3 per cent. two rooms, while only 7·1 per cent. of the population lived in these abnormally small houses; the great majority of the houses, 73·8 per cent. had four or more rooms.

Overcrowding in Scotland was necessarily widespread and acute. In 1911 almost a quarter of the population, 1,006 thousand, were overcrowded on the

[1] *Report of the Royal Commission on the Housing of the Industrial Population of Scotland Urban and Rural.* 1917. Cd. 8731. p. 346.

basis of a standard of more than three persons per room; on the basis of the English Census standard of more than two persons per room, the total overcrowded mounted up to 2,077 thousand, that is 45·1 per cent. These figures do not indicate the full horrors of the congestion, for a very large number of the overcrowded houses, particularly those with only one or two rooms, had no domestic offices. They were not in any real sense of the words houses or flats at all, for they were always without kitchens, and frequently without sculleries; individual w.c's or privies were by no means the rule, nor were individual piped water supplies even in the towns. Finally, in the towns the custom of building in tenements reduced to a minimum the light, sunshine and fresh air available, and added extreme density of population per acre to congestion indoors.[1]

The Commission estimated that to make any impression on this situation about 121 thousand new houses were needed immediately, half to replace houses totally unfit for human habitation and half to abolish overcrowding on the more than three persons per room standard. In order to raise housing standards to any reasonable level, however, at least half of the one-roomed houses and 15 per cent. of the two-roomed houses needed replacement. This would bring the total number of new houses required to 236 thousand,[2] equivalent to 21 per cent. of the houses existing in 1911. Private enterprise would not, in the Commission's judgment be able to provide these new houses, which should all have at least three rooms as well as proper domestic and sanitary conveniences.

" We are driven to the conclusion," the Report explained, " that the sources and forces that were available for the provision of working-class houses had—and this is quite apart from the difficulties brought about by the war—failed to provide anything like a sufficiency of houses, and that in particular they had failed to provide houses of a reasonable standard of accommodation and habitability. . . . Private enterprise was practically the only agency that undertook the building of houses, and most of the troubles we have been investigating are due to the failure of private enterprise to provide and maintain the necessary houses sufficient in quantity and quality."[3]

The Commission recommended that the state should put the responsibility for seeing that sufficient houses were built on to the local authorities. It should provide from central sources the funds necessary to make up the differences, believed to be inevitable, between the economic rents of the houses and the actual rents obtained by the local authorities. The Commission were opposed, taking into account the behaviour of builders, landlords and landowners in the past, to any attempt to get private enterprise to tackle the job with the aid of subsidies.[4]

The shortage of houses actually due to the lack of building during the Great War, and the policy adopted, must be considered against the background of these conclusions of the Commission. The actual shortage of houses attributable to the war was in 1921 about 95 thousand, but between 1921 and 1931 an additional 36 thousand were needed to balance increases in the number of families. The total was thus 131 thousand, equivalent to 11 per cent. of the number of houses in 1911; about 87 thousand of these houses would be needed for working-class families.[5] It will be noticed that the number of houses needed to counterbalance the war shortage, and carry on up to 1931, was only slightly greater than the number required by the Commission for remedying the worst housing conditions. The total number of houses required on these two counts together was equivalent to 22 per cent. of the number of houses in 1911—a proportion slightly smaller than that represented by the requirements for additional houses in England and

[1] Ibid. Chap. III, et seq., and the *Population Censuses of 1911* for England and Wales and Scotland.
[2] *Report* op. cit. pp. 8 and 9.
[3] Ibid. p. 292.
[4] Ibid. pp. 293 *et seq.* and Chapter XXXV.
[5] These estimates have been made in the same way as those for England and Wales (see pp. 10-11 above) and make no allowance for the reoccupation of houses vacant in 1914, see p. 264 below. The very small increase in the number of families in Scotland between 1921 and 1931 was due to the loss of population by emigration.

Wales up to 1931 without any allowance for replacements or diminution of overcrowding.

Post Great War housing policy as laid down in Acts of Parliament for Scotland was with a few exceptions the same as that for England and Wales.[1] It started with the Addison subsidy on the lines recommended for dealing with the inherited arrears of bad housing in Scotland. As time went, however, it diverged from these recommendations. Although it must have become clear that the relative magnitude of the need for additional houses, to make good the war shortage and keep pace with increases in the numbers of families, was much smaller than in England and Wales, the main subsidies provided by the Chamberlain and Wheatley Acts were intended to encourage the provision of additional houses rather than replacement or decrowding. The only subsidy available for slum clearance was that provided by the Chamberlain Act, by which losses were equally divided between the Treasury and the local authorities. Even in 1930 when the Greenwood subsidy for slum clearance was introduced, no consideration appears to have been given to the urgent need both for powers and financial assistance for decrowding in Scotland. These were not made available until 1935, eighteen years after the Royal Commission's Report.

Although the special problems of Scotland were placidly ignored by Parliament, it must in fairness be stated that the Department of Health for Scotland never became complacent. Its Annual Reports were full of criticisms of the progress made by local authorities. It attempted with all the means in its power to induce them to build more quickly and to deal with their slums. It did not hesitate to press home its arguments with descriptions of the worst types of conditions that continued to exist.

The powers of the Department were limited however. It was able, for instance, to resist only with slight success the wishes of the authorities to build two and three-roomed houses instead of four-roomed houses. Though it argued that an additional room only cost between £20 and £30 to build, and that Parliament had shown its disapproval of new houses with less than three rooms,[2] the rent argument was too strong to be entirely overcome. In the original plans made for building with the Addison subsidy 50·5 per cent. of the houses were to have more than three rooms, 48·2 per cent. were to have three rooms and the balance two; in fact, of the houses actually built with this subsidy only 41 per cent. had more than three rooms.[3] Finally, in 1929, the Department was obliged to agree that 25 per cent. of the houses built with the Wheatley subsidy might have only two rooms.[4] The local authorities were always able to argue that even with the subsidies the rents for houses with more than two rooms, a fortiori those with more than three rooms, involved too large an increase over the rents of the old houses, which normally had less than three rooms. The importance of this argument can be illustrated from the Board of Trade Inquiry into the Cost of Living in 1912. In ten towns in Scotland in 1912 the predominant range of rents, including rates, for two-roomed houses was from 2/- to 5/-. In England and Wales families of the same type as those living in two rooms in Scotland occupied, in general, four-roomed houses for which the predominant range of rents, including rates, was from 4/- to 6/-.[5] (The predominant range of rents for three-roomed houses was

[1] For an account of this housing policy see Part I, Chapters II, III and VII above. The main exceptions to the uniformity of policy referred to in the text were as follows: (a) The loss on housing operations, under the Housing and Town Planning, etc., Act, 1919, to which local authorities were liable in Scotland was 4/5ths of a penny rate instead of a penny rate. (b) The ordinary subsidies under the Chamberlain and Wheatley Acts were left unchanged until their complete abolition in 1933. In England and Wales both were reduced as from October, 1927, and the former abolished as from October, 1929.
[2] Annual Reports of the Scottish Board of Health (later the Department of Health for Scotland), 1920, p. 164; 1924, pp. 48–9; 1926, p. 48; 1929, p. 10. The codifying Housing (Scotland) Act, 1925, laid down that plans for private building of houses with less than three rooms were to be approved only in exceptional circumstances.
[3] Annual Reports, 1921 and 1927.
[4] Annual Report, 1929.
[5] Op. cit. The lower rents in Scotland are not explicable merely on the ground that the occupier in Scotland even in the case of working-class houses, only pays part of the rates in his gross rent.

from 3/- to 5/- ; there were, however, much fewer of these). Usually, therefore, the change over to the new houses with four rooms meant a larger increase in weekly expenses in Scotland than in England and Wales.[1] It was as a result of these difficulties that the Department of Health was obliged to give way on this matter of the number of rooms in new houses; by 1938 only 28 per cent. of all the local authority houses had more than three rooms, 61 per cent. had three rooms, and 11 per cent. had less, usually two.[2] The houses had, however, individual domestic offices and it was some improvement that the great majority had more than two rooms.

It will be convenient, before going further, to survey the actual progress made with building. By the spring of 1931 about 121 thousand houses had been built by local authorities and private enterprise together (excluding those used for the replacement of slums), compared with the requirements of 131 thousand for overcoming the war shortage and keeping pace with the increase in the number of families from 1921 to 1931. There was thus still an apparent shortage of about 10 thousand houses.[3] At the beginning of the Great War, however, it was generally agreed that there were an abnormally large proportion of houses vacant. If some credit is taken for the re-occupation of some of these, it may fairly be considered that the shortage of houses had more or less disappeared by 1931. There is little doubt that requirements in the limited sense were more easily met between 1921 and 1931 in Scotland than in England and Wales. It is not possible to estimate the number of additional new houses needed from 1931 to the outbreak of this war, for emigration from Scotland continued. There is little doubt, however, that the number of houses built from 1932 to 1938, averaging 12,265 a year (excluding those earmarked for replacement of slum houses), has been as great as the increase in the number of families.

It is important to notice other features of house building in Scotland. Of the houses built up to the end of the Second Experiment, that is up to 1934, the great majority, 83·9 per cent., were built with the aid of a subsidy, including 61·1 per cent. provided by the local authorities. In England and Wales the corresponding figures were 48·8 per cent. and 31·0 per cent.[4] There appear to be several reasons for the difference in the importance of subsidised building north and south of the Border. It seems that a considerable number of the more expensive local authority houses were occupied by families not generally defined as working-class, for the Department of Health remarked in one of its reports that the local authorities had interpreted the term " working-class in no narrow sense."[5] It must be remembered that the local authority four-roomed houses were superior to some of the old middle-class houses. Thus the Wheatley subsidy, under which the local authorities built almost exclusively for ordinary purposes benefited some families for whom it was not intended. Similarly the size of houses, which could be built by private enterprise with the aid of the Chamberlain subsidy (available in Scotland up to 1934), was adequate by Scottish standards for better-off families than in England and Wales. These factors naturally diminished the demand for unsubsidised houses. Moreover, there are really only two towns in Scotland, Glasgow and Edinburgh, which are large enough to stimulate any strong movement, into the surrounding country and create demands for suburban houses.

[1] In 1938 the rents of local authority houses in Scotland were similar to those in England and Wales in 1936. 35·7 per cent. were let at rents (excluding rates) less than 5/10, 41·2 per cent. from 5/11 to 8/10, and the rest at rents over 8/10. In England and Wales the rents for half the local authority houses were between 5/1 and 8/1, corresponding therefore to the biggest group in Scotland; fewer, only, 13 per cent., however, came into the lowest rent group under 5/1 and more into the highest, i.e. over 8/-. *Annual Report of the Department of Health or Scotland*, 1938, Appendix 8, and *Rents of Houses and Flats in England and Wales*, op. cit.
[2] *Annual Report of the Department of Health for Scotland*, 1938, Appendix 3.
[3] All the figures relating to houses built are taken from the Annual Reports of the Department of Health for Scotland.
[4] Excluding houses built in replacement of slums. The corresponding percentages up to 1929 (i.e., up to the repeal of the Chamberlain subsidy, and the reduction of the Wheatley subsidy, in England and Wales) were 87·9 per cent. and 67·2 per cent. respectively, in Scotland, and 65·0 and 36·7 per cent. respectively, in England and Wales.
[5] *Annual Report*, 1932.

Even after 1934, when some considerable expansion of private building took place, the middle-class replacement factor does not seem to have been so important as in England and Wales. Thus it is probable that indirect improvements in housing standards by filtering up into good houses, abandoned by their normal occupants, were less widespread. Direct improvements by the replacement of slum houses by the local authorities was on a relatively larger scale in Scotland. Up to 1930 they had built 12·5 thousand houses for this purpose, nearly as many as were built in the whole of England and Wales, and equivalent to 13·9 per cent. of local authority building instead of 2·2 per cent. Under the more favourable conditions provided by the Greenwood Act of 1930, building for this purpose expanded much more rapidly in Scotland than in England and Wales. By 1933 building under this Act was sufficiently important to offset the decline of local authority building under the Wheatley Act since 1929, and in 1935 more houses were built by the local authorities, 18·8 thousand, than in any previous year since the Great War.[1] In England and Wales similar developments did not take place till two or three years later. By the end of 1938 the Scottish local authorities had closed, or demolished, nearly 55 thousand out of the 63 thousand houses included in their 1934 programmes; over 40 thousand had been built for replacement purposes and there were 27 thousand built but unallocated between replacement, decrowding and ordinary needs. Progress with decrowding had, however, been much slower. The survey of 1936 had shown that 260 thousand houses were overcrowded on the definition of the Housing Act of 1935, that is about a quarter of all working-class houses. By 1938, however, only 36 thousand families had been removed from overcrowded houses,[2] while in England and Wales overcrowding had been diminished by about a third. The difference was due mainly to the much greater possibility of re-allocating houses in England and Wales, where overcrowding was concentrated among the unusually large families and the unusually small houses. In Scotland the normal working-class house was apt to be too small for the normal working-class family, thus decrowding could only be achieved effectively by building new houses.

There are four outstanding questions which we must try to answer. Was it possible to claim at the outbreak of this war that at least the minimum programme of the Royal Commission had been carried out? Could more have been done than was in fact done? What will be the outstanding housing needs of Scotland at the end of this war, and will they necessitate a housing policy for Scotland different to that in England and Wales?

The first question is fairly easy to answer definitely. The Commission had required that at least 60 thousand houses unfit for human habitation should be replaced. Between the end of the Great War and the end of 1938, this requirement was exceeded by about 7 thousand. The Commission had also required that, in addition to houses needed to make good the shortage due to the war and to keep up with subsequent increases in the number of families, another 60 thousand houses should be provided to abate overcrowding. This requirement had not been satisfied by the provision of additional working-class houses. Between 1919 and the spring of 1931 about 81 thousand houses were built by local authorities;[3] even if these were all occupied by working-class families there were too few to leave any surplus for decrowding purposes.[4] It is not possible to be so precise about the years 1931–38, but it is unlikely that the surplus over current requirements exceeded thirty thousand houses, including those built specifically for decrowding under

---

[1] The first peak in local authority building in Scotland was reached in 1922 with 9·5 thousand houses; this was followed, as in England and Wales, by a recession followed in turn by a new expansion, which reached a maximum in 1927 with 15·8 thousand houses. In Scotland building remained at a high level, i.e., between 14 and 15 thousand, in 1928 and 1929. The next recession came in 1930 with only 7·9 thousand houses built, but a gradual recovery started in 1931 with an increase in the number of houses built under slum clearance schemes.

[2] *Annual Report*, 1938.

[3] Excluding houses built to replace slums.

[4] See p. 264 above.

S

the special subsidy. Overcrowding probably was abated to some extent indirectly, however, by rehousing of overcrowded families in houses included in slum clearance schemes, by some reshuffling of families among the existing working-class houses, and by filtering up into such better class houses as were left vacant by their former occupiers moving into new houses. In view of the Department of Health's comments on the progress made with decrowding it seems unlikely that these indirect methods had results of major importance.[1] Thus it is clear that though the Commission's minimum requirements as to slum clearance had been satisfied, this had not been so in the case of decrowding.

The answer to the second question cannot be given in such precise terms. Judged by the scale of house-building in England and Wales between 1919 and 1939, the total of 311·5 thousand houses built in Scotland was disappointing. It was equivalent only to 28 per cent. of the total number of houses in 1911. In England and Wales, however, the total number of new houses built was equivalent to 52 per cent. of the number of houses in 1911. It has already been explained that the nature of the demand for new houses in Scotland after the Great War was different to that in England and Wales. On the one hand, the migration out of old middle-class houses into new ones in the suburbs was relatively unimportant; on the other, the need for organised slum clearance and decrowding was of overwhelming importance. The first difference meant that the opportunity for indirect improvements in working-class housing standards, through filtering up, were more limited in Scotland than in England and Wales. The second meant that increased powers and financial assistance for local authorities for slum clearance and decrowding, for the direct attack on low housing standards, were more urgently needed in the former. These were not available until 1930 and 1935, respectively. It was not surprising that the output of new houses in Scotland was relatively much smaller, as the figures just quoted demonstrate, than that in England and Wales. It should not be forgotten that the Department of Health's criticisms of the local authorities, already referred to,[2] suggest that nevertheless the local authorities could have done more than they did, especially after 1930. Naturally with the scale of house-building so much smaller in Scotland, the building industry was also relatively smaller than in England and Wales. For instance, in 1931 there were only 16·1 insured workers in the building industry for every thousand persons in the population in the former, compared to 19·1 per thousand in the latter. If the industry in Scotland had been on the same scale as in England and Wales, there would have been about 15 thousand, that is 19·2 per cent., more men in it in 1931 than there were.[3] There is no reason to doubt that, if prospects of employment in the industry had been as favourable north of the Border as south of it, its personnel would have increased appropriately. The answer to the second question is therefore clear. Undoubtedly much more might have been achieved in Scotland if an appropriate policy had been introduced early enough, and if the local authorities had made the most of their opportunities.

The third question is perhaps the easiest of all to answer. The Scottish Housing Advisory Committee has estimated the number of houses needed in Scotland immediately after this war.[4] In order to complete slum clearance and decrowding, as defined during the 'thirties, 321 thousand houses are needed. This number is

---

[1] See p. 265 above.
[2] See page 263 above.
[3] The actual rate of increase in the number of insured building workers appears to have been about the same in both countries, about 19 per cent. between 1923 and 1931 and between 42 and 45 per cent. for the whole period for which it is possible to calculate the increase, i.e., 1923 to 1938. The actual figures are probably not quite accurate for the form of the insurance statistics in 1923 was slightly different from that for the later years, and changes took place in the scope of unemployment insurance between 1923 and 1938. There is little reason to think that these factors altered the degree of similarity in the increases however. It should be explained that the Scottish building industry was extremely depressed just before the Great War and its personnel had been decreasing rapidly. In consequence, at the end of the Great War, it was still relatively smaller than in England and Wales. As it then increased at about the same pace as in England and Wales this disparity did not disappear. (For an account of the pre-Great War state of the Scottish building industry, see the *Report of the Royal Commission on Housing in Scotland*, op. cit.)
[4] *Planning Our New Homes.* 1944.

equivalent to 29 per cent. of the houses existing in 1911 and it accounts for 68 per cent. of the total number of new houses required by the Committee. 66 thousand of the houses are needed to replace houses known to be unfit for human habitation in 1938, but not included in the programmes drawn up in 1934; 55 thousand are needed to replace houses which have become similarly unfit between 1938 and 1943; 200 thousand are needed to complete the abolition of the overcrowding which existed in 1938. The maximum number of houses built in any year between the Great War and the present war by local authorities and private enterprise was 26 thousand. At a similar rate of building after this war it would take about thirteen years to complete this programme. In addition to these requirements, however, the Committee estimated that 148 thousand houses are needed for general purposes and to balance increases in the number of families between 1938 and 1943.[1] These would take another six years to build, quite apart from any additional houses needed for further increases in the number of families after 1943. The grand total of houses required amounts to 469 thousand, equivalent to 42 per cent. of the number existing in 1911, and about nineteen years would be needed to build them—that is to complete the reforms implicit in the sanitary policy of the 'thirties and make good the shortage inherited from this war. We estimated that in England and Wales, apart from the arrears of repairs to houses damaged in air-raids, it would be possible at the same rate of building as in the years just before this war *not only* to complete the sanitary policy programmes for slum clearance and decrowding, to make good the shortage of houses due to the war and to keep pace with increases in the number of families, *but also* to replace all the working-class houses which fail to satisfy modern standards in less than nineteen years.[2] In considering this contrast it must be remembered that, owing to the state of Scottish housing, slum clearance and decrowding as defined by the sanitary policy is bound to be on a larger scale in Scotland than in England and Wales. Almost certainly, therefore, completion of the sanitary programmes would result in the replacement of a larger proportion of old houses in the former than in the latter. Thus the scale of the rest of the rebuilding necessary to bring all houses up to modern standards would be relatively smaller than in England and Wales, though it would almost certainly be substantial.[3]

To sum up—after the Great War Scottish housing problems were different to those of England and Wales. This was not recognised and practically the same policy was applied both north and south of the Border. We have seen that uniformity of policy even in England and Wales led to a considerable number of difficulties owing to differences in the economic circumstances of different districts. In Scotland, where there was a peculiarly difficult group of housing problems as well as economic depression, this blind devotion to uniformity of policy led to serious delay. As a consequence, the housing problems facing Scotland to-day are again different to those facing England and Wales. More than two-thirds of the houses urgently required in the former, immediately after this war, are needed for the completion of the programmes covered by the terms of the sanitary policy of the 'thirties. The number of houses required for this purpose alone amounts to 29 per cent. of the total number of houses existing in 1911 and exceeds the number of houses of all sorts built between 1919 and 1939. In addition houses are needed for general purposes and to balance increases in families between 1938-43. A programme of this scale must inevitably require

[1] An explanation of this estimate is given in Chapter VIII of the Committee's Report, *Planning Our New Homes*. The total figure is made up as follows: (a) 64 thousand houses needed for general purposes and to replace the houses destroyed by raids (approximately 7 thousand), *plus* (b) 134 thousand houses required to balance the net increase of families between December, 1938, and December, 1943 (this item is particularly large owing to the increase in the number of marriages each year since 1938) *minus* (c) 50 thousand houses built between December, 1938, and December, 1943. As the Committee admits there are a large number of factors affecting these requirements about which it is at present only possible to guess, the total cannot be regarded as final.
[2] See pp. 195-6 above.
[3] Unfortunately it is impossible to estimate this from the existing published information.

as its basis firm decisions on the numerous unsettled principles of housing policy, and also decisions on some of the matters which, though not primarily housing problems, influence them.

These subjects have already been discussed at great length in Part II; all that needs to be pointed out here is the necessity of decisions being reached, at least as far as Scotland is concerned, without delay. In our opinion, it may be taken for granted that any housing policy more limited than that just outlined will not be acceptable in Scotland. On the other hand there is a choice of policy in England and Wales, apart from the rebuilding of houses destroyed in the Blitz, between what would be a relatively small building programme based on the sanitary policy of the 'thirties and a general rebuilding programme. For the former it is unnecessary to solve all the unsettled questions. Although we have argued that, as the war has created a shortage of houses and necessitated a larger immediate programme, it is desirable that these should be settled whatever the ultimate choice of policy may be, this is an issue about which reasonable people can argue. There is every possibility of considerable delay before decisions are reached in England and Wales. There is thus a case for considering housing problems, and their related problems, separately for Scotland in order to avoid delay in the preparation of plans. This case is all the stronger since there is, as we have shown, no practical justification for further attempts to apply the same housing policy automatically to Scotland as to England and Wales. There are, however, two difficulties which may be thought to limit the possibility of considering the Scottish problem independently. During the emergency period immediately after this war resources, including temporary houses, will have to be shared between the two countries; but this need not affect the preparation of plans to be put into operation immediately this period of absolute shortage of resources is over, and preliminary work on some sites could be started during this period. Second, housing policy in the long run must be affected by the location of industry, but location of industry policy cannot be settled for Scotland in isolation. It can, however, be argued with a great deal of force, that in any case the number of houses included in the programme under discussion will be needed in Scotland. It follows that this apparent obstacle to the independent consideration of the Scottish housing problem to avoid delay cannot be regarded as serious.[1]

----

[1] A rather similar problem arises in connection with the distribution of industry within Scotland itself. It must be remembered, however, that the number of permanent houses likely to be built in Scotland in any one place in the first few years after this war is likely to be too small in relation to needs ever to become redundant. It can also be argued that preparation for, and even completion of, at least some major rehousing schemes can be carried through without any real risk that their position will turn out to be unsuitable to the future location of industry within Scotland. By the time these safe projects have been completed the general lines of the future lo tion of industry, whether settled by the Government or not, are likely to be forseeable.

APPENDIX II

STATISTICAL NOTES AND TABLES

TABLE 1.—Private Families and Houses[1] in England and Wales, 1911 to 1939.
(*Thousands.*)

| Date (1) | Private Houses[2] | | Private Families[3] | | Excess or Deficit of Net Increases of Houses over Net Increase of Families[3] (6) |
	Total[3] (2)	Net Increase over 1911 (3)	Total (4)	Net Increase over 1911 (5)	
Census 1911 ..	7,691	—	7,953	—	—
Jan. 1919 ..	7,929	238	8,801	848	−610
Census 1921 ..	7,979	288	9,046	1,093	−805
March 1923 ..	8,181	490	9,265	1,312	−822
Census 1931 ..	9,399	1,708	10,140	2,187	−479
Sept. 1934 ..	10,101	2,410	10,490	2,537	−127
March 1939 ..	11,263	3,572	10,940	2,987	+585

[1] Including flats, etc. ; all structurally separate private dwellings (as used in the Population Census) are included under the general heading of houses throughout the tables.

[2] Including vacants.

[3] See Notes in Estimates below.

NOTES ON THE ESTIMATES IN TABLE 1.

(1) ESTIMATES OF THE NUMBERS OF PRIVATE HOUSES.

(i) *Census Years, 1911, 1921 and 1931.*—The numbers of houses are those given in the Housing Volume of the Population Census of 1931.

(ii) *January, 1919.*—The number of houses at the beginning of the month has been taken as the number at the 1921 Census *less the number built between January 1, 1919 and March 31, 1921*, on the assumption that there was no net wastage of houses in the period owing to the acuteness of the shortage. The estimate may be slightly wrong for two reasons. First, that the number of unsubsidised houses built is not known and was guessed from the Ministry of Health estimate of the number of such houses built between January 1, 1919 and September, 1922. (*See* note, Table II below). Second, the Census in 1921 was taken in June, so that the numbers of houses subtracted from the Census total ought to have been the new houses built up to June instead of up to the end of March, 1921. The former figure is not available however. Neither of these errors is significant in relation to the total number of houses existing or even in relation to the net increase between 1911 and 1919.

(iii) *March, 1923.*—This estimate has been made simply by adding on the number of houses built between March, 1921 and March, 1923, again assuming that there was no net wastage. The sources of error are the same as in the case of the 1919 figure, but are even less important.

(iv) *September, 1934 and March, 1939.*—In each case the estimates have been made by (*a*) adding the number of houses built (excluding those built under Slum Clearance Schemes) after March, 1931, to the total according to the Census, 1931, which was taken in the first week of April, and (*b*) by subtracting an estimated, or rather guessed, figure for net wastage. The net wastage allowance was reached as follows : It was assumed that all the net wastage between 1921 and 1931 (for which an estimate can be

269

derived from the Census's and the amount of new building), took place after 1923. The average annual amount of net wastage for these years has been adopted as the annual average from 1931 to 1939. Finally, for each period, 1931–1934 and 1934–1939, the excess or deficit of replacement houses built under slum clearance schemes over slum houses closed or demolished was added, or subtracted.   The net wastage figures so reached are almost certainly underestimates but there is no basis for better ones.   It is important to remember that in consequence the numbers of houses shown as existing in 1934 and 1939 are probably too high.

(2) Estimates of the Numbers of Private Families.

Census Years, 1911, 1921 and 1931.—The Registrar General's estimates according to his method " C," given in the Housing Volume of the 1931 Census, have been used. Method " C " is based on the calculation of increases in the numbers of private families defined in the following way :—The increase in the number of married women, *plus* the increases in the numbers of widows, widowers and divorcees under 65 years of age, *plus* 10 per cent. of the increase in single persons between 20 and 45 years of age.

Intercensal Years, 1919, 1923, 1934 and 1939.—These have all been interpolated on the assumption that, if the rate of marriages, etc., had not been disturbed by the Great War, the housing shortage and the Great Depression of the early 'thirties, the increase in the number of families in each year would have been equal to the annual average in each intercensal period.   This assumption has been made as the total increase in each intercensal period, 1911–21, 1921–31 and 1931–41 (as estimated) were very nearly the same.

(3) The Housing Shortage.

The figures in column (6) have been taken throughout as equivalent to the general housing shortage.   This means that the fact that about a million and a quarter families were sharing houses in 1911* has not been allowed for in the shortage, but that it has been assumed that each of the additional families since then required a separate house. There is no satisfactory statistical evidence of the extent to which separate families in fact share as a matter of preference rather than necessity.   The shortages indicated by the figures in this column are thus based on the assumption that the numbers of families sharing because they preferred to do so since 1911 was the same as the number actually sharing then.   This assumption is referred to in the text.

*Registrar-General's estimate—see Housing volume of 1931 Census.

(4) The Inclusion of Vacant Houses.

Vacant houses have been included throughout the tables together with the occupied. There are two reasons for this, one practical the other theoretical.

The practical reason is that the information is exceedingly unsatisfactory as to the number of genuinely vacant houses which were suitable for occupation.   In the Censuses of 1911 and 1921 the figures of vacant or unoccupied, and occupied houses include houses lived in by non-private families, *e.g.*, boarding-houses, schools, etc. Still more serious, any house which happened to be vacant on the Census nights was counted as vacant, irrespective of the reason for the absence of inhabitants.   In consequence, houses empty because the owners were temporarily away on holiday or business, for instance, were included with those in which no one was living at all. Similarly, houses empty because they were owned by people who lived in them part of the year and had a second house which was in use at Census time are included.   The totals of vacant houses thus includes houses which were not available for use by any families needing them.   The totals also include, of course, houses in outlying or remote areas which were empty because the population was declining ; these cannot be regarded either as potential additions to the supply of houses available to alleviate the shortage. At the 1911 Census there were about 440 thousand houses empty for these and other reasons ; by 1921 the total had fallen by about 264 thousand.   There is no means of knowing what part of the decline was due to the demolition of houses empty at the earlier date, and what part to re-occupation.   As the number of occupied houses in 1921 had increased by about 500 thousand, compared to an increase in the total number of houses by 288 thousand, however, it is reasonable to assume that some of the 1911 vacants had become occupied in the interval.   The actual shortage in 1921, calculated on the basis of changes in the numbers of occupied houses would have been about 600 thousand instead of about 800 thousand calculated from the changes in the total number

TABLE 2.—NUMBERS OF HOUSES BUILT IN ENGLAND AND WALES
between January 1, 1919 and March 31, 1939. (Thousands)†

In year ending March 31st	BY LOCAL AUTHORITIES (c)									BY PRIVATE ENTERPRISE (e)								GRAND TOTAL
	1st Exp. Housing etc. Act, 1919	2nd Exp. Housing Acts			3rd Exp. Housing Acts				TOTAL Local Authorities	Subsidised						Unsubsidised	TOTAL Private Enterprise	Local Authorities and Private Enterprise
										1st Exp. Housing etc. and Addit. Powers Acts, 1919(d)	2nd Exp. Housing Acts			3rd Exp. Housing Acts 1930 to 1938	TOTAL			
		1923	1924	TOTAL	1930, 1936 and 1938 Slum Clearance	1935, 1936 and 1938 De-crowding	1925, 1936 and 1938 General	TOTAL			1923	1924	TOTAL					
(1)	(2)	(3)	(4)	(5)	(6)	(7)	(8)	(9)	(10)	(11)	(12)	(13)	(14)	(15)	(16)	(17)	(18)	(19)
1920(a)	0·6	—	—	—	—	—	—	—	0·6	0·1	—	—	—	—	0·1	53·8 (f)	97·5 (f)	252·0 (f)
1921	15·6	—	—	—	—	—	—	—	15·6	13·0	—	—	—	—	13·0			
1922	80·0	—	—	—	—	—	—	—	80·8	20·3	—	—	—	—	20·3			
1923	57·5	—	—	—	—	—	—	—	57·5	10·3	—	—	—	—	10·3			
1924	10·5	3·8	—	3·8	—	—	—	—	14·3	—	4·3	—	4·3	—	4·3	67·5	71·8	86·1
1925	2·9	15·3	2·5	17·8	—	—	—	—	20·7	—	47·0	—	47·0	—	47·0	69·2	116·2	136·9
1926	1·1	16·2	26·9	43·1	—	—	—	—	44·2	—	62·4	0·4	62·8	—	62·8	66·4	129·2	173·4
1927	0·9	14·1	59·1	73·2	—	—	—	—	74·1	—	78·4	1·2	79·6	—	79·6	63·9	143·5	217·6
1928	0·2	13·8	90·1	103·9	—	—	—	—	104·1	—	73·1	1·5	74·6	—	74·6	60·3	134·9	239·0
1929	—	5·1	50·6	55·7	—	—	—	—	55·7	—	48·4	0·7	49·1	—	49·1	64·7	113·8	169·5
1930		5·6	54·6	60·2	—	—	1·6	1·6	61·8	—	49·1	1·6	50·2	—	50·2	90·1	140·3	202·1
1931		—	52·5	52·5	—	—	3·4	3·4	55·9	—	—	2·6	2·6	—	2·6	125·4	128·0	183·9
1932		—	65·2	65·2	2·4	—	2·5	4·9	70·1	—	—	2·3	2·3	—	2·3	128·4	130·7	200·8
1933		1·4(b)	47·1	48·5	6·0	—	1·4	7·4	55·9	—	—	2·4	2·4	0·1	2·5	142·0	144·5	200·4
1934		—	44·8	44·8	9·0	—	2·2	11·2	56·0	—	—	2·8	2·8	—	2·8	207·9	210·7	266·7
1935		—	11·1	11·1	23·4	—	5·7	29·1	40·2	—	—	0·8	0·8	0·3	1·1	286·4	287·5	327·7
1936					39·1	—	14·4	53·5	53·5					0·2	0·2	271·7	271·9	325·4
1937					54·7	2·0	15·1	71·8	71·8					0·8	0·8	274·4	275·2	347·0
1938					56·8	7·3	13·9	78·0	78·0					2·6	2·6	257·1	259·7	337·7
1939					74·1	14·3	12·5	100·9	100·9					4·2	4·2	226·4	230·6	331·5
TOTAL Armistice to March 31st, 1939	170·1	75·3	504·5	579·8	265·5	23·6	72·7	361·8	1111·7	43·7(d)	362·7	15·8	378·5	8·2	430·4	2455·6 (g)	2886·0	3997·7

† Sources : *Ministry of Health Annual Reports* and the six-monthly report *Housing*.
(a) Including three months January to March, 1919.
(b) Houses transferred from the Housing Act, 1924.
(c) Excluding 15,365 houses built to house persons displaced under reconstruction and improvement schemes under the 1890 and 1925 Acts.
(d) All the houses included in this column were built under the *Additional Powers Act*, except for 4·5 thousand.
(e) Excluding houses with rateable values exceeding £78 (£105 in the Metropolitan Police Area).
(f) Including houses built by unsubsidised private enterprise up to October, 1922, estimated by the Ministry of Health as 30 thousand.
(g) Including 21·5 thousand houses built by private enterprise with Local Authority guarantees under the *Housing (Financial Provisions) Act*, 1933, not shown separately for individual years.

of houses.   Unfortunately, it is evident that the lower figure is too unreliable to use as representing the full magnitude of the shortage.

In the 1931 Census, genuinely vacant houses were distinguished from temporarily and the figures were altogether better.   Unfortunately they are not comparable with those for earlier years and cannot therefore be used in the estimates.

The theoretical reason for basing estimates of the shortage on changes in the total numbers of houses rather than changes in the numbers of occupied houses is very simple. It is essential there should always be a considerable pool of genuinely vacant houses, for if there is not it becomes very difficult for people to move house and mobility is restricted.   Thus the partial using up of the margin of vacants during the Great War can only be regarded as providing a temporary addition to the supply of houses; the vacants of 1911 were not really surplus to the market.

It seems then that there would be little justification, either on practical or on theoretical grounds, for using changes in the numbers of houses occupied instead of changes in the total numbers as the basis of the estimates of the housing shortage. Actually, of course, it can be argued that the estimates ought to be increased to allow for an increase in the pool of vacants proportionate to the increase in the number of houses required.   To do so, however, would simply mean adding an entirely hypothetical figure to the estimates.   It seems preferable to keep in mind that to overcome the shortage entirely some margin over our estimates might be needed in practice.

TABLE 3A.—Rateable Values of Houses Built* January, 1919
to March, 1939 (a)—England and Wales.

Rateable Values (b) (1)	Numbers of Houses Built (*thousands*)					
	Up to £13			£14 to £78 (Private Enterprise)		All Houses
	Local Author. (2)	Private Enterpr. (3)	Totals (4)	£14 to £26 (5)	£27 to £78 (6)	(7)
Jan. 1919–Mar., 1931 (c)	585	14	599	707	354	1,660
Apr., 1931–Sept., 1934 (d)	178	255	433	276	90	799
Total to Sept., 1934	763	269	1,032	983	444	2,459
Oct., 1934–Mar., 1939 (e)	84	433	517	601	147	1,265
Total, 1919–1939	847	702	1,549	1,584	591	3,724

(a) Excluding all houses built for slum clearance schemes (see Table 2).

(b) In the Metropolitan Police Area the corresponding rateable values are :—Up to £20, £21–£35, and £36–£105, respectively.

(c) *Rateable Values up to £13 :*—The Ridley Report, p. 13, gives a total of 600 thousand houses in the up to £13 category as an amplification of the estimates in the Marley Report, p. 19.   The split in the table between private enterprise and local authority houses is based on the generally accepted belief that the great majority of the latter are in this rateable value class.   As there is no information as to the number falling outside it, all the local authority houses in the table are included in it though this involves some over-estimation.   It has been decided that the private enterprise houses most likely to come into this class, as well, are the 14 thousand built under the Addison subsidy of the Housing and Town Planning Act of 1919, and the Wheatley subsidy of the 1924 Act.   This makes up a total practically the same as that given in the Ridley Report.

Rateable Values £14 and Over :—These figures have been obtained from comparison of the total for houses up to £13 and the estimates in the Marley Report, p. 19.

(d) The same assumptions as for the earlier period have been made for local authority houses (*see* note (c) above).   The other figures are derived from a comparison of the estimates in the reports referred to above (note (*c*)) with the published figures of the rateable values of houses built by unsubsidised private enterprise. (Apart from houses built for slum clearance, there were no subsidies available for private enterprise during these years.)

(*e*) The same assumption as before has been made for local authority houses. The figures for private enterprise houses are those published in the Ministry of Health six-monthly report, *Housing*. The few odd houses built by private enterprise for decrowding purposes are included with those in the up to £13 group.

* *Note on Sources and the Significance of the Rateable Value Classes.*

The only complete records of the rateable values of houses built since 1919 relate to those built by unsubsidised private enterprise. From October, 1929, therefore they cover all houses built by private enterprise except the very small number built for decrowding and slum clearance ; the latter are not included in the table. Unfortunately up to October, 1934, the figures relate only to two broad categories, viz. : houses with rateable values up to £26, and houses with rateable values £27–£78. (Up to £35 and £36–£105 respectively, in the Metropolitan Police District.) From October, 1934 onwards houses with rateable values up to £13 have been shown separately in the publication *Housing* op. cit. The earlier figures were published in the *Ministry of Health's Annual Reports*. There are no complete figures of the rateable values of houses built by private enterprise with subsidies, or for any houses built by local authorities. The Marley and Ridley Committees on the Rent Restriction Acts gave estimates in their reports (1931, Cmd., 3911 and 1937, Cmd., 5621, respectively) of the numbers of new houses in each main rateable value category. These have been used in making the estimates in the table.

The ordinary new working-class houses in this country are houses below the rate compounding limit (*i.e.*, rateable values up to £13). Although relatively few non-working-class families live in new houses in this group, some working-class families from choice or necessity, have occupied the more expensive types. The houses under the compounding limit may be regarded as working-class therefore, but those just above are marginal, though in general the houses in the intermediate class (£14–£26), are the typical houses of the lower-middle class. Houses with rateable values over £26 are primarily the houses of the well-to-do. The rateable value categories thus on the whole correspond to the main broad classes of occupiers.

TABLE 3B.—All Houses in 1919, and New Houses 1919–1939, classified by Rateable Values. (Percentages)—England and Wales (*a*).

Houses in each Rate-able Value Group as Percentages of (1)	Rateable Values (*b*)					All Houses (7)
	Up to £13			£14 to £78 (Private Enterprise)		
	Local Author. (2)	Private Enterpr. (3)	Totals (4)	£14 to £26 (5)	£27 to £78 (6)	
All houses in 1919 (*c*)	—	—	67·6	20·9	11·5	100
New Houses Built : Jan., 1919–Sept., 1934	31·0	10·9	41·9	40·1	18·0	100
Oct., 1934–Mar., 1939	6·7	34·2	40·9	47·5	11·6	100
All, 1919–1939	22·7	18·9	41·6	42·5	15·9	100

(*a*) and (*b*) *See* corresponding notes to Table 3A above.

(*c*) Calculated from the estimates of the numbers of pre-war houses in each class in the Marley Report, op. cit., p. 19, on the assumption that the distribution of the small number of houses built during the war was similar.

TABLE 3C.—Percentage Increase in Number of Houses (a) in each Rateable Value Class, 1919–1939. England and Wales (1919=100) (b).

From January, 1919, to : (1)	Ratable Values (c)			All Houses (5)
	Up to £13 (2)	£14 to £26 (3)	£27 to £78 (4)	
March, 1931	11	43	38	21
September, 1934	19	60	48	31
March, 1939	29	96	65	47

(a) See corresponding note to Table 3A above.

(b) The numbers of houses in each category in 1919 have been obtained by applying the percentages in the first line of Table 3B above to the total number of houses in England and Wales in 1919, given in Table 1 above. (The totals shown in the Marley Report are too low.)

(c) See note (b) and Table 3A above.

TABLE 3D.—Rateable Values of Houses Provided by Unsubsidised Private Enterprise. (England and Wales)†

Nos. of Houses Built (Thousands).

Rateable Values* (1)	Up to £13 (2)	£14 to £26 (3)	£27 to £78 (4)	Houses Built for Letting included in cols (2) and (3)	
				Up to £13 (5)	£14 to £26 (6)
Armistice to Mar., 1930	388·6		149·1	* *	* *
During year ending March, 1931	104·9		27·7	* *	* *
1932	109·6		17·3	* *	* *
1933	121·9		21·5	* *	* *
1934	183·9		25·9	* *	* *
1935	105·5	148·9	34·0	33·2	22·5
1936	99·1	138·8	33·5	35·3	24·8
1937	98·2	140·9	34·0	39·9	31·3
1938	94·8	129·7	32·6	42·4	31·9
1939	83·3	114·0	29·1	38·2	30·0

† Sources : Ministry of Health Annual Reports and Housing, op. cit.

* The corresponding rateable values in the Metropolitan Police Area are : up to £20, £21 to £35 and £36 to £105, respectively.

* * Not available.

TABLE 4A.—Unemployment among Bricklayers and Changes in Wage-rates during the First Experiment.

Date (1)		Unemployed Bricklayers (a)		Index of Weekly Wage-rates (b)	
		% of Insured (2)	Thousands (3)	Bricklayers (1914=100) (4)	Bricklayers' Labourers (1914=100) (5)
1919	January	*	*	172	207
	February	*	*	175	212
	March	*	*	176	215
	April	*	*	176	215
	May	*	*	185	224
	June	*	2·3	185	224
	July	*	1·4	185	224
	August	*	0·8	186	226
	September	*	0·6	186	226
	October	*	0·7	186	226
	November	*	0·8	193	238
	December	*	0·7	197	246
1920	January	*	0·6	201	251
	February	*	0·4	202	253
	March	*	0·3	203	254
	April	*	0·2	206	260
	May	*	0·2	215	267
	June	*	0·2	228	288
	July	*	0·1	235	300
	August	*	0·1	235	303
	September	*	0·2	237	303
	October	*	*	237	303
	November	*	0·3	237	303
	December	*	0·5	237	303
1921	January		0·6	237	303
	February	1·3	0·7	237	303
	March	1·6	1·0	237	303
	April	2·5	1·4	237	303
	May	4·5	2·6	237	303
	June	4·7	2·9	222	278
	July	5·4	3·4	222	265
	August	4·8	3·0	214	252
	September	4·2	2·6	207	239
	October	4·9	3·0	207	239
	November	7·7	4·9	206	239
	December	10·2	6·5	206	239
1922	January	13·6	8·6	206	239
	February	14·1	9·0	202	234
	March	11·6	7·4	202	234
	April	11·2	7·1	184	208
	May	10·3	6·5	184	208
	June	10·2	6·4	168	185
	July	10·0	6·3	168	185
	August	8·7	5·5	168	185
	September	8·3	5·2	168	185
	October	8·7	5·4	168	185
	November	9·9	6·1	168	185
	December	11·1	6·8	168	185
1923	January	12·8	7·9	168	185
	February	12·1	7·5	168	185
	March	9·0	5·6	168	185

(a) Source : *Ministry of Labour Gazette*. Owing to changes in the scope of the Unemployment Insurance statistics the figures before October, 1920, are not strictly comparable with those after.

(b) Prof. A. L. Bowley's Index numbers.

* Not available.

TABLE 4B.—Tender Prices accepted for Local Authority Houses(a) and Numbers of Subsidised Houses built(b) during the First Experiment (England and Wales).

Period (c) (1)	Average Tender Prices Accepted (c) £ (2)	Period (3)	Nos. of Houses built	
			By Local Authorities (4)	Total Subsidised (5)
1919	728	} Jan., 1919–March, 1920	576	715
March, 1920..	836			
August, 1920	930	April, 1920–Sept., 1920	2,962	5,412
March, 1921..	700	Oct., 1920–March, 1921	12,659	23,137
April, 1921 ..	697			
May, 1921 ..	697			
June, 1921 ..	693	} Apr., 1921–Sept., 1921 ..	34,992	44,808
July, 1921 ..	665			
Aug., 1921 ..	612			
Sept., 1921 ..	594			
Oct., 1921 ..	573			
Nov., 1921 ..	577			
Dec., 1921 ..	514	} Oct., 1921–March, 1922	45,791	56,263
Jan., 1922 ..	494			
Feb., 1922 ..	494			
March, 1922..	463			
		Apr., 1922–Sept., 1922	40,185	49,902
		Oct., 1922–March, 1923	17,350	17,951

(a) *Ministry of Health Annual Reports* for 1920–21 and 1921–22.

(b) Ibid. Details of the numbers of unsubsidised houses built by private enterprise are not available for this period. According to the Ministry of Health estimates about 30 thousand were built between the beginning of 1919 and Sept., 1922 ; in the following six months 23·8 thousand were built. See Table 2.

(c) Statistics of average tender prices are only available for the periods shown in the table. Those for 1919 refer to the whole year, but for 1920–22 they refer to the individual months. It is important to appreciate that the actual cost of building during 1919 and 1920 was in practice well above the tender prices, and apparently reached in some months £1,000. The 1919 and 1920 averages include all types of local authority houses, but for 1921 and 1922 include only non-parlour houses. Figures are not available for the months April, 1922 to March, 1923. The cost of land is excluded throughout.

TABLE 4C.—Changes in Prices of Materials, etc. during the First Experiment.

Year	Wholesale Prices of Industrial Materials and Manufactures (Bd. of Trade Index)	Wholesale Prices of Building Materials (Jones' Index) (a)
1913	100	100
1918	*	205
1919	*	271
1920	328	298
1921	191	311
1922	155	242

(a) See G. T. Jones *Increasing Returns*, Cambridge University Press, p. 269, "Index of Prices of Materials on the Building Industry," converted to base 1913 = 100.

* Not available.

TABLE 5.—Index Numbers of Building Costs, Prices of Materials and Wages 1924-44 (1930 = 100).

Year	Building Costs		Wholesale Price (Board of Trade Index Numbers)		Weekly Wage-Rates (e)		
	Local Authority Average Contract Prices (a)	Economists' Index	Building Materials (d)	Industrial Materials and Manufactures	Building Industry		General Index
					Bricklayers	Labourers	
(1)	(2)	(3)	(4)	(5)	(6)	(7)	(8)
1924	125·8 (b)	109·6	—	144·0	104	105½	102
1925	129·3 (c)	106·4	—	134·0	104	105½	102
1926	129·3	106·8	—	125·0	104	105½	102
1927	120·5	105·0	—	118·0	104	105½	102
1928	106·2	103·1	—	116·0	102	103½	101
1929	101·5	100·0	—	114·0	102	103	101
1930	100·0	100·0	100·0	100·0	100	100	100
1931	97·9	96·4	96·4	87·4	97½	98	99
1932	89·6	94·2	94·5	84·6	95	95	97
1933	85·5	91·0	92·5	87·2	92½	93	96
1934	85·3	90·7	92·6	89·7	92½	93	96
1935	88·0	97·2	93·8	90·0	93½	93	97
1936	92·1	100·9	96·7	95·7	97	98	98
1937	104·6	107·2	104·2	112·0	99½	100	103
1938	107·9	107·2	104·1	103·5	102	103½	106
1939	109·1	107·5	104·8	105·5	102½	104	107
1940	—		121·8	138·4	109	113	119
1941	—		139·4	155·8	117	122½	130
1942	—		144·9	160·1	120	127	139
1943	—		149·6	164·0	125½	131	146
1944	—		153·0(f)	169·1(f)	126½(f)	132(f)	151(f)

(a) Annual averages of quarterly average prices of contracts let for ordinary three-bedroom non-parlour houses, excluding cost of land.

(b) Average of average prices of contracts let in March, June, September and December.

(c) Average prices for March included in place of those of first quarter which are not available.

(d) Not available before 1930.

(e) Prof. A. L. Bowley's Index Numbers. Annual averages except in the case of Bricklayers and Labourers for 1924 for which the December rates have been used. The length of the working week remained unchanged during the whole period.

(f) Average first 8 months.

TABLE 6.—Average Capital Costs, Average Local Authority Rents and estimated Weekly Costs of Buying a Three-bedroom, non-parlour House, 1925–38.

Year	Average Capital Cost (a)	Rate of Interest on Local Loans	Weekly Rents of Local Authority Houses				Building Society Rates of Interest (f)	Weekly Cost of buying (g)	
			Economic Rents (b)	Subsidised Rents possible under				without Subsidy	with Chamberlain Subsidy
				Chamberlain Act (c)	Wheatley Act (d)	Greenwood Act (e)			
(1)	(2)	(3)	(4)	(5)	(6)	(7)	(8)	(9)	(10)
	£	%	s. d.	s. d.	s. d.	s. d.	%	s. d.	s. d.
1925	510	4¾	12 0	10 6	7 4	—	6	12 1	10 7
1926	510	5	12 5	10 11	7 9	—	6	12 1	10 7
1927	481	5	11 10	10 4	7 2	—	6	11 4	9 10
1928	432	5	10 10	9 10	7 0*	—	6	10 0½	9 0½
1929	416	5	10 6	9 6	6 8*	—	6	9 9	8 9
1930	411	5	10 5		6 7*	—	6	9 9	
1931	404	4½–5	9 7 to 10 3		5 9* to 6 5	5 3 to 5 11	5·9	9 4	
1932	375	4½–5	9 0 to 9 7		5 2* to 5 9	4 8 to 5 3	5·9	8 7	
1933	362	4–4¾	8 2 to 9 1		4 4* to 5 3	3 10 to 4 9	4·9	7 8	
1934	361	3½	7 9		3 11*	3 5	5·2	7 10	
1935	371	3½	7 10			3 6	4·5	7 8	
1936	384	3½	8 0			3 8	4·5	7 11	
1937	427	3½	8 8			4 4	4·5	8 10	
1938	438	3⅞	9 0			4 8 or 6 3	†	†	

(a) *Ministry of Health Annual Reports* and *Report on Local Expenditure, 1932.* op. cit. Average Capital Cost is taken as the average all-in cost of building by local authorities, i.e. annual averages of average quarterly prices for contracts let for 3-bedroom non-parlour houses (excluding flats) plus £70 for land and drainage, etc., as taken in the Report, op. cit.

(b) The economic rents are calculated as in the *Report on Local Expenditure* as the weekly capital charges on a 60-year basis *plus* 2/1 for repairs and management expenses.

(c) The Chamberlain Subsidy on a 60-year basis amounted to 1/6 a week for houses built by September 30, 1927, and 1/- subsequently.

(d) The Wheatley subsidy on a 60-year basis amounted to 4/8 a week for houses built by September 30, 1927, and 3/10 subsequently.

(e) The Greenwood subsidy is taken on a 60-year basis for a family of four persons rehoused in an ordinary cottage dwelling. On this basis which applied up to the reduction in 1938, it was equivalent on an average to 4/4 a week per house. The higher figure for 1938 is the subsidised rent for any house qualifying only for the reduced rate of subsidy under the Amendment Act of that year.

(f) From 1928 the rates of interest shown are the average rates of interest charged by building societies on new advances (slightly rounded off), as given in the Annual Reports of the Chief Registrar of Friendly Societies. For the earlier years there is no information as to rates on new advances as distinct from average rates on all advances outstanding; as, however, changes in rates of interest on all advances outstanding were negligible in these years it is reasonable to assume that rates on new advances were for all practical purposes also the same as these were up to 1928. It is important to remember that all the rates are average rates, and that the rates charged by individual societies were not all the same and varied for each society according to the type of advance.

(g) The weekly cost of purchase is calculated on the ordinary formula for payments of interest and repayment of capital by instalments over a period of twenty years, this being the usual term for advances for house purchase. The amount of advance has been taken as 70% of the capital costs shown in column 1, slightly rounded for convenience in calculation. The resulting calculated cost of buying a house shown in the table is the cost of buying a house of the local authority three-bedroom non-parlour type and may reasonably be taken as the minimum cost of purchase of the smallest type of house that could be realised. These figures have been calculated solely for the purpose of comparison between the economic and/or subsidised rents of local authority houses and the cheapest terms on an average of buying such a house. In practice, people starting to buy houses tended to buy rather more elaborate houses, e.g. with parlours, gables, etc., and the terms on which advances were in fact obtained varied from those used as the basis of the calculations with the variations in the practise of different building societies.

* If the Wheatley subsidy had not been reduced as from October 1927, the average possible subsidised rents for new houses would have been 6/2, 5/10, 5/9, 5/3, 4/8½, 3/11½ and 3/1, from 1928 each year to 1934 consecutively.

† Not available.

TABLE 7A.—The Growth of Building Societies, 1924–37.*

Year (1)	Number of Share-holders thous. (2)	Number of Deposi-tors thous. (3)	Liabilities to Share-holders £mn (4)	Liabilities to Deposi-tors (a) £mn (5)	Number of Borrowers thous. (6)	Balance due on Mortgages at end of year £mn (7)	New Advances on Mortgages during year £mn (8)
1924	†	†	109·0	28·1	†	119·7	40·6
1925	†	†	127·8	27·3	†	145·9	49·8
1926	†	†	147·7	30·5	†	171·2	52·2
1927	†	†	172·8	33·4	†	197·7	55·9
1928	1,130·1	356·5	213·2	36·0	553·9	227·5(b)	58·7(b)
1929	1,265·3	393·8	250·2	38·9	628·9	268·1	74·7
1930	1,449·4	428·3	302·8	44·6	720·4	316·3	88·8
1931	1,577·9	465·2	341·8	50·4	802·5	360·2	90·3
1932	1,692·2	545·6	380·9	61·5	868·8	388·4	82·1
1933	1,748·0	631·4	395·5	75·5	948·5	423·5	103·2
1934	1,857·6	695·5	424·3	97·3	1,067·1	476·2	124·6
1935	1,938·7	763·8	447·2	114·8	1,180·2	529·7	130·9
1936	2,010·6	776·9	480·7	128·4	1,295·2	586·6	140·3
1937	2,083·9	794·3	517·5	143·3(c)	1,392·1	636·4	136·9

* Source : *Annual Reports of the Chief Registrar of Friendly Societies*, Part 5. Report for 1938 not available.

† Not available.

(a) Includes " Other Creditors."

(b) In 1928, the date of the year-end up to which statements are abstracted was advanced from 31st December to 31st January. The change brought in later returns for 38 building societies and expanded the balance due on mortgages by £2mn. The advances on mortgages made by these societies, but not brought into the account owing to the change amounted to £11·2mn.

(c) Includes £1·9 mn. previously included under " Other Liabilities."

TABLE 7B.—Advances on Mortgage not exceeding £1,000 made by Building Societies, 1928–37 (a).

Year	Advances on Mortgages not exceeding £1,000		
	as % of balance due on Mortgages at end of year	as % of new advances on Mortgages (b)	Average value of new advances on Mortgages (b) £
(1)	(2)	(3)	(4)
1928	81·4	79·5	425
1929	81·3	78·1	440
1930	81·7	78·7	469
1931	82·1	79·3	471
1932	83·3	82·0	446
1933	84·1	80·4	446
1934	85·1	81·7	446
1935	85·2	79·1	449
1936	84·9	78·6	458
1937	84·6	77·3	463

(a) *Annual Reports of the Chief Registrar of Friendly Societies, Part 5.*
(b) Not available before 1928.

TABLE 8A.—Numbers of Insured Workers in the Building Industry, 1924–39. (Males aged 16–64).* *Thousands.*

In July	Total (all skilled and unskilled)	Bricklayers	Carpenters	Plasterers
(1)	(2)	(3)	(4)	(5)
1924†	721·6	58·0	124·0	16·1
1925†	754·1	65·1	114·0	17·9
1926†	801·0	72·2	126·5	19·7
1927†	847·9	75·8	134·5	22·1
1928	816·6	73·9	127·1	23·4
1929	826·0	75·6	126·7	24·4
1930	832·3	73·8	125·7	24·3
1931	858·2	79·0	131·1	26·5
1932	856·9	81·3	134·3	28·1
1933	883·8	85·2	137·8	29·7
1934	928·3	86·7	137·6	30·2
1935	976·8	88·9	140·0	31·6
1936	1,019·7	97·6	142·7	34·6
1937	1,035·3	102·3	146·2	36·1
1938	1,050·1	110·6	153·2	38·2
1939	1,041·6	‡	‡	‡

* Source : *Ministry of Labour Gazette.*
† 16 years and over ; from 1928 onwards unemployment insurance figures covered only men from 16–64 years.
‡ Not available.

TABLE 8B.—Unemployment in the Building Industry, in certain years (summer months).*

Average May to July	Total (all skilled and unskilled)		Bricklayers		Carpenters		Plasterers	
	Thousands†	%‡	Thousands†	%‡	Thousands†	%‡	Thousands†	%‡
(1)	(2)	(3)	(4)	(5)	(6)	(7)	(8)	(9)
1924 ..	63·2	8·9	0·8	1·4	2·9	2·4	0·3	2·0
1927 ..	56·2	6·7	1·0	1·4	4·2	3·1	0·4	1·8
1931 ..	154·4	18·0	8·6	10·9	22·4	17·2	4·6	17·5
1934 ..	142·5	15·4	4·2	4·8	13·2	9·6	2·3	7·7
1936 ..	111·3	11·0	2·8	2·9	5·8	4·1	1·5	4·3
1939 ..	122·5	11·8	8·6	§	7·1	§	5·6	§

* See note † to Table 8A above.
† Source : *Ministry of Labour Gazette.*
‡ Calculated as % of the numbers insured in June each year. The numbers insured in June have been interpolated by taking eleven twelfths of the difference between the number insured in the July of each preceding year and the July of each year shown in the table.
§ Not available.

TABLE 9A.—Regional Distribution of Requirements(a) for Additional Houses, 1921–31, and of New Houses Built,(b) 1921–31, 1931–34, and 1934–39.

Percentages of Totals for England and Wales*

Regions†	Home Counties	Midlands	Textile Counties	North East England	South Wales and Mons.	Rest of England and Wales	Total England and Wales
(1)	(2)	(3)	(4)	(5)	(6)	(7)	(8)
Requirements, 1921–31	36·6	17·0	21·2	3·8	3·3	18·1	100
Deficits in 1931	41·1	17·8	16·6	3·6	3·8	17·1	100
Houses built 1921–31							
By Local Authorities (c)	24·3	20·9	27·5	6·1	3·3	17·9	100
By Private Enterprise :							
Subsidised (d).. ..	24·1	19·9	26·8	5·2	4·0	20·0	100
Unsubsidised (e) ..	51·8	8·4	15·5	2·4	2·1	19·8	100
Total	40·6	13·1	20·1	3·5	2·9	19·8	100
All Houses Built, 1921–31	34·7	15·9	22·7	4·5	3·1	19·1	100
Houses built April 1931– September 1934							
By Local Authorities ..	21·1	21·4	28·3	7·8	1·6	19·8	100
By Private Enterprise ..	45·0	13·9	18·8	3·8	1·2	17·3	100
Houses built October 1934—March 1939 (f)							
By Private Enterprise ..	39·2	17·1	20·6	4·1	1·3	17·7	100

(a) Including shortage outstanding in March 1921 as well as current requirements 1921–31.

(b) Excluding houses built for slum clearance purposes and for the abatement of overcrowding.

(c) Including 16,161 houses built before March 31, 1921.

(d) Including 13,103 houses built before March 31, 1921.

(e) Excluding houses built before September 30, 1922, for which particulars of the regional distribution are not available. The total number of houses omitted is 30,000 according to the estimate of the Ministry of Health. (*Ministry of Health Annual Report, 1922–3.*)

(f) Regional figures for unsubsidised building by local authorities during these years are not available. All subsidised building was either for slum clearance or for the abatement of overcrowding. See Table 2 above.

* The percentages are calculated from statistics of the numbers of houses built by local authorities and private enterprise, these have been provided by the Housing Department of the Ministry of Health. Since 1935, the statistics have been published in detail in the six-monthly statistical statement *Housing.*

† The Counties in each Region are as follows : *Home Counties* : Beds., Berks., Bucks., Essex, Herts, Kent, London, Middlesex, Surrey, Sussex. *Textile Counties:* Cheshire, Lancs., W. Riding of Yorks. and York City. *Midlands :* Derby, Leicester, Northants., Notts., Staffs., Warwicks., Worcestershire. *N.E. England :* Durham, Northumberland. *S. Wales and Mons. :* Glamorganshire, Mons. *Rest of England and Wales :* All other counties.

TABLE 9B.—Additional Houses required in each Region(a), 1921–31, as Percentages of Houses in 1921, and Additional Houses provided by Local Authorities and Private Enterprise(b), 1921–31, and Deficits in 1931 as Percentages of Requirements.

Regions	Require-ments 1921–31 as % of Houses in 1921	Percentage of Requirements provided by			Deficit in 1931 as % of Require-ments	Total of cols. (3) to (6)
		Local Authorities (c)	Private Enterprise			
			Subsidised (d)	Unsubsi-dised (e)		
(1)	(2)	(3)	(4)	(5)	(6)	(7)
Home Counties	33·1	18·2	13·0	41·1	27·7	100
Midlands ..	27·4	34·9	24·2	15·0	25·9	100
Textile.. ..	19·4	34·8	24·8	20·9	19·5	100
N.E. England	15·9	37·2	23·2	15·6	24·0	100
S. Wales and Mons. ..	20·2	27·9	24·7	19·3	28·1	100
Rest of England and Wales ..	18·1	26·0	20·8	29·9	23·3	100

(a) See note (a) Table 9A. (c) See note (c), Table 9A. (e) See note (e), Table 9A.
(b) See note (b), Table 9A. (d) See note (d), Table 9A.

TABLE 10.—Averages, Deviations and Correlation Coefficients referred to in Chapter IV, Section III (*b*).

Note : The following notation is used—

w = Rate of Requirements for additional houses, 1921–31, and w* the average rate.

b = Rate of Total Supply of additional houses, 1921–31, and b* the average rate.

l = Local Authority rate of supply of additional houses, 1921–31, and l* the average rate.

p = Private Enterprise rate of supply of additional houses, 1921–31, and p* the average rate.

l_1 = Addition to supply of houses made by Local Authorities as % of requirements, 1921–31, and l_1* the average rate.

p_1 = Addition to supply of houses made by Private Enterprise as % of requirements, 1921–31, and p_1* the average rate.

Averages†

$$w* = 22\cdot9; \sigma = \pm 9\cdot4$$
$$b* = 17\cdot8; \sigma = \pm 7\cdot9$$
$$l* = 6\cdot0; \sigma = \pm 2\cdot0$$
$$p* = 11\cdot9; \sigma = \pm 7\cdot3$$
$$l_1* = 28\cdot4; \sigma = \pm 9\cdot6$$
$$p_1* = 49\cdot5; \sigma = \pm12\cdot9$$

Correlation Coefficients††‡

$$r_{wl} = + 0\cdot45 \pm 0\cdot13$$
$$r_{wp} = + 0\cdot92 \pm 0\cdot03$$
$$r_{wb} = + 0\cdot96 \pm 0\cdot02$$
$$r_{lp} = + 0\cdot19 \pm 0\cdot15$$
$$r_{wl_1} = - 0\cdot58 \pm 0\cdot11$$
$$r_{wp_1} = + 0\cdot43 \pm 0\cdot13$$
$$r_{p_1l_1} = - 0\cdot61 \pm 0\cdot10$$

Coefficient of variation of l = 33·2%
Coefficient of variation of p = 61·6%

† When London, Middlesex, Essex, Kent and Surrey are excluded the following main results are obtained (using the same notation) : w*=20·7 ; b*=16·4 ; l*=6·0 ; p*=10·4 ; l_1=29·5 ; p_1=48·4 ; r_{wl}=+0·62 ; r_{wp}=+0·86 ; r_{lp}=0·25 ; r_{wl_1}=—0·42 ; r_{wp_1}=+0·29 ; $r_{l_1p_1}$=—0·59 ; $r_{wl.p}$=+0·82 ; $r_{wp.l}$=+0·92 ; $r_{lp.w}$=—0·70.

‡ Partial Correlation Coefficients : $r_{wl.p}$=+0·74 ; $r_{wp.l}$=+0·96 ; $r_{lp.w}$=—0·66.

Regression Equations : l=0·42w—0·42p ; p=0·81w—1·02l.

Note on the Calculations in Tables 10 and VI and VII.

When the original calculations were made for my paper *Local Authorities and Housing Subsidies*, read to the Manchester Statistical Society in 1942, the calculations of requirements, etc., were based on the numbers of houses *occupied* according to the Census's of 1921 and 1931. Since then I have decided that it is more appropriate to base all calculations on the total numbers *both occupied and unoccupied*. (See p. 270 n. 4.) above). All the figures have been recalculated on this new basis and, at the same time, revised figures of the numbers of houses built, kindly provided by the Ministry of Health, have been utilised. In fact, the new calculations do not affect the conclusions to be drawn, but the revisions provided by the Ministry of Health have made more difference to the detailed figures than the inclusion of *unoccupied* houses in the basis of calculations of requirements, etc.

It will be noticed that the deficits outstanding in 1931 have been calculated as the actual deficits on the basis of the Census of 1931, i.e. that is after allowing for wastage of houses through net demolition. This affects the sizes of the rates of supply of private enterprise and the local authorities to the same extent and does *not* affect comparison between them. In some cases it affects, however, the comparisons between individual counties, again to the same extent for private enterprise and local authorities. This course has been adopted in the interests of statistical accuracy and because it seemed more realistic.

One point of detail should be mentioned. The figures for private enterprise exclude unsubsidised houses before September, 1922, as the county figures were not available before that date. Those for the local authorities, however, include building between 1919 and 1921 as separate annual figures are not available. The numbers involved in each case are too small to affect the calculations. (See Table 9A notes (c) (d) (e) above.)

GEORGE ALLEN & UNWIN LTD

LONDON: 40 MUSEUM STREET, W.C.1
CAPE TOWN: 58–60 LONG STREET
TORONTO: 91 WELLINGTON STREET WEST
BOMBAY: 15 GRAHAM ROAD, BALLARD ESTATE
WELLINGTON, N.Z.: 8 KINGS CRESCENT, LOWER HUTT
SYDNEY, N.S.W.: BRADBURY HOUSE, 55 YORK STREET